EXTENDING DEONTIC LOGIC FOR THE FORMALISATION OF LEGAL RULES

Law and Philosophy Library

VOLUME 36

The titles published in this series are listed at the end of this volume.

LAMBÈR M.M. ROYAKKERS
Eindhoven University of Technology,
The Netherlands

EXTENDING DEONTIC LOGIC FOR THE FORMALISATION OF LEGAL RULES

SPRINGER-SCIENCE+BUSINESS MEDIA, B.V.

A C.I.P. Catalogue record for this book is available from the Library of Congress.

ISBN 978-90-481-5008-3 ISBN 978-94-015-9099-0 (eBook)
DOI 10.1007/978-94-015-9099-0

Printed on acid-free paper

Originally published by Kluwer Academic Publishers in 1998
Softcover reprint of the hardcover 1st edition 1998

Preface

This book is an adaptation of my PhD thesis *Representing L∃g∀l Rules in Deontic Logic* [Royakkers, 1996]. The main alterations are:

- The addition of chapter 2 concerning the semantics of deontic logic based on valuations. In this chapter I extend the Beth tableau method, which is originally developed for the propositional calculus, to also be applicable for deontic logic. For those who are not familiar with deontic logic or with the axiomatic deduction, this method is a useful tool to check whether a formula is valid or not.
- The addition of the notion of commitment in chapter 5, and the notion of weak and strong permission in chapter 7.
- The omission of the chapter concerning *defeasible deontic logic*, of which a revised version is published in [Nute, 1997].
- Chapter 6 has been revised rather thoroughly. Here I introduce the logic of enactment based on epistemic logic and local reasoning to express normative inconsistencies in a consistent way.

I wish to thank John-Jules Meyer, Giovanni Sartor and Marek Sergot for their suggestions and criticisms of my PhD thesis, which have improved this book. Heleen Neggers and Jan Draisma deserve credit for the layout.

Special thanks go to Frank Dignum for his continuous support and inspiring suggestions.

Contents

Chapter 1

Introduction

1.1 Logic and law

Formal logic is an indispensable instrument of analysis of the interpretation of legal texts and the assessment of the validity of legal reasoning. This is clear from the vast amount of work produced in the area of logic and law [see e.g. the journal of Artificial Intelligence and Law]. In practice formal logic is not often used by lawyers. However, there is a growing demand among lawyers and legislators for legal expert systems to support their work. There is a close connection between expert systems and logic. Expert systems are able to reason with complex rules as well as simple facts and several systems are available that can understand subjects of natural language [cf. Frost, 1986, p. 1] and are usually based on some form of formal logic. The nature of *legal* expert systems is in part determined by the logical formalism used for the representation of the legal rules involved.

The formalism of *deontic logic* is particularly suited for this purpose. Deontic logic is a branch of philosophical logic involving reasoning about norms: obligations, prohibitions and permissions. It has its roots in the philosophy of law. The state of the art in the field of deontic logic - the logic of norms: obligations, prohibitions and permissions - in legal knowledge representation is described in handbooks dating back to the seventies [cf. Alchourrón and Bulygin, 1971; Føllesdal and Hilpinen, 1971; Kutschera, 1973; Reisinger, 1977; Brouwer, Soeteman, and Wild, 1982]. For more recent publications see [Martino and Natali, 1986, especially part two], [Soeteman, 1989; Brouwer, 1990] and the ΔEON-proceedings [Meyer and Wieringa, 1991; Jones and Sergot, 1993b; Brown and Carmo, 1996].

In practice, it turns out, however, that the results from modern deontic logic concerning the logical structure of legal rules and of legal reasoning are not (explicitly) taken into account in the construction of expert systems. Classical two-valued predicate calculus is considered to be strong enough by many and is supposed to be adequate to cope with the problem of the representation of legal rules and legal reasoning [see Koers, Kracht, Smith,

Smits, and Weusten, 1989]. This presupposition, however, has been seriously questioned [cf. McCarty, 1986, 1989; Herrestad, 1991].

If one considers the representation and consistency of legal rules by themselves, then it might be sufficient to use predicate calculus. However, if one also considers the use of legal rules in actual situations, a formalisation of deontic notions is required. In these cases a discrepancy can arise between the ideal situation (described by the legal rules) and the actual situation. When such *violations* have to be accounted for [cf. Jones, 1990], the use of deontic logic is unavoidable. To express violations consistently, one has to distinguish between what ought to be done and what is the case. If this distinction cannot be made, the concurrent occurrence of a rule and the violation (which then is represented as the negation) of that rule would render the system inconsistent. Susskind expresses an even stronger point of view:

> The necessity for the inclusion of some deontic logic within a legal inference engine would seem beyond dispute. [Susskind, 1987, p. 225]

Bench-Capon [1989] disputes the necessity of deontic logic. He refers to some successful systems that have represented legal knowledge without deontic concepts, such as the Prolog program of the British Nationality Act of 1981 developed by the logic programming group at the Imperial College [Sergot, Sadri, Kowalski, Kriwaczek, Hammond, and Cory, 1986]. In this approach, legislation is viewed as a set of definitions rather than a set of norms issued by authorities. In other words, the norms are never compared with the actual situation. The system is only used to detect inconsistencies between and incompleteness of the rules. We support the idea of Sergot:

> for certain purposes, many fragments of law can be represented adequately without deontic logic, but that there are other fragments, and other purposes, where an adequate representation would demand a deontic logic. [Jones and Sergot, 1992, p. 47]

The purpose of this book is not to investigate which fragments of law can be represented by deontic logic, but to investigate the current limitations of deontic logic for the representation of legal rules and to develop some extensions of deontic logic that may allow for some improvements in the representation of legal texts and of legal knowledge in general.

This inquiry is meant to improve the usefulness of legal expert systems in law by taking into account deontic logic in representing legal rules - without regarding how the proposed formalisms would be implemented in a working legal expert system. The scientific interest of this book therefore lies in the application of results from a science of a highly theoretical and abstract nature (such as deontic logic) to an applied science as legal informatics by considering various ways of applying formal tools (focused on deontic logic) in the legal domain.

There are two types of deontic logic: one for *Ought-to-be statements* and one for em Ought-to-do statements. Both approaches have their own merits. Unfortunately, at present these approaches have not yet been combined into one formalism.[1] Therefore, the extensions that are developed in this book are based on both types of deontic logic: 'standard deontic logic' for Ought-to-be statements (see chapter 2) and 'dynamic deontic logic' for

[1]For a first attempt of a formal approach of the relation between the Ought-to-do and Ought-to-be we refer to [Altan, Meyer, and Wieringa, 1993].

Ought-to-do statements (see chapter 3). The difference between Ought-to-be and Ought-to-do will also be discussed in chapters 2 and 5. We will not make a formal comparison between Ought-to-be and Ought-to-do. Neither do we aim to construct a combination of the two approaches in this book. This would take us beyond the main goal of the book and, therefore, we leave it for future research.

In this book, we will extend the two deontic logics with some new concepts. These concepts are:

- (Groups of) actors (chapters 4 and 5)
- Authorities/enactment (chapter 6)
- Authority hierarchy/applicability (chapter 7)

With these extensions of deontic logic, the deontic logic becomes more powerful at representing normative rules, since its expressibility increases. The latter two concepts relate to the notion of normative inconsistency, which is a very relevant area for AI-and-Law research, since rules used in a legal domain often are conflicting.

In order to illustrate the importance of the formalisation of legal rules and the role of the above-mentioned extensions, we present an in-depth discussion in the next section of a case of conflicting speed limits on the basis of a judgement by the Supreme Court. This case is a good example of the type of problems that are encountered in representing legal rules and reasoning with legal rules. It illustrates the motivation for our research to new concepts in deontic logic as is pursued in the rest of this book. In chapter 8, we will analyse and formalise these problems on the basis of the concepts discussed in the other chapters.

1.2 Conflicting speed limits

In this section, based on [Royakkers, 1995], we give an extensive description of an example from the Dutch Traffic Regulation to illustrate the types of problems we try to model in this book.[2]

The amendment of the Dutch Traffic Regulation 1966 ('Reglement Verkeersregels en Verkeerstekens 1966' - RVV 1966) has led to a great deal of largely justified criticism. The Dutch Traffic Regulation 1990 was supposed to become the political showpiece of deregulation. Compared to the 1966 Act, the Dutch Traffic Regulation 1990 showed that a simplification and reduction of regulations in the critical field of road traffic was possible. The aim of the legislature was to increase the credibility of the rules. According to Otte [1993], however, the Dutch Traffic Regulation 1990 turned into a total fiasco as regards simplicity, accessibility and comprehensibility. Also, in a number of articles for the Dutch journal Verkeersrecht, Otte and Simmelink [1993] discussed some of the structural flaws in various rules of the Dutch Traffic Regulation 1990. In one of their so-called 'Kronkels in het RVV 1990' (Twists in the Dutch Traffic Regulation 1990),.they question the

[2]The reason for choosing the Dutch Traffic Regulation that this part of Dutch law contains a minimum of fuzzy concepts. Therefore, it seems to lend itself for formalisation.

effectiveness of the speed limit rules. They discuss this on the basis of a case such as the following.

1.2.1 A false note in the composition of the Dutch Traffic Regulation 1990

On a national route road A28, within the city limits of Zwolle, a lorry from the firm H.I. drove at a speed of 96 km/h. H.I. was imposed an administrative sanction on the ground of 'a lorry exceeding the speed limit by 15 to 20 km/h'. An appeal was lodged with the public prosecutor and the subdistrict court judge, because H.I. was of the opinion that, on the road in question, traffic signs indicating a speed limit of 100 km/h were in force, and that, therefore, no sanctionable act had been committed, for traffic signs override traffic rules.[3]

Otte and Simmelink:[4]

> Our advice is twofold. The subdistrict court judge has no choice but to pronounce the appeal by the lorry driver valid and to quash the court order by the public prosecutor. When the Dutch Traffic Regulation is evaluated - or sooner - the legislator will have to amend the Dutch Traffic Regulation. (...) Neither is it desirable to amend arts. 21 and 22 of the Dutch Traffic Regulation. The solution should be sought in amending Article 63 of the Dutch Traffic Regulation 1990.

The subdistrict court judge:[5]

> In Article 22 of the Dutch Traffic Regulation 1990,[6] it is laid down that for lorries the special speed limit of 80 km/h holds. In Article 63 of the Dutch Traffic Regulation 1990, it is laid down that traffic signs override traffic rules, in as far as these rules are incompatible with the signs. From the text it appears that traffic signs only override traffic rules if they are in conflict with the traffic rules. This is, according to the subdistrict court judge, not the case here. Traffic sign A1 indeed indicates the speed limit, but as this is not in conflict with the traffic rule as stated in Article 22 of the Dutch Traffic Regulation 1990, the latter rule remains in force. Traffic sign A1 is a regulatory sign (a speed limit of 100 km/h in this case) and does not imply a higher speed limit in force for particular vehicles such as lorries.

The accused:

> The court shares my view that traffic signs have a higher rank than traffic regulations. However, in my case matters are reversed and traffic regulations supersede traffic signs. This can only be true if an indication is given beneath said traffic sign that it does not apply to freight traffic.

---

[3]Art. 63 of the Dutch Traffic Regulation 1990: Traffic signs override traffic rules in as far as specific rules are incompatible with specific signs.

[4][Otte and Simmelink, 1993, p. 167].

[5]Subdistrict courtnumber ZW) 33/92 (CJIB-number 568418).

[6]Art. 22 of the Dutch Traffic Regulation 1990: In as far as no lower speed limits have been set in other articles, the following special speed limits hold for the following vehicles: a. for lorries, buses and vehicles with trailers 80 km/h; (...).

The Advocate-General Meijers:[7]

> According to Article 63 of the Dutch Traffic Regulation 1990, the prohibition of Article 22 preamble and sub a, Dutch Traffic Regulation 1990, would, for a lorry driver, be lifted by a traffic sign if that traffic sign were to imply a compulsory minimum speed limit of 81 km/h on that particular section of the road. Only in such a case would there be incompatibility of rule and sign.

The Supreme Court:

> The appeal to the court of cassation of H.I. has to be rejected.

1.2.2 Article 63 and incompatibility

In what situations are traffic signs and traffic rules incompatible? To answer this question, we will first take a close look at the notion of 'incompatibility'. Two rules are incompatible if, and only if, they lead to contrary results or conclusions. Let us consider the following example. Car driver A is on a major road and approaches a junction, where car driver B approaches from the left. According to Article 15 of the Dutch Traffic Regulation 1990, B has to give way to A, who approaches the junction from the right. Also, according to the right-of-way signs (A6 and A9), B has to give way to A. So, it will be clear that there is no incompatibility between traffic rule and traffic signs in this case. However, we do not know exactly on the basis of which B has to give way. In the case of an offence in such situations, it does not matter whether the violation of a traffic rule or a traffic sign is held against the suspect. Now, suppose that B approaches the junction from the right. On the basis of Article 15 of the Dutch Traffic Regulation 1990, A has to yield right of way and, according to the right-of-way signs (A6 and A9), B has to yield right of way as well. In a logical sense, there is no incompatibility between signs and rule here; there is a deadlock, however: both drivers have to yield right of way. The relevant rules and signs do not lead to contrary conclusions. However, we may also apply a different interpretation to the situation. On the basis of the *principle of trust*, we may assume that the obligation of one means the right of the other. 'Trust' here means that a road user can, in principle, expect the other road users to observe the rules [cf. Simmelink, 1995]. On the grounds of the rule in Article 15 and the principle of trust, B has right of way, and A does not; on the grounds of the right-of-way signs and the principle of trust, A has right of way, and B does not. In this formulation A both has right of way and has not, which is clearly a case of incompatibility. So, on the basis of Article 63, B has to yield to A. Strictly speaking (considering the letter of the law), there is no incompatibility; when considering the underlying aims, there is indeed incompatibility between signs and rule.

The necessity of the condition 'in as far as specific rules are incompatible with specific signs' in Article 63 lies in the fact that, should this condition be lacking, a traffic rule could suspend all rules in force at that moment, meaning that no rules are in force as long as there are traffic signs, which is absurd, to say the least. For example, A drives his car at the speed of 100 km/h within a built-up area, and is halted by a policeman, because A is not permitted

[7] HR 61-93-V, (DD, 94.137).

to drive faster than 50 km/h. A can, however, refer to the fact that there was a traffic sign (for example a 'right-of-way' sign) and that this sign overrides the rule, so that the rule (speed limit of 50 km/h) is no longer in force. In the case mentioned above, this would mean that the lorry driver would be in the right, because the sign overrides the rule, which is thus suspended.

1.2.3 Speed limit

Opinions differ as to the question whether rules and signs pertinent to the speed limit are incompatible or compatible, as can be seen from the motivation by the district court judge, which was not in line with Otte and Simmelink's advice. The explanatory memorandum to the Dutch Traffic Regulation 1990 indicates that there is incompatibility in this case:[8]

> The systematic structure of Article 63, according to which traffic signs override traffic rules, implies that a different maximum speed indicated by traffic signs - such as 30 or 70 km/h inside a built-up area - need not be incorporated into the rules of this section.

Let us consider the meaning of traffic sign A1, which indicates that a speed limit of 100 km/h holds for that particular part of a motorway.[9] This only means that each car doing over 100 km/h breaks the law. We obey the law if we drive at a speed of 10 or 20 km/h. But this does not mean that we also observe other possible prohibitions or obligations concerning speed, for example that drivers must adjust their speed to the traffic situation or to weather conditions. Taking weather conditions into account may mean that our maximum speed should be 80 km/h, which implies that, when driving at a speed of 90 km/h, we may observe the former prohibition, but not the latter order. This example shows that the prohibition to drive faster than 100 km/h can only mean that every speed under 100 km/h is permitted in as far as one does not have to take other speed orders or prohibitions into account. The prohibition to drive faster than 100 km/h only means that we will, in any case, break the law if we drive at a greater speed than 100 km/h. This implies that a traffic sign indicating the prohibition of any speed over 100 km/h is not in conflict with the prohibition in the rule to drive at a greater speed than, for example, 80 km/h. For, if it is not permitted to drive faster than 80 km/h, it is certainly not permitted to drive faster than 100 km/h.

The prohibition to exceed the speed limit of 100 km/h clearly does not imply that it is by definition permitted to drive at a speed of 96 km/h: one has to take other speed prohibitions and orders into account, such as Article 25 of the Traffic Act.[10] It would be absurd to stick to this meaning when one considers the following example. There is a traffic jam on the motorway, and a car is driving at a speed of 100 km/h. The driver breaks the law in this situation, and he cannot maintain that it was permitted to drive at a speed of 100 km/h on this section of the road. The Supreme Court and the Advocate-General are in agreement on the meaning of the prohibition to exceed the 100 km/h limit in the case presented above.

---

[8] *Bulletin of Acts and Decrees*, 1990, 459, Explanatory memorandum, p. 103.

[9] Hereafter, this traffic sign will be referred to as 'A1 (100)'.

[10] Art. 25 of the Traffic Act: On the road, it is prohibited to act in such a way that the freedom of traffic is hindered without necessity or that road security is jeopardised or may reasonably be expected to be jeopardised.

What are the consequences of traffic sign A1 (100) for car drivers? On motorways outside built-up areas, a speed limit of 120 km/h is in force. On the approach of the A1 (100) traffic sign, the maximum speed of 100 km/h holds for car drivers, not, however, because the traffic rule is incompatible with the traffic sign. The speed limit of 120 km/h still holds, because cars are still not permitted to drive faster than 120 km per hour. The prohibition is, however, restricted by another prohibition, namely the prohibition to drive faster than 100 km per hour. The traffic sign has a *speed-reducing effect on the rule*. For lorry drivers traffic sign A1 (100) has no meaning: for them this sign carries superfluous information, because they are not permitted to drive faster than 80 km/h, so not faster than 100 km/h anyway. The result is that Article 63 of the Dutch Traffic Regulation 1990 can never be applicable as regards speed limits, because speed limits do not conflict.[11]

1.2.4 Undesirable consequences

The motivation by the district court judge, which was supported by the Supreme Court, poses problems, however. In many cities, so in built-up areas, there are, for example, A1 traffic signs on circular roads, indicating that it is prohibited to drive faster than 70 km/h. Many drivers will, and justifiably, take this sign to mean that it is permitted to drive at a speed of 70 km/h. This is, however, in disagreement with the motivation by the district court judge and the Advocate-General. According to Article 20 of the Dutch Traffic Regulation 1990, a speed limit of 50 km per hour holds for motor vehicles inside built-up areas. Traffic sign A1 (70) does not imply that on that particular section of the road the minimum speed is 51 km/h. So, there is no conflict here between traffic rules and traffic signs, with the result that traffic sign A1 (70) is totally superfluous and has no other meaning than that it is not permitted to drive at a greater speed than 70 km/h. This we already knew, because it is not permitted to drive faster than 50 km/h anyway. In this case, the district court judge will reason as follows: 'Traffic sign A1 (70) is a regulatory sign (meaning that it is prohibited to drive faster than 70 km/h) and does not imply that the speed limit in force for motor vehicles in built-up areas is raised.'

There is a similar problem in the case of national routes and motorways inside built-up areas. From the above it follows that it is prohibited to drive faster than 50 km/h on such roads, because they are inside built-up areas. It was, of course, the intention of the legislator to indicate that the prohibition to drive faster than 50 km/h is no longer in force, and that on such roads it is prohibited to drive faster than 100 or 120 km/h, respectively. In the Dutch Traffic Regulation 1990, however, the legislator did not define the speed limit on national routes and motorways inside built-up areas.[12]

---

[11] Traffic signs and traffic rules can only be incompatible in situations concerning right of way and changing lanes.

[12] Cf. Arts. 20 and 21. The maximum speed limit on motorways has only been set outside built-up areas.

1.2.5 Article 63a

The regulation has suffered much criticism since the time of its inception in 1990. The legislator was not entirely satisfied either, as appears from the fact that the former Minister of Transport and Public Works Maij had the Dutch Traffic Regulation revised in 1993. These revisions, introduced in 1996, were very marginal however. The most important change was concerned the addition of Article 63a regarding the maximum speed limit, since the maximum speed limit was not regulated adequately or accurately enough. By adding this new article matters did not improve and the composition of the Dutch Traffic Regulation now contains a cacophony of dissonant sounds. Article 63a is as follows:

> Traffic signs indicating a maximum speed do not supersede the maximum speeds determined in Articles 20, section b, 21, section b, 22, in as far as these signs indicate a higher maximum speed.

Article 63a is an exceptional provision for Article 63. The reason Article 63a was added, was to prevent misunderstandings from occurring according to the explanatory memorandum. Here, we shall see that the provision itself is another big misunderstanding and that the argument used in favour of 63a is specious. By means of the analysis an alternative solution will be presented that will not allow for misunderstandings by road users and lawyers.

During the discussion of Article 63 it has become clear that maximum speeds cannot be in conflict. The consequence is that traffic signs indicating a maximum speed never override traffic regulations that define a set maximum speed. This proves the absurdity of Article 63a. This regulation reiterates something that already results from the law and therefore is totally unnecessary. It is striking that Article 20, section a is missing.

How did the legislator manage to produce such an absurd regulation? In the explanatory memorandum the following is said about this:

> Traffic signs override traffic regulations in as far as these regulations are incompatible with the signs. As a result of this ranking the question has been raised whether this would lead to the conclusion that traffic signs indicating a maximum speed override the special maximum speeds listed in section 8. The consequence of that would be that a maximum speed of 100 km/h indicated by a sign on motorways would override the general maximum speed of 80 km/h listed in section 8 for lorries. To avoid any misunderstanding on this point Article 63a has been included.

Despite the case cited above, the legislator still bases himself on the notion that maximum speeds can be in conflict. The legislator believes that lorry drivers, for example, who see a sign with a maximum speed of 100 km/h will take this to mean that the set maximum speed of 80 km/h has been superseded. To avoid this from happening, the legislator has specified that traffic signs indicating a maximum speed do not override the set maximum speed given in Article 22 for lorry drivers. Analogies are made for the cases mentioned in Article 20, section b, Article 21, section b, and other cases in Article 22. It is obvious that Article 63a adds nothing, since traffic signs never override the set maximum speeds listed in Articles 20, section b, 21, section b, and 22.

Perhaps we should make use of the interpretative argumentation scheme: *a contrario argument*.[13] Article 63a makes no mention of the case regulated in Article 20, section a; this case appears to have no essential points of agreement with the cases regulated in Articles 20, section b, 21, section b, and 22. Thus, Article 63a does not hold for the case in Article 20, section a. That would mean traffic signs indicating a maximum speed do override the maximum speed set down in Article 20, section a. However, Article 63a can never be applied, since it is an exceptional provision for Article 63. In its turn Article 63 never applies to maximum speeds. Or should we read 'whether or not there is incompatibility' into this argument? That would be a very roundabout way of thinking. In addition, we should consider whether an a contrario argument is an admissible argumentation scheme and whether or not it can be applied correctly [cf. Eemeren and Grootendorst, 1992]. We shall not go into detail here, but in all probability there are objections to the application of an a contrario argument in relation to Article 63a. This is especially true as traffic signs indicating a maximum speed never override traffic regulations concerning the maximum speed. The legislator could have sufficed with the following stipulation:

> Traffic signs indicating a maximum speed override the maximum speed indicated in Article 20, section a.

In this stipulation it is explicitly stated that a traffic sign overrides a traffic regulation (regarding the maximum speed) without the presence of incompatibility. With this stipulation everything is formulated correctly. The problem of the lorry driver is solved because maximum speeds cannot be in conflict and Article 63 therefore cannot be applied. The problem of the car driver who sees a traffic sign on the ring road that indicates a maximum speed of 70 km/h also is solved by this new stipulation.

1.2.6 Emergency service vehicles

There is one case in which Article 63 has a nasty consequence, as Otte and Simmelink [1993] described in their 'Kronkels in het RVV 1990', 'The regulation concerning so-called "emergency service vehicles"', with regard to Article 50 of the Dutch Traffic Regulation 1990.[14] They discuss the following situation. A passenger car driving on a major road approaches a junction, and at the same time a police car with flashing light and sirens approaches from the right. On the ground of a traffic rule (Article 50 of the Dutch Traffic Regulation 1990), the driver of the passenger car has to give way to the driver of the police car, but on the ground of the right-of-way signs, the driver of the police car has to give way to the driver of the passenger car. As signs and rule are incompatible in this case, the driver of the passenger car has right of way on the ground of Article 63. Otte and Simmelink, therefore, conclude that the position of emergency service vehicles is not adequately provided for. It is clearly the intention of Article 50 that police cars, fire engines and ambulances with operating signals should always have right of way, but this cannot be concluded from the systematic structure of the Dutch Traffic Regulation 1990. This problem can easily be solved by replacing Article 50 by:

[13] For an extensive discussion of the a contrario argument the reader is referred to [Kloosterhuis, 1994].

[14] Art. 50 of the Dutch Traffic Regulation 1990: Road users are obliged to give way to drivers of emergency service vehicles.

> Yielding right of way by road users to drivers of emergency service vehicles overrides traffic lights and traffic signs and rules that regulate right of way.

This sentence could, systematically, best be incorporated in the section 'General provisions' of chapter 3 of the Dutch Traffic Regulation 1990, which also contains Article 63.

1.2.7 Coda

The composer in the shape of the legislator who conceived Dutch Traffic Regulation goes to great pains to harmonise all the false notes in the Dutch Traffic Regulation concerning the maximum speed. The result however is a cacophony. It is a consequence of the addition of a totally superfluous stipulation, namely Article 63a. The political hobby horse of the deregulation - which RVV 1990 was intended to be - had already stumbled, but the addition of Article 63a clearly demonstrated the hobby horse would never again enter the arena. The addition has injured the credibility of the regulations in the important area of traffic regulation, while it was the intention of the legislator to achieve the opposite. The superfluous addition is based on the improper application of Article 63 in combination with Article 1 of the Penal Code.

In this section we have demonstrated how the problems surrounding the maximum speeds can be solved quite simply, in a way that suits the letter of the law and agrees with the spirit of the law. Moreover, we have shown in what situations Article 63 can be applicable and the uselessness of Article 63a. An annoying consequence of Articles 50 and 63 was also solved through a simple alteration to Article 50.

The solution I propose to the problems surrounding Article 63 is as follows: Replace Articles 50, 63, and 63a with the following article:

> **Article 63.** 1. Giving right of way to priority vehicles overrides traffic lights, traffic signs, and traffic regulations pertaining to the right of way.
> 2. Traffic signs concerning the right of way and getting into lane override traffic regulations in as far as these signs are incompatible with these regulations.
> 3. Traffic signs that indicate a maximum speed override the maximum speed set down in Article 20, section a.

We may conclude that rules and signs that provide speed limits can never be in conflict. The ruling of the district court judge in the case discussed is correct, but leads to undesirable situations concerning the speed limit inside built-up areas. As a consequence, the letter of the law with regard to the speed limit is not in agreement with the spirit of the law in the Dutch Traffic Regulation 1990. This does not contribute to the credibility of the law. The reason for this lies in the distinction that is made between driving inside and outside built-up areas, and the lack of clarity about the notion of incompatibility. By means of the solution given above and by clarifying the notion of 'incompatibility' the problems concerning speed limits can be solved.

1.3 Evaluation

From the above case, the following aspects arrest our attention:

1. The soundness of the standards of argumentation used by the designers of the Dutch Traffic Regulation 1990 leaves much to be desired. However, proper arguments play an important role if one wishes to make a particular legal point acceptable. In this book, we pose that logic, and especially deontic logic, can be a very helpful tool for making an acceptable legal argument. In the last chapter, we show that the problem of the 'the speed limit' case easily can be solved by the formalisation of that case and that our stipulation is a (logical) valid legal argument.

2. The legislator sometimes makes use of the room offered by inconsistencies as a legislative technique. Here, inconsistency means that contradictory conclusions can be drawn from information taken from a specific case, i.e. both a particular conclusion and the negation thereof can be deduced. Thus, Article 63 first is a handy way to invalidate traffic regulations that are incompatible (inconsistent) with traffic signs, without explicitly stating that traffic regulations do not apply in a particular case. Second, it is a way to separately include traffic regulations and traffic signs in the law. Article 63 gives a ranking, much like the adage 'Lex Posterior Derogat Legi Priori' or 'Lex Specialis Derogat Legi Generali.' So, the law is not merely a set of norms, but a hierarchical system.

   In chapter 7, we introduce a hierarchical system on the basis of the competencies of normative authorities who enact the norms, which can be used to determine which norm should be followed in cases of normative conflicts. However, we shall see that such an authority-hierarchy does not resolve all conflicts. In chapter 6, we describe the logic of enactment based on local reasoning and epistemic logic to reason consistently in the presence of conflicting enacted norms.

3. The misunderstanding that a prohibition to exceed the speed limit of 100 km/h implies by definition the permission to drive 90 km/h is based on a poor comprehension of the range of the Feuerbach principle 'nullum crimen, nulla poena sine praevia lege poenali', stated in Article 1 sub 1 of the Dutch Penal Code: 'No act is a penal act unless it be by virtue of a prior legal penal clause'. This stipulation determines that the predicates penally not illegal and penally permissible are equivalent by definition. In jurisprudence this principle is usually labelled as 'sealing legal principle', often formulated as 'whatever is not forbidden, is permitted' [cf. Tammelo, 1969], see also [Brouwer, 1979]. We call these systems *closed legal systems*, also called universal normative systems. Within these systems there is a positive legal norm - a general closure rule - governing all acts that are not subject to other legal norms.

   A consequence of the *postulated universality* by 'sealing legal principle' is that, if we want to talk about criminal law, we have to take into account the difference between two types of permission. There are permissions that are enacted by competent normative authorities: *strong permissions*, and permissions that are not enacted, but follow from a 'sealing legal principle' (or from the absence of prohibitions): *weak permissions*.

In chapter 7 we will investigate the nature of the permission with respect to the universality of the Dutch criminal law, and the formalisation of the strong and weak permission. The formalisation rests on the relation between enacted norms and applicable norms. Within this, we are concerned with two concepts of validity: membership (enactment) and applicability. A norm can be said to be valid in the sense that it belongs to or is a member of a legal system: membership (see chapter 6). A norm is often also said to be valid in the sense that it is obligatory or has a 'binding force': applicability (see chapter 7). Both of them play a central role in law and in legal theories [cf. Bulygin, 1982].

4. Norms are directed to addressees: actors or groups of actors. However, most norms are not directed to all actors, but to actors who belong to a certain set of actors. For example, Article 22, section a of the Dutch Traffic Regulation 1990 (see previous section) is directed to lorry drivers. In the chapters 4 and 5 we add actors to deontic logic, so that we can indicate to whom a norm is directed in our logic and that our logic is not 'impersonal' anymore.

1.4 The structure of this book

In this book, we will address the problems indicated in the previous section by extending two deontic logics. In the chapters 2 and 3, we discuss these two deontic logics: SDL and DDL and some modifications of these systems. In chapters 4 and 5, relativised deontic modalities are investigated in SDL and DDL, respectively. We will see that the addition of actors and groups of actors gives new expressive power, and the formulas of these relativised deontic logics acquire new meanings, not expressible in SDL and DDL. They are, therefore, subject to new intuitions. The systems developed in chapters 4 and 5 will be extended to authorities in chapter 6. Authorities are responsible for the establishment of norms and supervising the enactment of the norms. With the addition of authorities to a deontic system, we can consistently express conflicting norms enacted by (sets of) authorities. The theory is based on epistemic logic and local reasoning. However, this does not determine which norm should be followed in cases of conflicting norms: this will be discussed in chapter 7. In chapter 7, we introduce the term 'authority hierarchy' to overcome this problem. The authorities are used to prioritise the norms they enacted. In this chapter, we also discuss some related issues such as promulgation, derogation and universality. Finally, in chapter 8, we apply the concepts - investigated in chapters 2 up to and including 7 - to some cases related to the case of 'conflicting speed limits', discussed in this chapter. Finally, some areas for future research are indicated.

Chapter 2

Standard Deontic Logic

2.1 Introduction

Deontic logic[1] is a branch of philosophical logic concerning reasoning about norms, or in other words, about normative versus non-normative behaviour. It is the logic of obligations, prohibitions and permissions. As such, it is relevant for the foundations of ethics and law. Deontic logic has been used to analyse the structure of normative law and normative reasoning in law.[2] In this book, we will use deontic logic as a tool for representing legal rules.

Not much is certain in deontic logic, in contrast to, for example, propositional and predicate calculus. There are not many principles, in whatever deontic system, which are undisputed; i.e. which cannot be accepted as rational reconstructions of normative reasoning. There is, nevertheless, a formal system on which several other systems are based, although it has been disputed as a whole as well as with regard to its theorems. Most other systems can be regarded as extensions of standard deontic logic. One may, therefore, to a certain extent, rightly speak of a 'standard system of deontic logic'. This is even more justified by the fact that alternative systems have often been developed as a reaction to this system. In this chapter we discuss this standard system.

Before we discuss the standard deontic logic (SDL), which is a normal modal logic with a Kripke-style semantics using the operator O as the basic 'necessity operator', we shall discuss system S_n. This system has the same rules and axiom schemes, but with a semantics based on valuations. The reason for doing this is to extend the Beth tableau method for deontic logic. The Beth tableau method is a simple alternative method to find

[1] The adjective deontic is derived from the Greek word '$\delta\epsilon o\upsilon\tau\omega\varsigma$', which means 'as it should be'.

[2] However, as so many subjects in philosophical logic and philosophy in general, the subject was also picked up by computer scientists and AI (artificial intelligence) researchers. Deontic logic promises to be relevant for such prosaic matters as authorisation mechanisms, decision support systems, database security rules, fault-tolerant software and database integrity constraints. Thus, this will take it outside the area of legal analysis and legal automation. A survey of applications can be found in Meyer and Wieringa [1991].

out whether a well-formed formula of the propositional calculus is valid or not. We will show that the extension is an excellent tool for checking whether a well-formed formula of standard deontic logic is a theorem or not. Furthermore, we discuss some philosophical questions concerning the application of formalisms and the representation of normative rules: *consistency, universality, paradoxes of deontic logic* and *Ought-to-be versus Ought-to-do.*

This chapter is structured along the following lines. In section 2.2 we present informal propositional calculus to introduce the Beth tableau method. Section 2.3 presents the informal deontic logic and the normative tableau method to find out whether a well-formed formula is valid or not. The formal deontic logic is discussed in section 2.4. In this section we present the axiom schemes and the rules of system S_n (that correspond with standard deontic logic) and we give some theorems. In section 2.5 standard deontic logic is presented as a normal modal logic. Some philosophical questions concerning legal knowledge representation are discussed in section 2.6. We finish with some conclusions.

2.2 Informal propositional calculus

2.2.1 Language L_s

A logical system presumes a logical language. This section gives an example of a logical language, i.e. L_s, in which 'L' refers to the language and 's' refers to statement. It is a language in which the logical relations between statements can be analysed. Such a structure is also known as a syntax: in a manner of speaking grammar determines which formulas belong to a language. They are well-formed and belong to language L_s if they arose through the application of the syntactical rules of this language. The set of syntactically well-formed formulas W_s can be determined with the following definitions.

Definition 2.2.1 *The set P is the set of simple formulas (abbreviated as sfs). Its elements are indicated with the letters $p, q, r, s,$ or t with a possible index number where necessary.*

Using the simple formulas and the connectives $\neg$ and $\rightarrow$ the compound formulas (abbreviated as cfs) can be formed.

Definition 2.2.2 *The set W_s of well-formed formulas of L_s is defined as follows:*

1. *Every simple formula (pf) is a well-formed formula (wf).*
2. *If A is a wf, then $\neg A$ is a wf.*
3. *If A and B are wfs, then $A \rightarrow B$ is a wf.*
4. *All that can be formed in a finite number of steps with 1 and 2 is a wf.*

The wf $\neg A$ can be read as 'not A' and the wf $A \rightarrow B$ as 'if A, then B'.

2.2.2 Semantics

Syntactical rules (grammar rules) of a language prescribe how sentences or formulas have to be written. Semantic rules, however, have to do with the relation between the meaning of sentences (or the formulas for those sentences) and the actual (objective) state of affairs. If there is agreement between the two a sentence (formula) is true, if there is no agreement it is false.[3] We attribute the truth value 1 (for true) and value 0 (for false) in these cases to the formulas or sentences. The classic logical analysis only works with these two relations: agreement and non-agreement. In non-classic logic other values are known, such as irresolvable, undecided, undetermined, etc. In this section we shall introduce a classic logical semantics to language L_s.

Definition 2.2.3 *A valuation is a function* v *that attributes value 1 or 0 to any sf.*

The set theory notation of this is: $v : P \rightarrow \{1, 0\}$, in which P is the set of sfs.

The truth value of a wf A will be defined as follows:

Definition 2.2.4 *Let* v *be a valuation. The* truth value *given* v *is a function* $W_v : W_s \rightarrow \{0, 1\}$ *defined by*

1. $W_v(p) = v(p)$, *if* $p \in P$ *(*p *is an* element of P*)*
2. $W_v(\neg A) = 1$ *if and only if (iff)* $W_v(A) = 0$, *if* $A \in W_s$
3. $W_v(A \rightarrow B) = 0$ *iff* $W_v(A) = 1$ *and* $W_v(B) = 0$, *if* $A, B \in W_s$

Note the distinction between *valuation* and *(truth) value*: the value of $p \rightarrow (q \rightarrow r)$ is 1 for the valuation $v(p) = 1$, $v(q) = 0$ and $v(r) = 1$.

Definition 2.2.5 *A valuation* v *is a model of a wf* E *if* $W_v(E) = 1$, *and is a counterexample if* $W_v(E) = 0$.

In our semantics we distinguish three types of wfs: tautologies, contradictions and contingencies:

Definition 2.2.6

1. *A wf* E *is a tautology (is valid) iff every valuation is a model of* E.
2. *A wf* E *is a contradiction iff every valuation is a counter example of* E.
3. *A wf* E *is a contingency iff* E *is not a tautology and not a contradiction.*

How do we find out whether a wf E is a tautology, a contradiction or a contingency? To answer this question we first introduce the following definitions:

Definition 2.2.7 *Two valuations* v *and* v' *for a wf* E *are equal iff* v *and* v' *attribute the same value to all sfs which occur in* E.

Now we can easily derive the following theorem:

Proposition 2.2.8 *The number of different valuations for a wf* E *in which* n *different sfs occur, is equal to* 2^n.

---

[3] Despite its purely mathematical nature, the truth table method has a philosophical origin.

2.2.3 Beth tableau method

Besides the usual truth tables' method, there is another method to decide whether a wf is a tautology, a contradiction or a contingency. This alternative method was developed by the Dutch logician Beth [1971].[4] The Beth tableau method works with a hypothetically assumed value of the wf one must decide upon. On the basis of this value w (either 1 or 0) for a wf E, one can determine whether there are valuations ν for which $W_\nu(E) = w$ applies. If this is the case the valuations that function can be listed.

We would like to note that the set of valuations $\{\nu | W_\nu(E) = w\}$ is easy to determine.[5] If E is a sf to which we attribute the hypothetical value w, the set will consist of the valuations ν for which $\nu(E) = w$ applies (see definition 2.2.4).

If E is a wf and not a sf, then we can determine the valuations the assumed value w of E implies as follows:

- If $E = \neg A$, then the assumption that $W_\nu(E) = 1$ is equal to the assumption that $W_\nu(A) = 0$. The assumption that $W_\nu(E) = 0$ is equal to assumption $W_\nu(A) = 1$.
- If $E = A \rightarrow B$, then the assumption that $W_\nu(E) = 0$ is equal to the assumption that $[W_\nu(A) = 1$ and $W_\nu(B) = 0]$ and the assumption that $W_\nu(E) = 1$ is equal to the assumption that $[W_\nu(A) = 0$ and/or $W_\nu(B) = 1]$.
- If we then depict the value(s) of A (and B) in terms of the values of formulas that A (and B) are composed of and repeat this process, we shall eventually arrive at the assumption that $W_\nu(E) = w$ is given in terms of the values of the sfs of E, and thus in terms of valuations. The finiteness of this procedure stems from the fact that the number of sfs that occur in the wf E is finite (see definition 2.2.2).

For a general survey of the procedure (which is desirable if a large number of connectives occur in the wf E) tableaus are introduced. A tableau is a scheme consisting of a 1-side and a 0-side. On the 1-side the values $W_\nu(\ldots) = 1$ are written down and the 0-side the values $W_\nu(\ldots) = 0$ are. Moreover, the lines are numbered to increase insight into the procedure.
Example The decision procedure for $\wedge \neg p \rightarrow q$ can be depicted as follows in a tableau:

1	line	0
	1	$p \wedge \neg p \rightarrow q$
$p \wedge \neg p$	2	
	3	q
p	4	
$\neg p$	5	
	6	p
$p(4)$	7	$p(6)$

- In line 1 it is assumed that $W_\nu(p \wedge \neg p \rightarrow q) = 0$.

[4] With this method, not all values of a wf are calculated, which is the case for the truth table method.
[5] $\{\nu | W_\nu(E) = w\}$ stands for the set of valuations ν for which $W_\nu(E) = w$ applies.

- Lines 2 and 3 follow from line 1 on the basis of equality:

$$W_\nu(p \wedge \neg p \rightarrow q) = 0 \text{ iff } [W_\nu(p \wedge \neg p) = 1 \text{ and } W_\nu(q) = 0]$$

- Lines 4 and 5 come from line 2 on the basis of:

$$W_\nu(p \wedge \neg p) = 1 \text{ iff } W_\nu(p) = 1 \text{ and } W_\nu(\neg p) = 1]$$

- Through the application of $W_\nu(\neg p) = 1$ iff $W_\nu(p) = 0$ on line 5 we can derive line 6.

We underline the tableau above after line 6 to indicate that the hypothetical assumption is depicted in terms of values of sfs. In line 7 the finding is made that the assumption from line 1 leads to a contradiction: p has to be true (line 4) and false (line 6). If a contradiction is found the tableau is underlined twice to signify it is closed. There is no valuation ν for which $W_\nu(p \wedge \neg p \rightarrow q) = 0$ holds. The wf $p \wedge \neg p \rightarrow q$ therefore does apply.

A tableau is not always closed, as becomes clear in the following example.
Example An example of a tableau that cannot be closed:

1	line	0
	1	$p \rightarrow (\neg q \rightarrow r)$
p	2	
	3	$\neg q \rightarrow r$
$\neg q$	4	
	5	r
	6	q
$p(2)$	7	$r(5),q(6)$

Line 7 gives the valuation ν that is equivalent to the hypothetically assumed value from line 1. Since this tableau does not contain a contradiction, it is not closed so there is no double underlining.

- If a tableau of E starts with the hypothetical assumption $W_\nu(E) = 0$ and the tableau is closed, then E is a tautology.
- If a tableau of E starts with the hypothetical assumption $W_\nu(E) = 0$ and the tableau is not closed, then the valuations found with the values of the sfs are all counterexamples of E. In the tableau above the last line contains all counterexamples for $p \rightarrow (\neg q \rightarrow r)$.
- If a tableau of E starts with the hypothetical assumption $W_\nu(E) = 1$ and the tableau is closed, then E is inconsistent. It appears there is no valuation ν for which the value meets $W_\nu(E) = 1$. According to the tableau below the wf $\neg(p \rightarrow p)$ is inconsistent:

1	line	0
$\neg(p \to p)$	1	
	2	$p \to p$
p	3	
	4	p
$p(3)$	5	$p(4)$

- If a tableau of E starts with the hypothetical assumption $W_\nu(E) = 1$ and the tableau is not closed, then the valuations found with the values of the sfs are all models of E (see definition 2.2.5).

In the equations below both 'and/or' and 'or' occur on the right-hand side of the 'iff':

1. $[W_\nu(A \vee B) = 1]$ iff $[W_\nu(A) = 1$ and/or $W_\nu(B) = 1]$
2. $[W_\nu(A \to B) = 1]$ iff $[W_\nu(A) = 0$ and/or $W_\nu(B) = 1]$
3. $[W_\nu(A \wedge B) = 0]$ iff $[W_\nu(A) = 0$ and/or $W_\nu(B) = 0]$
4. $[W_\nu(A \equiv B) = 1]$ iff $[W_\nu(A) = W_\nu(B) = 1$ or $W_\nu(A) = W_\nu(B) = 0]$
5. $[W_\nu(A \equiv B) = 0]$ iff $[[W_\nu(A) = 1$ and $W_\nu(B) = 0]$ or $[W_\nu(A) = 0$ and $W_\nu(B) = 1]]$

If we make use of these equations in a tableau, the tableau must be split up into two subtableaus each consisting of a 1-side and a 0-side. If we test the consequences of $W_\nu(A \vee B) = 1$, then we have to check what the consequence is of $W_\nu(A) = 1$ in one subtableau and what the consequence of $W_\nu(B) = 1$ in another. All three of the possibilities of $W_\nu(A \vee B) = 1$ can be checked in this fashion. It is easier to understand that the fourth line of the list of formulas above leads to two subtableaus: the one checks what the consequence is if A and B (left in subtableau (1)) are both true for example. The other checks the consequence if A and B (right in subtableau (2)) are both false for example. These two statements are encapsulated in the statement $W_\nu(p \vee \neg p \equiv q) = 1$ in the first line of the tableau below. To avoid confusion about the sides and the subtableaus, the subtableaus are numbered. While numbering care is taken to make sure the 1-side and 0-side of a subtableau have the same number.

Example Take the hypothetical assumption $W_\nu(p \vee \neg p \equiv q) = 1$.

1			line	0		
$p \vee \neg p \equiv q$			1			
(1)		(2)		(1)		(2)
$p \vee \neg p$			2			
q			3			
			4			$p \vee \neg p$
			5			q
(11)	(12)			(11)	(12)	
p			6			
	$\neg p$		7			
			8		p	
			9			p
			10			$\neg p$
		p	11			
$p(6),q(3)$	$q(3)$	$p(11)$	12		$p(8)$	$p(9),q(5)$

The hypothetical assumption $W_\nu(p \vee \neg p \equiv q) = 1$ is equal to $[W_\nu(p \vee \neg p) = W_\nu(q) = 1$ or $W_\nu(p \vee \neg p) = W_\nu(q) = 0]$. Subtableau (1) is a representation of the procedure in which it is decided whether there are valuations ν with $W_\nu(p \vee \neg p) = W_\nu(q) = 1$ and subtableau (2) is a representation of the procedure in which it is decided whether there are valuations ν with $W_\nu(p \vee \neg p) = W_\nu(q) = 0$. This division is justified by the fourth of the five equations listed above. Subtableaus (11) and (12) are necessary because the assumption $W_\nu(p \vee \neg p) = 1$ is equal to $[W_\nu(p) = 1$ and/or $W_\nu(\neg p) = 1]$. In subtableau (2) it appears that the assumption $W_\nu(p \vee \neg p) = W_\nu(q) = 0$ implies a contradiction: $W_\nu(p) = 0$ (in line 9) and $W_\nu(p) = 1$ (in line 11). To indicate the contradiction both sides of the tableau are closed with double underlining. From the tableau above we may conclude there are two valuations ν for which $W_\nu(p \vee \neg p \equiv q) = 1$, namely $\nu_1(p) = 1$, $\nu_1(q) = 1$ and $\nu_2(p) = 0$, $\nu_2(q) = 1$.

Now we can introduce the following ten tableau rules that determine which manipulations are permitted on the one hand and allow us to indicate which equations of values have been used in a tableau (see examples below). The reader should refer to the five equations listed above to answer the question why a tableau is split up into subtableaus.

NR (Negation Right): If an unclosed (sub)tableau occurs on the 0-side of a wf with the shape $\neg A$, the A can be added to the 1-side of the same (sub)tableau. This tableau rule can be depicted with the following scheme:

1	line	0	rule
	1	$\neg A$	
A	2		NR(1)

We shall only give the schematic representation of the following tableau rules:

NL (Negation Left):

1	line	0	rule
$\neg A$	1		
	2	A	NL(1)

IR (Implication Right):

1	line	0	rule
	1	$A \to B$	
A	2		IR(1)
	3	B	

IL (Implication Left):

1		line	0		rule
$A \to B$		1			
(1)	(2)		(1)	(2)	IL(1)
	B	2			
		3	A		

CR (Conjunction Right):

1		line	0		rule
		1	$A \wedge B$		
(1)	(2)		(1)	(2)	CR(1)
		2	A		
		3		B	

CL (Conjunction Left):

1	line	0	rule
$A \wedge B$	1		
A	2		CL(1)
B	3		

DR (Disjunction Right):

1	line	0	rule
	1	$A \vee B$	
	2	A	DR(1)
	3	B	

DL (Disjunction Left):

1		line	0		rule
$A \vee B$		1			
(1)	(2)		(1)	(2)	DL(1)
A		2			
	B	3			

ER (Equivalention Right):

1		line	0		rule
		1	$A \equiv B$		
(1)	(2)		(1)	(2)	ER(1)
A		2			
		3	B		
	B	4			
		5		A	

EL (Equivalention Left):

1		line	0		rule
$A \equiv B$		1			
(1)	(2)		(1)	(2)	EL(1)
A		2			
B		3			
		4		A	
		5		B	

Example Take the following hypothetical assumption:

$$W_\nu((\neg p \vee q) \rightarrow ((q \rightarrow r) \rightarrow (p \rightarrow r))) = 0$$

We can see that every subtableau in table 2.1 is closed: there does not appear to be a valuation ν for which $W_\nu((\neg p \vee q) \rightarrow ((q \rightarrow r) \rightarrow (p \rightarrow r))) = 0$ and therefore the formula is a tautology. Subtableau (2) can already be closed after line 9 according to the guideline that a (sub)tableau can be closed with a double underlining as soon as there is a wf in the (sub)tableau to which both value 1 and 0 can be allocated.[6] There is no way in which a valuation can be found with this tableau.

We conclude the treatment of the Beth-tableau method with some remarks:

- It is wise to consider whether a tableau rule can first be applied that does not double the number of subtableaus during the construction of a tableau (these are tableau rules NR, NL, IR, CL, and DR). This results in the clearest possible tableau.

[6] After line 8 the tableau cannot be closed, because then the application of rule IL(4) would be interrupted as it were.

1			line	0			rule
			1	$(\neg p \vee q) \rightarrow ((q \rightarrow r) \rightarrow (p \rightarrow r))$			
$\neg p \vee q$			2				IR(1)
			3	$(q \rightarrow r) \rightarrow (p \rightarrow r)$			
$q \rightarrow r$			3				IR(3)
			5	$p \rightarrow r$			
p			6				IR(5)
			7	r			
(1)		(2)		(1)		(2)	IL(3)
		r	8				
			9	q			
(11)	(3)			(11)	(3)		DL(2)
$\neg p$			10				
	q		11				
			3	p			NL(10)
$p(6)$	$q(11)$	$r(8)$	13	$p(3)$	$q(9)$	$r(7)$	

Table 2.1: Tableau for $W_\nu((\neg p \vee q) \rightarrow ((q \rightarrow r) \rightarrow (p \rightarrow r))) = 0$

- In an incomplete (sub)tableau a tableau rule is applied to each wf in principle. For rough calculations it is handy to cross out the wfs a rule has been applied to. This makes it easier to see whether a value for a wf has been converted into equivalent values.

- Once a subtableau has been closed, only one sf has to be listed below the double underlining to indicate why a tableau has been closed. If it does not close, all the sfs that occur in the subtableau have to be mentioned at least once.

- The value of a wf may only be crossed out if the value has been replaced by an equivalent value (or combination of values). This is not always possible when the Beth-tableau method is applied to predicate calculus [cf. Beth, 1971].

2.3 Informal deontic logic

2.3.1 Language L_n

To be able to analyse normative systems, we have to extend the statement logical language L_s (from the previous section), so that a new artificial language is created: the normative logical L_n in which 'L' refers to the language and 'n' refers to normative. L_n differs from L_s in two ways:

- The set of basic signs is extended with the capital letter 'O'.

- The rules for the formulation of well-formed formulas (wfs) is altered to allow formulas with the shape '$O(A)$' to exist too. Here 'A' stands for a wf of L_s, which is referred to as the argument of the operator 'O'.

These agreements can be put more formally:

Definition 2.3.1 *If W_s is the set of all wfs of L_s and W_n is the set of all wfs of L_n, then $E \in W_n$ iff*

1. *E is an element of W_s or*
2. *E has the shape $O(A)$, with $A \in W_s$, or*
3. *E has the shape $\neg A$ or $A \rightarrow B$, with $A, B \in W_n$*
4. *All that can be formed in a finite number of steps with 1, 2, and 3 is a wf.*

From this we can deduce that

- $p \wedge q$
- $p \rightarrow O(q)$
- $O(p \rightarrow q)$

are all wfs of L_n. But this does not apply to $O(O(p))$, for $O(p) \notin W_s$. Here it becomes clear that formulas which correspond to 'it is obligatory, that it is obligatory, to do something in such and such a way' do not occur in L_n.

The new language L_n has three kinds of simple formulas. This distinction is of major importance if we are to explain certain techniques, such as the normative tableau method. We distinguish the following:

- The simple formulas of the arguments of normative operators. For this purpose we introduce the abbreviation 's_af'.
- The simple formulas of L_s that are also simple formulas of L_n but are not $s_a$fs. The abbreviation sf will be used for these.
- The normative logical simple formulas with the shape $O(A)$, with $A \in W_s$. For this purpose the abbreviation s_nf will be used.

In accordance with this agreement it holds that

$$p \rightarrow O(q \rightarrow r)$$

p is a sf, $O(q \rightarrow r)$ is a s_nf, and q and r are $s_a$fs. $O(A)$ can be read as 'A is obligatory' or 'It is obligatory that A'. Using the following definitions, we shall introduce the normative logical (deontic) operators F, P, and I.

Definition 2.3.2 $F(A) := O(\neg A)$

'$F(A)$' is read as 'it is forbidden that A'.

Definition 2.3.3 $P(A) := \neg O(\neg A)$

'$P(A)$' is read as 'it is permitted that A'.

Definition 2.3.4 $I(A) := \neg O(A) \wedge \neg O(\neg A)$

'$I(A)$' is read as 'It is indifferent that A'. From definitions 2.3.2 and 2.3.4 it follows that it is indifferent to accomplish that A is neither obligatory nor forbidden. According to definitions 2.3.2 and 2.3.3 it is not forbidden to accomplish that A if it is permitted. The formula $O(A) \rightarrow P(A)$, for example, is read as 'if it is obligatory to accomplish that A, then it is also permitted'. By reading formulas in this way it is easy to interpret them. These insights agree with the traditional interpretation of 'obligation', 'prohibition', and 'permission'. We would like to point out that the operator O was introduced as a *primitive*, with which we can define other primitives. We could just as easily have selected F or P as the primitive operator. The operator I is not suitable as a primitive operator, as $I(p)$ is equivalent to $I(\neg p)$.

2.3.2 Semantics

The semantics (interpretation) of normative logic is not as simple as that of propositional calculus. They bring about three types of connections:

- Formulations for situations (or actions) - arguments of normative logical operators - on the one hand and situations that are actually possible within a certain range (traffic actions for example) on the other.
- Normative statements (normative logical formulas) on the one hand and norms that apply within a given system.
- Normative and non-normative formulations. The latter constitute a condition for the validity of norms. This applies to the example sentence: 'if the light turns red, one must stop'.

In accordance with this a normative logical valuation determines three respective values: that of $s_a$fs, that of $s_n$fs, and that of the sfs. The values for the $s_n$fs, however, are implicitly determined by that of the $s_a$fs. First, we shall discuss the formal rules that determine the values of the formulas of L_n. The normative valuation (abbreviated to n-valuation) is defined as follows:

Definition 2.3.5 *A n-valuation for the wfs of L_n is an ordered pair $\langle v, A \rangle$, in which v is a function, which allocates exactly one value (1 or 0) to each sf (not a $s_a f$), and in which A is a non-empty set of a-valuations. An a-valuation is a function that allocates exactly one value (1 or 0) to each $s_a f$.*

In other words for a specific n-valuation n for the wf $p \rightarrow O(q)$ the value 1 is allocated to the sf p for example by the valuation ν_1 (or 0 by the valuation ν_2) and that a maximum of two values can be allocated to the saf q: the value 1 for example by the a-valuation a_1 and the value 0 by the a-valuation a_2. One of the two a-valuations a_1 and a_2 may be absent; they cannot both be absent according to the definition.

As regards the formulas above, there are two different valuations ν_1 and ν_2 and three different a-valuations and - in combination - six different n-valuations:

1. $\langle \nu_1, \{a_1\} \rangle$
2. $\langle \nu_1, \{a_2\} \rangle$
3. $\langle \nu_1, \{a_1, a_2\} \rangle$
4. $\langle \nu_2, \{a_1\} \rangle$
5. $\langle \nu_2, \{a_2\} \rangle$
6. $\langle \nu_2, \{a_1, a_2\} \rangle$

'$W_n(A) = 1$' is read as 'for the n-valuation n the wf A has a value of 1'. The value (truth value) of a wf $F \in L_n$ now is completely determined by the definitions 2.3.6, 2.3.7 and 2.3.8:

Definition 2.3.6 *Let a be a a-valuation. The* truth value *given a is a function* $W_a : W_s \rightarrow \{0, 1\}$ *defined by*

- $W_a(A) = a(A)$, *if A is a saf*
- $W_a(\neg A) = 1$ *iff* $W_a(A) = 0$, *if* $A \in W_s$
- $W_a(A \rightarrow B) = 0$ *iff* $W_a(A) = 1$ *and* $W_n(B) = 0$, *if* $A, B \in W_s$

Note that it follows from this definition that determining the value for an argument B for an a-valuation is similar to determining the wf B with a valuation from propositional calculus.

Definition 2.3.7 *If F is a snf with the shape* $O(B)$, *then* $W_{\langle \nu, A \rangle}(F) = 1$ *iff for each a-valuation* $a \in A$ *it holds that* $W_a(B) = 1$.

The last definition for the determination of the complete value is:

Definition 2.3.8 *Let n be a n-valuation. The* truth value *given n is a function* $W_n : W_n \rightarrow \{0, 1\}$ *defined by*

- $W_n(F) = \nu(F)$, *if F is a pf* ($F \in P$)
- $W_n(\neg F) = 1$ *iff* $W_n(F) = 0$, *if* $F \in W_n$
- $W_n(F \rightarrow F') = 0$ *iff* $W_n(F) = 1$ *and* $W_n(F') = 0$, *if* $F, F' \in W_n$

According to the definitions 2.3.6 and 2.3.8, the values for the sfs and those of the $s_a$fs are immediately determined by their respective valuations, as it was m.m.[7] in propositional calculus. As we have seen there are three different sets of a-valuations for the argument $p \to O(q)$: $A_1 = \{a_1, a_2\}$, $A_2 = \{a_1\}$ and $A_3 = \{a_2\}$, with a_1, a_2 as functions for which $a_1(q) = 1$ and $a_2(q) = 0$ applies. According to definition 2.3.7, $O(q)$ only has the value 1 for the n-valuation $\langle \nu, A_2 \rangle$.

We distinguish the n-valuation and n-value: the n-value of $p \to (O(q) \to r)$ is 1 for example for a n-valuation $\langle \nu, \{a_1\} \rangle$ for which $\nu(p) = 1, a_1(q) = 0$, and $\nu(r) = 1$ applies.

With the set of terms *model* and *counterexample*, we distinguish the n-valuations where a wf F is true for the n-valuations in which F is not true (cf. definition 2.2.5).

Definition 2.3.9 *A n-valuation n is a model of F if $W_n(F) = 1$, and n is a counter example if $W_n(F) = 0$.*

Similar to definition 2.2.6 we distinguish three types of wfs here too: formulas with models only (tautologies), formulas with counter examples only (contradictions), and the other formulas (contingencies). 'F is a tautology normatively' is abbreviated to $\models_n F$.

One example of a tautology is $O(p \vee \neg p)$, and therefore $\neg O(p \vee \neg p)$ is a contradiction.

Example The formula $F = p \to \neg O(q \to \neg p)$ is a contingency. There are 30 different n-valuations for this formula[8], since there are two different valuations for the sf p:

- $\nu_1(p) = 1$
- $\nu_2(p) = 0$

and four different a-valuations for the $s_a$fs p and q:

- $a_1(p) = 1, a_1(q) = 1$
- $a_2(p) = 1, a_2(q) = 0$
- $a_3(p) = 0, a_3(q) = 1$
- $a_4(p) = 0, a_4(q) = 0$

Note that the first p in the wf F is a sf and that the second p is a s_af. An a-valuation a_1 and a valuation ν need not allocate the same value to p. For the n-valuation $\langle \nu_2, \{a_1\} \rangle$ it holds that $\nu_2(p) = 0$ and $a_1(p) = 1$ for example.

[7]The abbreviation 'm.m.' stands for 'mutatis mutandis' (to change what has to be changed - due to a change in the system).

[8]The number of possible n-valuations for a formula F is $L(\nu, F)(2^{L(a,F)} - 1)$, in which $L(\nu, F)$ is the number of valuations ν for F and $L(a, F)$ is the number of valuations for F. The '-1' is the result of the requirement that the set of a-valuations may not be empty.

n-valuatie n_i	$W_{n_i}(F)$	n-valuatie n_i	$W_{n_i}(F)$
$n_1 = \langle \nu_1, \{a_1\}\rangle$	1	$n_{16} = \langle \nu_2, \{a_1\}\rangle$	1
$n_2 = \langle \nu_1, \{a_2\}\rangle$	0	$n_{17} = \langle \nu_2, \{a_2\}\rangle$	1
$n_3 = \langle \nu_1, \{a_3\}\rangle$	0	$n_{18} = \langle \nu_2, \{a_3\}\rangle$	1
$n_4 = \langle \nu_1, \{a_4\}\rangle$	0	$n_{19} = \langle \nu_2, \{a_4\}\rangle$	1
$n_5 = \langle \nu_1, \{a_1, a_2\}\rangle$	1	$n_{20} = \langle \nu_2, \{a_1, a_2\}\rangle$	1
$n_6 = \langle \nu_1, \{a_1, a_3\}\rangle$	1	$n_{21} = \langle \nu_2, \{a_1, a_3\}\rangle$	1
$n_7 = \langle \nu_1, \{a_1, a_4\}\rangle$	1	$n_{22} = \langle \nu_2, \{a_1, a_4\}\rangle$	1
$n_8 = \langle \nu_1, \{a_2, a_3\}\rangle$	0	$n_{23} = \langle \nu_2, \{a_2, a_3\}\rangle$	1
$n_9 = \langle \nu_1, \{a_2, a_4\}\rangle$	0	$n_{24} = \langle \nu_2, \{a_2, a_4\}\rangle$	1
$n_{10} = \langle \nu_1, \{a_3, a_4\}\rangle$	0	$n_{25} = \langle \nu_2, \{a_3, a_4\}\rangle$	1
$n_{11} = \langle \nu_1, \{a_1, a_2, a_3\}\rangle$	1	$n_{26} = \langle \nu_2, \{a_1, a_2, a_3\}\rangle$	1
$n_{12} = \langle \nu_1, \{a_1, a_2, a_4\}\rangle$	1	$n_{27} = \langle \nu_2, \{a_1, a_2, a_4\}\rangle$	1
$n_{13} = \langle \nu_1, \{a_1, a_3, a_4\}\rangle$	1	$n_{28} = \langle \nu_2, \{a_1, a_3, a_4\}\rangle$	1
$n_{14} = \langle \nu_1, \{a_2, a_3, a_4\}\rangle$	0	$n_{29} = \langle \nu_2, \{a_2, a_3, a_4\}\rangle$	1
$n_{15} = \langle \nu_1, \{a_1, a_2, a_3, a_4\}\rangle$	1	$n_{30} = \langle \nu_2, \{a_1, a_2, a_3, a_4\}\rangle$	1

Table 2.2: All n-valuations for $p \to \neg O(q \to \neg p)$

We can see how we determine the value for $p \to \neg O(q \to \neg p)$ for the n-valuation $\langle \nu_1, \{a_1, a_2\}\rangle$ (n-valuation n_5 in table 2.2. In table 2.2 we have all the n-valuations n_i for the wf including the calculated value $W_{n_i}(F)$.

The normative tableau method is an efficient method to clarify whether a wf F is a tautology or a contradiction or a contingency. In practice the difference between contingency, tautology, and contradiction are relevant for L_n. For a more detailed explanation it is important to keep in mind that norms gain their validity from an authority: the legislator (whoever that may be). What logically determines a normative authority? It determines that $O(q)$ is true, for example, by selecting a valuation in which the formula is true: a set A of a-valuations is chosen with the characteristic that $a_i(q) = 1$ for all $a_i \in A$, so that $O(q)$ are indeed true.

Only contingent (or compositions of) arguments can be made obligatory by an authority in a meaningful way. For if the arguments are tautologies, obligation is superfluous and each situation meets the requirement: obligations with tautologies as arguments do not form any kind of obligation! If they are contradictions then the arguments are not meaningful, since no situation can correspond to the contradictory combination, so that the norm is useless.

2.3.3 Normative tableau method

To decide about validity, we shall adapt the Beth tableaus introduced in the previous section to deontic logic. Considering we shall prove in the following sections that the terms 'validity' and 'provability' are equivalent in the deontic logic presented here, we can also make an implicit decision, using the tableau method, about whether a formula from the language L_n is provable.

A normative tableau meets m.m. the description from the previous section: it is a scheme consisting of a 1-side and a 0-side. On the 1-side the formulas F for which $W_n(F) = 1$ are recorded, and on the 0-side the F for which $W_n(F) = 0$. The tableau rules NR, NL, IR, IL, CR, CL, DR, DL, ER, and EL still are in force. Due to definition 2.3.6 these tableau rules can also be applied to the arguments of the obligation operator. The semantic rules from the previous subsection still require a few alterations, making the decision about the closure or non-closure of a tableau somewhat more complicated. We shall introduce two tableau rules for the normative logical operator O:

OL (O-operator Left):

1	line	0	rule
$O(B)$	1		
$W_a(B)$	2		OL(1)

for each random a-valuation $a \in A$.
So we can apply this rule continuously as long as we can draw new elements (a- valuations) from A.

The OL is based on theorem 2.3.10, which directly follows from definition 2.3.7:

Proposition 2.3.10 *Let n be the n-valuation $\langle v, A\rangle$ and F a snf, say $F = O(B)$. It then holds that if $W_n(F) = 1$, $W_a(B) = 1$ for each a-valuation $a \in A$.*

If it turns out that there is no a-valuation a for which $W_a(B) = 1$ (i.e. if the tableau closed), then there is no n-valuation for which $W_n(O(B)) = 1$, i.e. $O(B)$ is a contradiction.
Example $O(p \wedge \neg p)$

1	line	0	rule
$O(p \wedge \neg p)$	1		
$W_a(p \wedge \neg p)$	2		OL(1)
$a(p)$	3		CL(2)
$W_a(\neg p)$	4		
	5	$a(p)$	NL(4)
$a(p)$(3)		$a(p)$(5)	

The tableau rules from the previous section apply to the argument $p \wedge \neg p$ (of the operator O), since the determination of the truth values of the arguments for a-valuations is equivalent to the determination of these values for the valuations from the previous section. However, we must continue to indicate the a-valuation we selected, because the value for the argument depends on this a-valuation. In this way lines 3 and 4 can be deduced from the application of definition 2.3.6 ($W_a(p \wedge \neg p) = 1$ iff $W_a(p) = 1$ and $W_a(\neg p) = 1$) on line 2. In other words, by applying the tableau rule CL on the argument $p \wedge \neg p$ with the a-valuation a. Instead of $a(p)$ on line 3, we could also have written $W_a(p)$, since it holds that for a saf p that $W_a(p) = a(p)$. The tableau is closed due to the contradiction of lines 3 and 5: no a-valuation a meets $a(p) = 1$ and $a(p) = 0$. From this we can deduce that there is no n-valuation n for which $W_n(O(p \wedge \neg p)) = 1$, so $O(p \wedge \neg p)$ is a contradiction.

From definition 2.3.7 we can immediately deduce the following theorem:

Proposition 2.3.11 *Let n be the n-valuation* $\langle v, A\rangle$ *and F a snf, say* $F = O(B)$. *It then holds that if* $W_n(F) = 0$, *that there is an a-valuation* $a \in A$ *with* $W_a(B) = 0$.

From this we can derive the tableau rule OR:

OR (O-operator Right):

1	line	0	rule
	1	$O(B)$	
	2	$W_a(B)$	OR(1)

if the a-valuation a does not already occur in the tableau.
The hypothesis that there is a n-valuation $n = \langle v, A\rangle$ for which $W_n(O(B)) = 0$, leads to the assumption that there is an a-valuation $a \in A$ for which $W_a(B) = 0$ according to theorem 2.3.11 If such a valuation a does not exist (i.e. the tableau closes) then there is no n-valuation n for which $W_n(O(B)) = 0$, i.e. the snf $O(B)$ is a tautology.
Example $O(p \to q) \to (O(p) \to O(q))$

1		line	0		rule
		1	$O(p \to q) \to (O(p) \to O(q))$		
$O(p \to q)$		2			IR(1)
		3	$O(p) \to O(q)$		
$O(p)$		4			IR(3)
		5	$O(q)$		
		6	$a(q)$		OR(5)
$a(p)$		7			OL(4)
$W_a(p \to q)$		8			OL(2)
(1)	(2)		(1)	(2)	IL(8)
	$a(q)$	9			
		10	$a(p)$		
$a(p)$(7)	$a(q)$(9)		$a(p)$(10)	$a(q)$(6)	

After applying the IR rule twice, the lines 1 and 3 in the tableau can be crossed out. The tableau closes on the grounds that there is no n-valuation that is a counterexample for the wf $O(p \to q) \to (O(p) \to O(q))$, since there is no a-valuation a for which it holds that

- $a(q) = 0$
- $a(p) = 1$

- $W_a(p \to q) = 1$

Subtableau (1) closes because of the contradiction between lines 7 and 10. For there is no a-valuation for which $a(p) = 0$ and $a(p) = 1$. Subtableau (2) closes because of the contradiction between lines 6 and 9. So the wf is a tautology.

Example $(O(p) \to O(q)) \to O(p \to q)$

1		line	0		rule
		1	$(O(p) \to O(q)) \to O(p \to q)$		
$O(p) \to O(q)$		2			IR(1)
		3	$O(p \to q)$		
		4	$W_{a_1}(p \to q)$		OR(3)
$a_1(p)$		5			IR(4)
		6	$a_1(q)$		
(1)	(2)		(1)	(2)	IL(2)
	$O(q)$	7			
		8	$O(p)$		
	$a_1(q)$	9			OL(7)
		10	$a_2(p)$		OR(8)
$a_1(p)(5)$	$a_1(q)(9)$		$a_1(q)(6), a_2(p)(10)$	$a_1(q)(6)$	

Subtableau (2) closes because of the contradiction between lines 6 and 9. Subtableau (1) does not close, as the n-valuation $n = \langle v, \{a_1, a_2\}\rangle$, for which it holds that $a_1(p) = 1$, $a_1(q) = 0$ and $a_2(p) = 0$ is a counterexample. Thus, the wf is a contingency. Line 10 is a result of the application of tableau rule OR on line 8. Here, we see why the condition 'unless the a-valuation does not already occur in the tableau' is included in the tableau rule OR. If we had written $a_1(p)$ instead of $a_2(p)$ in line 10 (which is incorrect!), then the tableau would have closed, from which we would conclude that the formula was a tautology. This is incorrect because the a-valuation a_1 is already linked to the truth of q (see line 6). We can never say with certainty that the a-valuation a_1 also makes p true. For this reason we are obliged to make a choice for an a-valuation that does not occur in the tableau.

In order to know all counterexamples of $(O(p) \to O(q)) \to O(p \to q)$, a complete list of a-valuations is made:

$$a_1(p) = 1,\ a_1(q) = 0$$
$$a_2(p) = 0,\ a_2(q) = 0$$
$$a_3(p) = 1,\ a_3(q) = 1$$
$$a_4(p) = 0,\ a_4(q) = 1$$

The counterexamples of $(O(p) \to O(q)) \to O(p \to q)$ now are all n-valuations $n = \langle v, A\rangle$, in which A has to contain a_1, and a_2 or a_4 as elements.

From the above to examples it follows that $O(p \to q)$ is a stronger statement than $O(p) \to O(q)$.[9]

Considering each n-valuation unequivocally determines a wf in L_n, it is not always necessary to analyse the set A of a-valuations in detail. As soon as the same s$_n$f occurs on both sides of the tableau, it can be closed.

Example $(p \to P(q)) \vee (p \to F(q))$
First we eliminate the operators P and F using definitions 2.3.3 and 2.3.2. As a result we have $(p \to \neg O(\neg q)) \vee (p \to O(\neg q))$.

1	line	0	rule
	1	$(p \to \neg O(\neg q)) \vee (p \to O(\neg q))$	
	2	$p \to \neg O(\neg q)$	DR(1)
	3	$p \to O(\neg q)$	
p	4		IR(2)
	5	$\neg O(\neg q)$	
p	6		IR(3)
	7	$O(\neg q)$	
$O(\neg q)$	8		NR(5)
$O(\neg q)$		$O(\neg q)$	

Example $O(p \vee q) \to (O(p) \vee O(q))$
Consider the tableau of table 2.3. The counterexamples are all n-valuations $n = \langle v, A \rangle$, for which the a-valuation a_1 with $a_1(p) = 0$ and $a_1(q) = 1$ and the a-valuation a_2 with $a_2(p) = 1$ and $a_2(q) = 0$ both are elements of A.

We conclude our treatment of the normative tableau method with two remarks:

- If we take the hypothetical assumption $W_n(E) = w$ (where w has the value 0 or 1) for a tableau, we find all n-valuations with the extended Beth-tableau method in terms of values of sfs and s$_a$fs, for which $W_n(E) = w$. The finiteness of this procedure follows from the fact that the number of sfs and s$_a$fs in a wf E is finite (see definition 2.3.1).

- In contrast with the tableau method for the propositional calculus, the order of the application of the tableau rules is of importance in avoiding clumsy constructions. Let us illustrate this with an example:

[9] A statement A is *stronger* than statement B if and only if $A \to B$ is a tautology and $B \to A$ is not a tautology.

1			line	0			rule
			1	$O(p \vee q) \to (O(p) \vee O(q))$			
$O(p \vee q)$			2				IR(1)
			3	$O(p) \vee O(q)$			
			4	$O(p)$			DR(3)
			5	$O(q)$			
			6	$a_1(p)$			OR(4)
			7	$a_2(q)$			OR(5)
$W_{a_1}(p \vee q)$			8				OL(2)
(1)	(2)			(1)	(2)		DL(8)
$a_1(p)$			9				
	$a_1(q)$		10				
	$W_{a_2}(p \vee q)$		11				OL(2)
	(21)	(22)			(21)	(22)	DL(11)
	$a_2(p)$		12				
		$a_2(q)$	13				
$a_1(p)(9)$	$a_1(q)(10)$,$a_2(p)(12)$	$a_2(q)(13)$		$a_1(p)(6)$	$a_1(p)(6)$,$a_2(q)(7)$	$a_2(q)(7)$	

Table 2.3: Tableau for $W_\nu(O(p \vee q) \to (O(p) \vee O(q))) = 0$

1	line	0	rule
	1	$O(p) \to O(p \vee q)$	
$O(p)$	2		IR(1)
	3	$O(p \vee q)$	
$a_1(p)$	4		OL(2)
	5	$W_{a_2}(p \vee q)$	OL(3)
	6	$a_2(p)$	DR(5)
	7	$a_2(q)$	
$a_2(p)$	8		OL(2)

In this tableau the tableau rule OL was used superfluously on one occasion. We could have avoided this by first applying OR and then OL, as we have done in the tableau below:

1	line	0	rule
	1	$O(p) \to O(p \vee q)$	
$O(p)$	2		IR(1)
	3	$O(p \vee q)$	
	4	$W_{a_1}(p \vee q)$	OL(3)
	5	$a_1(p)$	DR(4)
	6	$a_1(q)$	
$a_1(p)$	7		OL(2)
$a_1(p)(7)$		$a_1(p)(5)$	

The clumsy procedures in the tableaus can be avoided by applying the following two guidelines:

- In the case we have to make a choice between several rules, the rules NR, NL, IR, IL, CR, CL, DR, and DL applied to constituent parts of the wf F in line 1 have priority before NR, NL, IR, IL, CR, CL, DR, and DL applied to the arguments of the obligation operator, and OR and OL.
- OR has priority over OL.

2.4 Formal deontic logic

In this section we shall make a start with formal logic. The axiomatic deductive method will be presented. In this method hypotheses are deduced from a limited number of axioms. Axioms are hypotheses that are held to be fruitful points of departure. The transition from the axioms to other hypotheses can be achieved by means of rules. The deduced hypotheses themselves then serve as the points of departure for new hypotheses. The importance of this axiomatic deductive method was recognised early on in history. To a large extent its application guarantees a scientific approach along the lines a thought that has been popular since the times of Aristotle (284-322 BC) and Euclid (around 300 BC). Ancient

Greek insights into this method may have been primitive compared to present insights, but the change of perspective has not undermined the importance of the method. On the contrary, most mathematicians and physicists and other scientists demand their discipline be axiomatically deductively systematised to guarantee an exact theory.

Axiom If a mathematician wishes to prove a hypothesis, he makes use of hypotheses he or a colleague has already proved. Those hypotheses in their turn were proved using other hypotheses, etc. This process cannot be repeated infinitely, unless circular logic was allowable: this would means that hypothesis H_1 can be proved by making use of hypothesis H_2, which itself was proved by making use of hypothesis H_1 directly or indirectly. A *circular proof* conceals the fact that H_1 and H_2 have no foundation. That is why this proof is viewed as one of the most serious mistakes a scientist can make. If the circular proof is rejected and the infinite process is essentially impossible, there is only road left to us: we have to accept some unproved first principles. Aristotle already reached this conclusion and Euclid defined the term axiom with this content.[10]

System When we apply the axiomatic deductive method on physics for example, all physical knowledge about a particular domain (e.g. mechanical phenomena) have to be reduced to a few elementary principles (axioms). It has to be possible for all other insights to be deduced directly or indirectly from these axioms. As a result there is a hierarchical system: the axioms and the hypotheses derived from them. The physical nature of an axiomatic system is guaranteed by adding some physical hypotheses to the purely mathematical system. This addition or extension is not the subject of this section. An axiomatic system in the sense we mean here is a set of wfs. The wfs consist of elements that are axioms or elements that can be found by applying expressly formulated rules on existing hypotheses. In the definitions 2.4.2 and 2.4.4 the most well-known (and in principle the only) rule of the propositional logic is formulated: the modus ponens. In the subsections that follow we shall become acquainted with another rule.

Truth of axioms We already stated that we assume that axioms can be proved. As far as this is concerned modern insights differ considerably from the Ancient Greeks. The assumption of unproved principles seemed a risky business to them. Therefore, Aristotle and Euclid (for physics and mathematics respectively) demanded that first principles had to be self-evident: anyone with knowledge of the subject had to accept them as true. This had important consequences for the development of physics and mathematics: the scientists did not dare move away from matters that were obviously clear and true, unless deduction justified it.[11]

---

[10]The term axiom is of a more recent date [cf. Freundenthal, 1971].

[11]One important development was the introduction of the mathematical symbols through Descartes' work (1596-1650). This allowed Newton (1642-1727) and Leibniz (1646-1716) to develop differential and integral calculus. The use of artificial languages allowed formal statement calculus to be applied (by Newton among others). However, Descartes did not discard the notion we already presented. Descartes prescribes a course of action

The fifth axiom of Euclid has always been a point of contention (the parallel axiom)[12]: on the one hand the truth of it has never been doubted and on the other the immediate evidence for it has never been defended. This has led to numerous attempts to prove it via other axioms.[13] Only in the nineteenth and twentieth century did it become clear that the fifth axiom is independent of Euclid's other axioms, i.e. neither axiom 5 nor its negation can be deduced from the other axioms.[14]

The result of this discovery was the insight that alternative systems of geometry could be developed. The ability to develop systems and to analyse them independent of the fact that the axioms can be accepted as true statements is connected to this too. Logic only profited from these insights in this century. In the twenties and thirties different kinds of logical systems were designed. In most systems (e.g. the classic system) principle $(A \vee \neg A)$ can be proved - in other words, is a theorem -, in other systems however (the intuitional system) it cannot. It also proved possible to separate the truth of axioms from other problems connected to the development of a logical system.

Independence of axioms An axiom unnecessary for a system (because it would be provable even if it were to be introduced as immediately provable) depends on the other axioms. As we saw earlier independence played an important role in the history of geometry: people tried to make the fifth axiom dependent on the others. The pursuit of the least number of mutually independent axioms was popular among the Greeks, since more axioms led to greater uncertainty. Certainty was required about every axiom. We shall not discuss the independence of axioms, or to be more precise of the axiom schemes.[15]

Consistency of systems A system can be rejected as soon as a contradiction can be deduced from it. Under the circumstances that one is not capable of deducing a contradiction, it cannot be concluded that the system in question is consistent. We shall see that all the systems we discuss are consistent.[16]

---

in which all scientific knowledge should be based on clearly true and precise insights. His first methodological principle in his *Discours de la Methode* [1637] is: nothing can be true that is not so evidently, so clearly, and so precisely true that I could hardly doubt it.

[12]This axiom from Euclidian geometry is: given a line l and a point p that is not on that line, there is a unique line through p that has no points in common with l.

[13]The most famous attempt is that of the Jesuit priest Gerolamo Saccheri (1667-1733). In his logic he based himself on the rejection of the axiom. This rejection led to various impossible hypotheses that were inconsistent with the traditional views in geometry. Later the hypotheses proved to be properly founded in non-euclidian geometry.

[14]To an important extent this development was a result of the works of Gauß, Lobatsjevski, Riemann, and finally Einstein.

[15]Nowadays the notion of 'independence' has less value. Proof of independence has not been found for many well-known systems.

[16]The consistency requirement has hardly been doubted throughout history. Only the representatives of the Greek school of Elea (Parmenides, Zeno) and Hegelians introduced various terms for the truth concerning matters of informal logic and thus went against the notion of the consistency requirement. In a time in which informal and formal statement calculus and the various levels of languages could not be distinguished, this led to a great deal of confusion.

Soundness and completeness of systems We we can deal with questions concerning the interpretation of a system independently of the problems related to the development of that system. In practice, however, this division cannot be maintained permanently. Once a system has been developed, one can ask very precise questions about its applicability. While applying the axiomatic deductive method people try to deduce all accepted insights from a certain field from the axioms or basic laws. We call a system *sound* if every theorem is a tautology, and *complete* if every tautology is a theorem.

2.4.1 System S_n

The logic in this section first deals with the question what requirements a wf from the language L_n has to meet to be provable in S_n. To prove or derive normative logical formulas, we shall make an extension to propositional calculus. This gives rise to system S_n, which is equivalent to the standard system of deontic logic, which had an enormous influence on later work on deontic logic. This system was the foundation for many other systems, which all can be viewed as extensions of S_n.

First we give the axioms of propositional calculus, i.e. system S_L. There are an infinite number of axioms, so we cannot list them all. However, we can specify all these axioms by three *axiom schemes.*

Definition 2.4.1 *The axiom schemes of* S_L *are:*
AS_1: $A \to (B \to A)$
AS_2: $(A \to (B \to C)) \to ((A \to B) \to (A \to C))$
AS_3: $(\neg A \to \neg B) \to (B \to A)$

The deductive nature of S_L follows from the following definition:

Definition 2.4.2 *A proof in* S_L *is a sequence of wfs* $A_1, \ldots, A_n$ *such that for each* i $(1 \leq i \leq n)$ *either* A_i *is an axiom of* L *or* A_i *follows from two members of the sequence, say* A_j *and* A_k $(j < i, k < i)$ *as a direct consequence using the rule of deduction MP. Such a proof will be referred to as a proof of* A_n *in* S_L*, and* A_n *is said to be a theorem of* S_L ($\vdash_{S_L} A_n$).

In S_L there is only one rule of deduction: *modus ponens* (abbreviated by MP). The rule states that B is a direct consequence from A and $A \to B$, if A and B are wfs of S_L. We denote this rule as follows:

$$\frac{A, A \to B}{B}$$

For every wf A of S_L it holds that A is a theorem of S_L if and only if it is a tautology [cf. Hamilton, 1988]. So, S_L is *sound* (every theorem of S_L is a tautology) and *complete* (every tautology is a theorem). If A can be deduced from a set Γ of wfs, we say Γ yields A and write $\Gamma \vdash_{S_L} A$ or $A \in Cn(\Gamma)$, with $Cn(\Gamma)$ the transitive closure of Γ with respect to the derivation.

System S_n is an extension of S_L. The axioms of S_L and the MP rule remain in force. Besides that, we introduce two axiom schemes and the O-necessitation rule.

Definition 2.4.3 *The axiom schemes of S_n are:*
AS_1: $A \rightarrow (B \rightarrow A)$
AS_2: $(A \rightarrow (B \rightarrow C)) \rightarrow ((A \rightarrow B) \rightarrow (A \rightarrow C))$
AS_3: $(\neg A \rightarrow \neg B) \rightarrow (B \rightarrow A)$
AS_{n_1}: $O(A \rightarrow B) \rightarrow (O(A) \rightarrow O(B))$
AS_{n_2}: $O(A) \rightarrow \neg O(\neg A)$

The O-necessitation rule is represented as

$$\text{if } \vdash_{S_L} A \text{ then } \vdash_{S_n} O(A)$$

The first three axioms will usually be noted as 'all tautologies of propositional calculus'.
The deductive nature of S_n follows from the following definition:

Definition 2.4.4 *A proof in S_n is a sequence of wfs $A_1, \ldots, A_n$ such that for each i ($1 \leq i \leq n$) either A_i is an axiom of L or A_i follows from two members of the sequence, say A_j and A_k ($j < i, k < i$) as a direct consequence using the rule of deduction MP, or A_i follows from a members of the sequence, say A_j ($j < i$) as a direct consequence using the O-necessitation rule. Such a proof will be referred to as a proof of A_n in S_n, and A_n is said to be a theorem of S_n.*

It can be proved that S_n is also complete and sound [see Kutschera, 1973]. Thus, if we want to check whether a wf A is a theorem of S_n, we can do this with the normative tableau method: If it turns out that A is a tautology, then A is a theorem; if A is a contingency or a contradiction, then A is not a theorem. For readers not familiar with the axiomatic deductive method of S_L and S_n, the (normative) tableau method is a very workable tool to check whether a wf A is a theorem or not.

Some theorems of S_n, which can easily be proved with the help of the normative tableau method:

1. $F(p \vee q) \equiv F(p) \wedge F(q)$
2. $F(p) \vee F(q) \rightarrow F(p \wedge q)$
3. $O(p) \vee O(q) \rightarrow O(p \vee q)$
4. $O(p \wedge q) \rightarrow O(p) \wedge O(q)$
5. $O(p) \wedge O(q) \rightarrow O(p \wedge q)$
6. $P(p \vee q) \equiv P(p) \vee P(q)$
7. $P(p \wedge q) \rightarrow P(p) \wedge P(q)$
8. $P(p) \equiv \neg F(p)$
9. $P(p) \equiv \neg O(\neg p)$

10. $F(p) \rightarrow F(p \wedge q)$

11. $O(p \wedge q) \rightarrow O(p)$

12. $O(p) \rightarrow O(p \vee q)$

13. $O(p \vee q) \wedge F(p) \rightarrow O(q)$

14. $F(p \wedge q) \wedge O(p) \equiv F(q) \wedge O(p)$

15. $F(p \vee (\neg p \wedge q)) \equiv F(p) \wedge F(q)$

16. $O(p \vee p) \equiv O(p)$

17. $O(p \vee \neg p)$

18. $F(p \wedge \neg p)$

19. $O(p) \rightarrow P(p)$

20. $I(p) \rightarrow P(p)$

21. $\neg O(p \wedge \neg p)$

22. $\neg(O(p) \wedge O(\neg p))$

23. $\neg p \rightarrow (p \rightarrow O(q))$

Among these theorems of the system, we find very familiar ones, both evident truths and more controversial assertions. In subsection 2.6.3 we discuss some of the controversial assertions (paradoxes).

2.5 Standard deontic logic

Standard deontic logic SDL is usually presented as a normal modal logic[17] consisting of the same axioms and rules as S_n. We will use the following alternative (equivalent) characterisation of S_n for SDL [cf. Chellas, 1980]:

(ROM) $\quad \frac{A \rightarrow B}{O(A) \rightarrow O(B)}$

(MP) $\quad \frac{A,\, A \rightarrow B}{B}$

together with the following axiom schemes:[18]

[17] By standard deontic logic, a modal (Kripke-style) version of the now so-called 'Old System' of Von Wright [1951], we mean the smallest normal KD-system of modal logic [cf. Chellas, 1980].

[18] Axiom ON was rejected by Von Wright, since he developed the *principle of deontic contingency*: 'A tautologous act is not necessarily obligatory, and a contradictory act is not necessarily forbidden' [Wright, 1951, p. 11]. We have to commit ourselves to this axiom, since otherwise we cannot view deontic logic as a branch of Kripke-style normal modal logic.

(PL)	All tautologies of the propositional calculus
(OC)	$(O(A) \wedge O(B)) \rightarrow O(A \wedge B)$
(ON)	$O(A \vee \neg A)$
(OD)	$\neg O(A \wedge \neg A)$

The theorems 5, 17 and 21 of S_n mentioned above correspond with axiom schemes (OC), (ON) and (OD), respectively, of SDL.

As with other modal logics, the semantics of SDL is based on the notion of possible worlds and can be given using the following model structure $M = (W, R, \nu)$ consisting of three elements:

1. The set of possible worlds $W = \{w_1, w_2, \ldots\}$.

2. The accessibility function R on W relates a world to a set of possible worlds: $R : W \rightarrow 2^W$.

3. A valuation function π, which assigns the values 'true' or 'false' to each proposition at each world in W.

The intuition behind the function R is that it yields the *deontically ideal worlds* (the worlds in which all norms are fulfilled) relative to a given world. The truth conditions for O and P can now formally be given as follows:

$$M, w \models O(p) \text{ iff } R(w) \subseteq [\![p]\!] \quad (2.1)$$

and

$$M, w \models P(p) \text{ iff } R(w) \cap [\![p]\!] \neq \emptyset, \quad (2.2)$$

with the function $[\![\,]\!] \in W_f \rightarrow 2^W$ and W_f the set of well-formed formulas of SDL.[19] Thus, $O(p)$ holds in w if and only if p is true in all ideal worlds with respect to w, and $P(p)$ holds in w if and only if there is at least one ideal world with respect to w in which p is true.

The following constraint (which gives schema (OD))

$$R(w) \neq \emptyset \text{ for all } w \in W \quad (2.3)$$

- which means that R is *serial* in w - will be added to validate the schema (OD). One can prove that the system SDL is sound and complete with respect to the model structure $M = (W, R, \nu)$ with R serial.

[19] $[\![p]\!] = \{w | \pi(w, p) = true\}$. It is easy to see that the following properties hold: $[\![p \vee q]\!] = [\![p]\!] \cup [\![q]\!]$, $[\![p \wedge q]\!] = [\![p]\!] \cap [\![q]\!]$ and $[\![\neg p]\!] = \overline{[\![p]\!]}$.

2.6 Applications of the logic of norms: normative realities

In the above we extended the propositional calculus with operators (O, F, P and I), axioms, and with a rule to obtain SDL. The aim of this extension is to have the ability to describe normative realities. Some example of normative realities are: a system of traffic regulations in a certain country, or the norms set for laws, such as the penal code. It may also be possible to analyse certain social norms of a group (e.g. university staff and students). In addition, matters of ethics can be dealt with, as was done by Kutschera [1982].

Applications in the these two fields (social norms and ethics) run into some sticky problems. The formal analysis becomes harder the poorer the interpretation of the formulations is. Problems related to the possible application of formal languages have been analysed for some decades now in the field philosophical logic, also known as logic theory or analytical language philosophy. The expression *philosophy* is justified here, since the problems have no clear-cut solutions.[20] Though it is true that they are related to formal languages, the interpretation and use is not exact in the sense that mechanical rules or formulas lead to the answer sought, as is the case with a proof or deduction. The interpretation and use of formal languages requires an innate sense of the relations between formal languages and languages of content. The determination of the relations between formulations and occurrences of content often are philosophical too. The jurisprudence as a source of inspiration for the determination of agreements between normative formulations and concrete actions is not based on exact guidelines from the legislator, but on professional estimation as we shall see later on.

Philosophical questions have the negative tendency to scare people off. Perhaps this is rightly so, since the solutions are not of a nature that allows us to say precisely whether something is good or bad. An application cannot strictly be called a mistake; determining a mistake presupposes one is able to observe a deviation from a valid rule. When applying formal systems one has to leave the field of exact rules. A system or one of its applications therefore is either felt to be adequate or less adequate.

The philosophical questions here concern the application of formalisms that are intrinsic to practical science. That is why we will not avoid them. Successively, we shall deal with (but not at length) the following subjects:

- Consistency
- Universality
- The paradoxes of SDL
- Ought-to-do versus Ought-to-be

[20] Physicists face similar problems while choosing a formal system for a theory. These choices should not be overrated. Usually one is forced to adapt to the tradition that largely determines the use of formalisms. Only geniuses in physics have been afforded a large measure of freedom.

2.6.1 Logical and normative consistency

The question whether a legal system (such as the traffic regulations) should be consistent is a valid one, since absurd systems cannot prescribe anything with any force. However, there are terminological problems here. We shall first try to avoid these by making certain agreements. The word 'system' has more than one meaning in this context. It is used in expressions like the 'traffic system' and 'logical system'; we shall avoid the first use here. As regards norms, we shall restrict ourselves to sets of norms, classes of norms, systems of norms, and normative order. The word 'system' will thus retain the logical meaning that was introduced. Furthermore, we distinguish three types of consistency:

- The consistency of the logical system that is used for the analysis of norm system. A system S is consistent if and only if there is no wf A such that A is a theorem and $\neg A$ is a theorem. The system SDL is consistent [cf. Sarlemijn and Royakkers, 1997].
- The logical consistency (L-consistency) of normative systems.
- The normative consistency (N-consistency) of normative systems.

In contrast with the first, the L-consistency and N-consistency depend on the characteristics of concretely given sets of norms. The two latter consistencies would be independent of each other, if it were possible to prescribe incompatible actions. We shall see, however, that this is out of the question. The L-consistency is related to the reasoning with which norms are presented, while the N-consistency is primarily connected to the content of the norms. The distinction is subtle and it will become clear that both terms are equivalent for the system SDL. Let us put it differently: it will become clear that it is out of the question that incompatible actions can be prescribed in a logically consistent fashion. To outline our reasoning more clearly, we shall now introduce the definitions for the terms mentioned.[21]
Use will be made of the following two abbreviations:

V_n: a set wfs from the language L_n.

$Cn(V_n)$: the set of formulas that can be derived from those of V_n.

Note that $V_n \in Cn(V_n)$.[22]

Definition 2.6.1 *V_n is L-consistent iff there is no wf $F \in W_n$ such that $F \in Cn(V_n)$ and $\neg F \in Cn(V_n)$.*

In the next chapters, we use 'consistent' instead of 'L-consistent'.

Definition 2.6.2 *V_n is N-consistent iff there is no wf $A \in W$ such that $O(A) \in Cn(V_n)$ and $O(\neg A) \in Cn(V_n)$.*

---

[21] For convenience, we only consider unconditional norms. For a discussion of the problems of the formalisation of the conditional norms, we refer to [Alchourrón, 1986].

[22] Let N be a set of norms. Then, we define $Cn(N)$ as the set of norms that includes N and all its consequences. Set N is called the basis of system $Cn(N)$. Thus, $Cn(N)$ is the transitive closure of N with respect to the derivation ($\vdash$).

The terms are equivalent [cf. Sarlemijn and Royakkers, 1997]:

Proposition 2.6.3 *For each V_n it holds that V_n is L-consistent iff V_n is N-consistent.*

The following theorem can easily be proved.

Proposition 2.6.4 *Assume that $O(A) \in Cn(V_n)$ or $F(A) \in Cn(V_n)$ or $I(A) \in Cn(V_n)$. If V_n is N-consistent (or L-consistent), then by exclusion it holds that*

- *either $O(A) \in Cn(V_n)$*
- *or $F(A) \in Cn(V_n)$*
- *or $I(A) \in Cn(V_n)$.*

This theorem stems directly from the fact that $O(A) \wedge F(A)$ and $O(A) \wedge I(A)$ and $F(A) \wedge I(A)$ result in N-inconsistency (L-inconsistency). The exclusion does not hold for $P(A)$, since it follows that $\vdash I(A) \rightarrow P(A)$ and that $\vdash O(A) \rightarrow P(A)$.

In many contemporary deontic logics the axiom (OD) is not accepted. From this it follows that the terms N-consistency and L-consistency are not equivalent in those logics. However, it does hold that N-consistency implies L-consistency. One point of criticism is that the statement $O(p) \rightarrow P(p)$ need not apply to a certain order of law. This may depend, for example, on whether a distinction is made in a normative system between the weak and strong permission [cf. Wild, 1979]. The first is the absence of a prohibition (absence of law) and the second is an explicit permission given by a body of authority (see chapter 7). Thus $O(p) \rightarrow P(p)$ holds for the strong permission but not for the weak permission. Another - more important - point of criticism is that the axiom excludes the logical possibility to express conflicting norms, such as $O(p) \wedge F(p)$ [cf. Meyer, Dignum, and Wieringa, 1994]. Though conflicting norms generally are felt to be undesirable, they do occur regularly in law. If authority a has enacted norm $O(p)$ and authority b norm $O(\neg p)$, we say that the two norms are conflicting, since p is obligatory and at the same time forbidden. This is the 'classical' notion of *normative inconsistency*. Two authorities promulgating (enacting) two contradictory or conflicting norms is a frequently occurring phenomenon, at least in certain areas like law [see Alchourrón and Bulygin, 1981]. The conflict arises when the norms become members of the same normative system, not if they belong to different systems. Such a system loses its meaning in a logical sense in the case of inconsistency: everything can be deduced and, in particular, all obligations, permissions, etc., are deducible (*ex falso sequitur quodlibet*). So, the main objection to this axiom (OD) is that it states that there is no conflict of duties, which is clearly not in line with situations in daily life.[23]

[23] In spite of this objection, some authors defend this schema for a deontic system. Bailhache [1981, 1991] defends this schema, so that he obtains a complete coherent deontic system, without conflicting obligations, and Horty [1994] defends this schema with the argument that the deontic systems are too weak without this schema (OD).

Alchourrón [1969] argues that schema (OD) is valid for a logic of norms (deontic logic) and invalid for a logic of normative propositions (normative logic), which is an extension of deontic logic. The elementary propositions of normative logic are propositions to the effect that some agent has issued a norm. The main difference between these two logics is that (OD) is a schema of deontic logic and not a schema of normative logic:

> This is so because normative systems may be inconsistent. (...) But it is interesting to observe that the definition of consistency has a similar structure as DL4 $[\neg(O(p) \wedge O(\neg p))]$: the structural similarity explains perhaps the basic intuitions that lie behind DL4. But whereas DL4 excludes the possibility of $O(p)$ and $O(\neg p)$ (both cannot be true), the definition only states the conditions under which the system is consistent without excluding the possibility of inconsistent systems. [cf. Alchourrón and Bulygin, 1984]

So, with respect to normative logic the incompatibility of obligation and prohibition does not hold. Prakken [1996] gives a pragmatic view on the effect of these normative inconsistencies:

> That in one particular situation a rule is dropped to maintain consistency does not mean that it has no binding force at all, since in other, unproblematic situations it can still be applied. I see no compelling reasons why the binding force of a deontic rule should be equated with its application to every single occasion.

According to Brouwer, who has been involved with the *coherence of law* in many publications[24], the requirement of consistency is a necessary condition for coherent law.[25] In Brouwer's view it therefore is impossible to speak of coherence without assuming that there are logical relations between (the contents) of norms, since consistency presumes logic. Brouwer does not tell us unequivocally whether the legal consequences of a set of norms can lead to inconsistencies or not. On the one hand, he states that even in relatively simple systems one cannot exclude the possibility of inconsistencies from occurring. On the other, none of these theoretical inconsistencies will ever occur in practice, since incompatible norms are made (or seem to be) compatible via certain tricks, such as methods of interpretation.

The Argentines Carlos E. Alchourrón and Eugenio Bulygin became famous with their fundamental work Normative Systems, in which they developed a new logical system for normative-logical analyses [Alchourrón and Bulygin, 1971]. In later publications they concentrated on problems of application. Thus, they came upon the fact that legal systems had severe drawbacks concerning accuracy. Their displeasure with the lack of accuracy of lawyers rings throughout their view regarding this matter [Alchourrón and Bulygin, 1977].

> Gerade im Bereich des positiven Rechts sind die Normenkonflikte keine Seltenheit; die Logik kann diese Tatsache micht Leugnen. (...) gerade das, was gelöst werden muß, d.h. der Normenkonflikt, ist der interessante Sachverhalt, der logisch charakterisiert werden muß. Es scheint zweckmäßiger zu sein, die Möglichkeit der gleichzeitigen Geltung logisch unverträglicher Normen (...) zu akzeptieren. (...)

[24] See, for example, Brouwer [1990, 1992].

[25] This is in contrast to MacCormick [1984], who denies the connection between consistency and coherence.

> Was die Lösung der Normenkonflikte betrifft (...) Die von den Juristen gebrauchten Regeln (lex posterior, lex superior, lex specialis) sind praktisch nützliche Hilfsmittel, aber logisch nicht gültig.

2.6.2 The logical possibility of universal norm systems

The question whether universality is possible can be rephrased as follows: is it possible that all situations (actions) that belong to a particular range (e.g. situations carried out in traffic) are normalised, i.e. can they be obligatory, prohibited, or left explicitly indifferent? Naturally, it is a requirement that the sets of norms in question be consistent. If there is inconsistency, the question of universality loses its sense. To answer this question, certain terms have to be introduced. It should be kept in mind that universality is related to three sets:

- The set V_n of norms through which situations (actions) are obligatory, prohibited, or left indifferent.
- The set H of situations that belong to the range intended (e.g. traffic)
- The set R of situations that are actually normalised (by the elements of V_n).

V_n is (normatively) universal if a norm applies for each action $A \in H$, such that $R = H$. Usually, R only is a subset of H: $R \subsetneq H$. Let us put it more precisely by means of a definition and a theorem that follows from it (see also theorem 2.6.4).

Definition 2.6.5 *V_n is universal if it (exclusively) holds that for each $A \in H$:*

- *either $O(A) \in Cn(V_n)$*
- *or $F(A) \in Cn(V_n)$*
- *or $I(A) \in Cn(V_n)$*

Proposition 2.6.6 *If V_n is universal, then V_n is N-consistent (L-consistent).*

We wish to prove that each N-consistent V_n can be extended to a universal. But because we logically work at a simpler level with the term 'maximality' rather than with the term 'universality', we replace the latter by the former. To this purpose we have the following definition:

Definition 2.6.7 *V_n is maximal if for every $A \in H$ it holds that either $O(A) \in Cn(V_n)$ or $\neg O(A) \in Cn(V_n)$.*

It should be noted that the statement an obligation regarding $A \in H$ is lacking' does not have the same meaning as 'A is not obligatory' in logic (legally matters are different). From the following theorem it appears that 'either $O(A)$ or $\neg O(A)$' is equivalent to 'either $O(A)$ or $F(A)$ or $I(A)$ [cf. Sarlemijn and Royakkers, 1997].

Proposition 2.6.8 *V_n is maximal iff V_n is universal.*

From this theorem it follows that we can construct a universal set if the procedure for a maximal set has no problems. To this purpose we describe 'extension to a given consistent set V_n to a maximal V_n^*' according to a specific procedure. We base ourselves on a consistent V_n and assert that $V_n = V_n^0$. Besides that we assume a countdown of all wfs A of SDL for which it holds that $A \notin V_n$, say $A_1, A_2, \ldots$. We now introduce a relation between the normative sets $V_n^1, V_n^2, V_n^3, \ldots$ and the countdown $A_1, A_2, A_3, \ldots$, for which it holds that:

- $V_n = V_n^0$
- $V_n^{k+1} = \left\{ \begin{array}{ll} V_n^k \cup \{A_{k+1}\} & \text{if } \neg A_{k+1} \notin Cn(V_n^k) \\ V_n^k & \text{if } \neg A_{k+1} \in Cn(V_n^k) \end{array} \right\}.$

We now assume that

$$V_n^* = V_n^0 \cup V_n^1 \cup V_n^2 \cup V_n^3 \ldots$$

With the help of this procedure we can easily prove the following theorem:

Proposition 2.6.9 *Each consistent set V_n can be extended to a maximal set V_n^*.*

From the theorems 2.6.8 and 2.6.9 we can deduce that every V_n can be extended to a universal. However, it is obvious from the above that the option is purely logical and that it is problematic in practice (e.g. the legislator who wishes to make the traffic regulations universal). V_n^* is not determined unequivocally concerning its content. This is reflected in the nature of the construction process of V_n^*. If we assume that $A_4 = O(p)$ and $A_5 = \neg O(p)$, it is possible that $O(p) \in Cn(V_n^*)$, while this was not the case for $A_4 = \neg O(p)$. On the basis of purely logical considerations, it is not possible to enforce a particular order on the countdown. We shall come back to these problems of interpretation in chapters 6 and 7.

2.6.3 Paradoxes and semantics of the deontic operators

Logicians with a lively interest in philosophy sometimes have a penchant for paradoxes. Deontic logic has been bothered by a number of paradoxes during its entire development. These paradoxes are logical expressions that have validity in a deontic system, such as SDL, but are counter-intuitive in a common sense context, or they are logical expressions that are inconsistent. The relative simplicity of the paradoxes is surprising. We shall discuss some of the most well-known paradoxes from deontic literature here, since their treatment helps us to gain intuitive insight into the relations between formal systems and systems of content. So, the theorems and axioms of SDL give rise to a further inspection of the semantics of the deontic operators. Here, three different kinds of aspects play a role:

- Aspects related to formalism.
- Aspects related to the interpretation of the axioms, rules, and formulas.
- Aspects related to the relation between what is mentioned in 1. and 2.

Ross paradox
From SDL it follows that $O(A \vee B)$ can be derived from O(A). $O(A) \rightarrow O(A \vee B)$ is known as the Ross paradox. The standard version of this paradox is:

> It is obligatory to post the letter implies that it is obligatory to post the letter or to burn it.

Ross [1941] uses the spoken language variant of $O(A \vee B)$ and then $O(A) \rightarrow O(A \vee B)$ is counter-intuitive.

However, this is not a proper anomaly; only if we make use of the intentional meaning of the word 'or', the theorem is contrary to our intuitions. But in our system, we make use of the extensional meaning of the word 'or', which we will call the *passive choice*: the choice between A and B is an underspecification, because it concerns A or B, without specifying which. Thus, $O(A \vee B)$ does not mean that the norm subject is free to choose between A and B.

> It merely means that the norm-subject is obligated to perform at least one of both acts. In this meaning $O(p \vee q)$ follows from $O(p)$, without it being paradoxical: if one is obliged to perform p, then one is also obliged to perform at least one of both p and q. By disobeying $O(p \vee q)$ thus by performing $\neg p \wedge \neg q$, $O(p)$ is disobeyed as well; therefore it follows from $O(p)$ that $[O(p \vee q)$ has to be obeyed. [Soeteman, 1989, p. 116]

With regard to the deontic status of q, nothing is said: q may be obligatory, forbidden or permitted. The Ross paradox is not really problematic and not actually a paradox.

McLaughlin's paradox
Analogously, we can discuss permission $P(p)$. $P(p)$ means that it is permitted to accomplish that p in at least one way. Probably, there are many ways of accomplishing p, some of which are forbidden; but if $P(p)$ holds, not all ways of accomplishing p are forbidden. This corresponds with McLaughlin's paradox: 'If one is permitted to walk in a public road and to wear clothes, then one is permitted to walk in a public road' ($P(p \wedge q) \rightarrow P(p)$). According to McLaughlin [1955] it is now also permitted to walk in the public road not wearing clothes, but McLaughlin misreads $P(p)$. This formula does not mean that one is permitted to accomplish p in *every* possible way. We are not permitted to walk in a public road simultaneously disregarding traffic rules, or not wearing clothes.

From the above, it does not follow that operators O and P behave identically within system SDL. In SDL, e.g. $P(p \vee q) \rightarrow P(p) \vee P(q)$ is valid, but $O(p \vee q) \rightarrow O(p) \vee O(q)$ is not, and $O(p) \wedge O(q) \rightarrow O(p \wedge q)$ is valid, but $P(p) \wedge P(q) \rightarrow P(p \wedge q)$ is not. This follows immediately from the semantics.

In contrast with $P(p)$ and $O(p)$, prohibition $F(p)$ means that *all ways* of accomplishing p are forbidden. This immediately follows from $F(p) \equiv O(\neg p)$. Thus, $F(p)$ means that we have to accomplish $\neg p$, and that we are in trouble if we accomplish p. If, e.g. it is forbidden to drive at a speed of more than 100 km/h, then every speed over 100 km/h is forbidden.

The Good Samaritan paradox

The following counter-intuitive example of the theorem $O(p \wedge q) \rightarrow O(p)$, is called the Good Samaritan paradox:

- One is obliged to help someone who has been robbed $(O(q \wedge p)$
- If one helps someone who has been robbed, this implies someone has been robbed $(q \wedge p \rightarrow p)$.

From these two rules we derive the absurdity that it is obligatory for someone to be robbed $(O(p))$. Castañeda [1981] believes there is a solution in the fact that we must make a distinction between propositions like 'someone has been robbed' and actions like 'to help'. It is Castañeda's view that only actions can be used as an argument of a normative operator and that propositions cannot be used. So the obligation 'one is obliged to help someone who has been robbed' cannot be formalised by $O(q \wedge p)$. This obligation is a conditional obligation and could be formalised as follows: $p \rightarrow O(q)$, so that the paradox is solved. Whatever the case may be, the paradox is based on the difficulties of translating actual norms into a normative-logical language.

Chisholm paradox

The Chisholm paradox[26] can be represented as follows [cf. Chisholm, 1963]:

- It ought to be that certain man go to the assistance of his neighbours $(O(p))$.
- It ought to be that if he does go he tell them he is coming $(O(p \rightarrow q))$.
- If he does not go, then he ought not to tell them he is coming $(\neg p \rightarrow O(\neg q))$.
- He does not go $(\neg p)$.

From an intuitive perspective these four sentences are consistent, but in the system SDL the formalisation of these four sentences is inconsistent. One could simply avoid this paradox by formalising the second line as $p \rightarrow O(q)$. However, we would have missed the point of this paradox: the four lines are no longer independent, because $p \rightarrow O(q)$ can be derived from the fourth line. According to deontic logicians [e.g. Åqvist, 1967] the solution to this paradox can only be a satisfactory solution if the four lines can be presented as independent lines. The solution of Castañeda for the Samaritan paradox by making a distinction between actions and propositions does not work for the Chisholm paradox, because p and q are actions and not propositions. This paradox and the Forrester paradox (the following paradox) are the result of *contrary-to-duty* obligations. Take for example the rule that you cannot make a U- turn on a motorway, if you are driving against traffic you are obliged to make a U-turn. The obligation to make a U-turn on the motorway is a contrary-to-duty obligation, because making a U-turn is an offence (against the prohibition

[26] A thorough investigation of this paradox can be found in Smith [1994].

that one may not make a U-turn on the motorway). In other words, in the Chisholm paradox, the obligation not to say that you are going if you are not going is a contrary-to-duty obligation, because not going is an offence (against the obligation to go). Deontic logic is not very good at dealing with these contrary-to-duty obligations, which are the source of many paradoxes.

Forrester paradox

The Forrester paradox or *gentle murderer paradox* can be represented as follows:

- It is forbidden to commit murder ($F(p)$).
- If a person murders someone, this must be done gently ($p \rightarrow O(p \wedge q)$).
- If someone is murdered gently, someone has been murdered ($p \wedge q \rightarrow p$).
- Someone is murdered (p).

Though these rules are meaningful in spoken language, this set of rules, say V_n, is inconsistent.

The Forrester paradox also involves contrary-to-duty obligations. One way to formalise these contrary-to-duty obligations is to use semantics based on preferences. In the Forrester paradox we can distinguish three situations:

- One cannot murder someone.
- One can murder someone in a humane way.
- One can murder someone and it can be done in a non-humane way.

Obviously, the first situation is the most desirable and the latter is the least desirable. We could order norms by the degree of punishment for example. Meyer [1987] did not use just one operator O but several operators for the obligation: $O_1, O_2, \ldots, O_n$, in which the index indicates the degree of punishment for an offence. The formalisation of the first two rules of the Forrester paradox is as follows:

- $F(p_1)$: it is forbidden to commit murder under penalty of sanction 1.
- $p \rightarrow O_2(p \wedge q)$: if one murders someone, one is obliged to do this in a humane way under penalty of sanction 2.

Now we can deduce $O(p_2)$, and it is not contradictory to $F_1(p)$. Moreover, we can deduce that $F_2(\neg q)$, so therefore $F_2(\neg q \wedge p)$ and also that $F_1(\neg q \wedge p)$, which means that the person who murders someone and does not do this in a humane way, does so under penalty of sanction 1 and 2. Sanction 1 is only applicable to someone who commits a murder in a humane fashion.

From the above it is clear that the solutions for the latter two paradoxes require more extended (or more adequate) systems. In the literature various approaches are given for the representation of such contrary-to-duty norms; each approach has its own pros and cons.[27] Most standard deontic systems, like SDL, lack sufficient expressiveness, so that the two latter paradoxes cannot be solved.

2.6.4 Ought-to-do and Ought-to-be

The expressions in deontic logic are read as 'it is obligatory (forbidden, permitted) *that* ...' followed by a descriptive sentence, or are read as 'it is obligatory (forbidden, permitted) *to* ...' followed by a verb (or verb phrase) for a category or type of *action* or *activity*.

The reading of the deontic operators with 'that' and 'to', respectively, may be said to answer to two different types of deontic logic. The first type is a logic of that which ought to, may or must not *be*, and the second a logic of that which ought to, may or must not be *done*. According to Castañeda:

> In short, deontic statements divide neatly into: (i) those that involve agents and actions and support imperatives, and (ii) those that involve states of affairs and are agentless and have by themselves nothing to do with imperatives. The former belong to what we used to call the *Ought-to-do* and the latter to the *Ought-to-be*. [Castañeda, 1970, p. 452]

The difference between Ought-to-do and Ought-to-be matters greatly. It depends on the interpretation of the norm content one uses, and is especially relevant for the analysis of legal rules, which mostly belong to Ought-to-do and not to Ought-to-be (the 'duties of care' constitute an exception to this). A system expressing Ought-to-do sentences fits better with the common-sense interpretation of legal rules, especially in criminal law[28], since norms are mostly concerned with behaviour, and are thus essentially related to individuals; they constitute somebody's obligation, permission or prohibition (see chapter 5).

In SDL, we cannot deal with actions; norms are expressed by applying a sentential operator O to sentence letters p. Now, $O(p)$ cannot be read as 'it is obligatory to do p', for then p would not be a sentential letter. In 'it is obligatory to feed the monkeys', 'to feed the monkeys' is not a sentence.[29] Thus, SDL is inadequate for representing Ought-to-do statements.

An approach to express Ought-to-do statements is system DDL (dynamic deontic logic), developed by Meyer [1988, 1989]. This system is an extension of SDL using the variant of SDL of Anderson [1967] with propositional dynamic logic. This system will be discussed in the next chapter.

[27] See [Torre, 1997] for a more extensive discussion about contrary-to-duty obligations.

[28] Criminal law is concerned with behaviour: if an illegal situation is mentioned in the description of an offence, the question is raised as to who created this situation (by action or omission) and who is responsible for continuing the situation. Thus, from the illegal situation a certain type of behaviour is derived, as it were.

[29] Wright [1951] interpreted the norm content as a description of an action ('act-qualifying properties'), by introducing 'performance-values' which are strictly analogous to the truth values in alethic logic and thus present the possibility of compound actions, e.g. action $p \wedge q$ is performed if and only if action p is performed and action q is performed. However, then system SDL as a logic of Ought-to-do is not satisfactory. The central point of this problem consists of the interpretation of the internal negation. For an analysis of this problem, we refer to Brouwer [1990].

2.7 Conclusions

In this chapter we have extended the Beth tableau method for propositional calculus to the normative tableau method for deontic logic. It is a very workable tool for finding out whether a well-formed formula of S_n is valid or not. Since S_n is complete, we can also use this method to check whether the formula is a theorem or not.

We also present SDL as a normal modal logic, with a Kripke-style semantics based on the notion of possible worlds. The axiom schemes and rules - an alternative (equivalent) characterisation of S_n - of SDL give rise to philosophical questions with respect to the representation of normative rules. A question with respect to consistency is, for example, how to overcome normative inconsistencies among the enacted norms. This problem will reveal itself frequently in the remainder of this book. The nasty paradoxes constitute another difficult point in SDL. Many researchers have tried to modify or extend SDL to avoid these paradoxes.

In SDL we can only represent ought-to-be statements and not ought-to-do statements. In the next chapter we present DDL (dynamic deontic logic), which provides means to deal with ought-to-do statements.

Chapter 3

Dynamic deontic logic

3.1 Introduction

The system DDL (Dynamic Deontic Logic) was developed by Meyer [1988, 1989]. Meyer defined DDL as a modal logic, following an article by Anderson [1967]. The basis for DDL is the logic framework of (propositional) dynamic logic. The reduction of deontic operators to dynamic ones makes use of Anderson's violation atom V to indicate that an action took place that violates one of the deontic constraints, i.e. that the performance of a forbidden action leads to a *bad state of affairs*. A *bad state of affairs* can be, e.g. a sanction, a liability to sanction or trouble. What exactly the consequences are of a *bad state of affairs* is another matter, and depends on the philosophy one adheres to. Our interpretation of the constant V is: the situation is in contravention of the law. Whether it leads to a sanction will be left aside here.

(Propositional) dynamic logic [e.g. Harel, 1984] consists of the normal propositional language extended with modal operator $[\beta]$ for every action β in the language. Expression $[\beta]\Phi$ means that Φ holds after β has been performed. The essential reason to describe deontic logic as a variant of dynamic logic is that actions and assertions can be strictly separated now, because:

- ... 'an action may change the current situation (world) and an assertion does not'.
- ... 'only assertions can be asserted and actions can be acted or performed. So it is meaningless to state the obligation $O\phi$ of some proposition ϕ, such as $OO\alpha$, where ϕ is taken to be the assertion stating that the action α is obligatory'.
- ... 'the fact that actions change situations implies some notion of passing time'.[1]

[1] A deontic system in which time is a central notion is given in [Eck, 1982]. The main difference between the temporal treatment in Van Eck's system and DDL is the definition of the accessibility relation. Van Eck defines this relation between worlds within one time-slice, and in DDL the relation is defined between worlds with different 'time-stamps'.

[Meyer, 1988, p. 109]

We can see $[\beta]\Phi$ as a refined version of the expression $\beta \to \Phi$ in traditional deontic logic, the difference being that actions and assertions are strictly separated, and a notion of time-lag is built in. In this approach, 'β is forbidden' ($F(\beta)$) is reduced to a dynamic expression as follows:

$$F(\beta) \equiv [\beta]V.$$

It is also easy to express the deontic modalities of 'permission' and 'obligation' in dynamic logic, once so-called negated actions (e.g. '$\overline{\beta}$') have been added to the syntax of actions. The negated action $\overline{\beta}$ expresses the *non-performance* of action β. This seems clear, however, we shall see that this notion is not trivial in a formal manner.

In this section, we present a formal introduction to the syntax and semantics of a simplified version of DDL. The simplification consists in the restriction to actions: we will not consider sequences of actions. The inclusion of sequences of actions does not lead to semantic difficulties, but complicates the syntax and semantics to the point that it would obscure the issues that we have tried to clarify in this book. Section 3.2 presents the language of actions. The language of DDL assertions and their formal semantics, and the formal system DDL itself are discussed in section 3.3.

3.2 Actions

Actions are the semantic counterparts of the action expressions used in dynamic logic (and thus used in DDL). The semantics of an action expression is a set of sets of actions. We will come back to this in subsection 3.2.3.

3.2.1 The syntax of actions

We define A as the set of action symbols. An atomic action is denoted by an underlined action symbol ($\underline{a}$). $\underline{A}$ is the set of atomic actions. Furthermore, we introduce a special action symbol *skip*, which is not an element of A[2] and a special action symbol δ, which is neither an element of A, and which models failure. Together, they constitute the set of semantic elementary actions.

The set of all action expressions Act can now be determined by the following BNF for its elements (β)

$$\beta ::= \underline{a}|\beta_1 \cup \beta_2|\beta_1 \& \beta_2|\overline{\beta}|\textbf{any}|\textbf{fail}|\textbf{skip}|\textbf{change}.$$

The meaning of $\beta_1 \cup \beta_2$ is a choice between β_1 and β_2, $\beta_1 \& \beta_2$ stands for the simultaneous performance of $\beta_1 \& \beta_2$, and $\overline{\beta}$ stands for the negation of action expression β. The **any** action expression indicates a universal or 'don't care which' action. The **change** action expression can then be characterised as a 'don't care which, but not the skip' action. The

[2]The *skip* symbol, introduced in [Dignum, 1989, p. 188], is comparable with the ϵ process in process algebra.

skip action expression stands for the empty action; that is, the action that has no effect ('does nothing'). Finally, the **fail** action expression expresses the action that always fails. After this action, the system stops and nothing can be done any more.

The performance of an atomic action $\underline{a}$ (e.g. to walk) involves the performance of a (semantic) elementary action a (to walk), possibly together with other elementary actions (e.g. to whistle, to look, etc.), and followed by an arbitrary performance of future actions (e.g. to run, to eat, etc.). Thus, we have to be careful not to confuse an atomic action (expression) $\underline{a}$ with the semantic elementary action a. The meaning (denotation) of $\underline{a}$ only stipulates (specifies) the performance of a corresponding semantic a, but we are free to perform any other set of elementary actions simultaneously with a.

3.2.2 The semantics of action expressions

We give the semantics of action expressions by sets of what are called *synchronicity* sets. These sets denote sets of elementary actions that are performed simultaneously. The following definitions formally describe the synchronicity sets and the ways they can be combined to form the semantic counterparts of the syntactic operators on action expressions.

Definition 3.2.1

- *Set* $\{\delta\}$ *is a synchronicity set (s-set).*
- *Set* $\{skip\}$ *is an s-set.*
- *Every non-empty subset of* A *is an s-set.*

We will use S, S_1, S_2, ..., S', ... to denote s-sets. The powerset of actions in A will be denoted by $\mathcal{S}$ (the set of non-empty s-sets). In concrete cases, we will write such a set using brackets. Thus, the s-set consisting of the action *skip* is written as $[skip]$ and the s-set consisting of actions a_1 and a_2 is written as

$$S = \begin{bmatrix} a_1 \\ a_2 \end{bmatrix},$$

and

$$\mathcal{S} = \{[a_1], [a_2], [a_3], \begin{bmatrix} a_1 \\ a_2 \end{bmatrix}, \begin{bmatrix} a_1 \\ a_3 \end{bmatrix}, \begin{bmatrix} a_2 \\ a_3 \end{bmatrix}, \begin{bmatrix} a_1 \\ a_2 \\ a_3 \end{bmatrix}\},$$

with $A = \{a_1, a_2, a_3\}$. Note that $\mathcal{S}$ does not contain s-set $[\delta]$ nor s-set $[skip]$.

Definition 3.2.1 prevents the simultaneous performance of the special actions *skip* and δ with other actions, because they are not in A. This is needed because it is, of course, not possible to perform an action and at the same time do nothing, or have a deadlock.

Since the language of action expressions contains a choice operator introducing non-determinism, we have to consider sets of s-sets as the semantics of an action expression. Moreover, non-determinism is introduced by using the open specification of actions, as we have seen in the intended semantics of $\underline{a}$. That is, $\underline{a}$ indicates a choice between all possible actions in which a is at least performed. Each s-set in such a set stands for a possible choice. We use $T, T_1, T_2, \ldots, T', \ldots$ to denote sets of s-sets.

Domain $\mathcal{A}$ of the action model is now given by:

Definition 3.2.2 *$\mathcal{A}$ is the collection of sets T consisting of s-sets.*

To give the denotation for all action expressions in Act, we define operations $\sqcup$, $\sqcap$ and $\tilde{}$ on domain $\mathcal{A}$, which we will use as semantic counterparts of the syntactic operators $\cup$, & and $\bar{}$, respectively, in the language Act. We first present a handy operator on sets of s-sets:

Definition 3.2.3 *Let T be a set of s-sequences. Then*

$$T^\delta = \begin{cases} T \setminus \{[\delta]\}, & \text{if } \exists_{S \in T} S \neq [\delta] \\ \{[\delta]\}, & \text{otherwise} \end{cases}$$

This operator is closely related to what is called *failure removal* in [Bakker, Kok, Meyer, Olderog, and Zucker, 1986]. The idea is that failure is avoided if possible, i.e. if there is a non-failing alternative. Such an interpretation of non-determinism, where a 'good' alternative is preferred to a 'bad' one, is sometimes called *angelic* non-determinism [cf. Broy, 1986].

Now we can define the semantic operators on $\mathcal{A}$. For the parallel operator $\sqcap$ we use a set-intersection $\cap$, which is almost the same as the normal set-interaction.

Definition 3.2.4 *For $T, T' \in \mathcal{A}$:*

$$T \sqcap T' = \begin{cases} T \cap T' & \text{if } T \cap T' \neq \emptyset \\ \{[\delta]\}, & \text{otherwise} \end{cases}$$

Definition 3.2.5 *For $T, T' \in \mathcal{A}$:*

$$T \sqcup T' = (T \cup T')^\delta.$$

Definition 3.2.6 *$\tilde{}$ is defined as follows:*

1. *For an s-set S,*

$$\tilde{S} = (\mathcal{S} \cup \{[skip]\}) \setminus S.$$

2. *For a non-empty set $T \in \mathcal{A}$,*

$$\tilde{T} = \sqcap\{\tilde{S} \mid S \in T\}.$$

Note that $\tilde{\mathcal{S}} = [\delta]$.

As was suggested in their notation, $\sqcap$ and $\sqcup$ resemble ordinary set-theoretical intersection $\cap$ and union $\cup$. The definition of operator $\tilde{}$ consists of two clauses. Clause (1) is straightforward: if we want to indicate that an s-set $S \neq [\delta]$ is not involved, we may express this by considering all other s-sets in $\mathcal{S}$, and if we want to indicate that one does not fail, any s-set is possible. Clause (2) states that the negation of a set T of s-sets considers all negations $\tilde{S}$ of s-sets $S \in T$ and takes the $\sqcap$-intersection of these sets.

3.2.3 S-set semantics of action expressions

With the above-mentioned definitions, we can now define the semantics of action expressions from Act.

Definition 3.2.7 *Semantic function* $[\![\ ]\!] \in Act \to \mathcal{A}$ *is given by:*

1. $[\![\underline{a}]\!] = \{S \in \mathcal{S} | a \in S\}$
2. $[\![\beta_1 \cup \beta_2]\!] = [\![\beta_1]\!] \sqcup [\![\beta_2]\!]$
3. $[\![\beta_1 \& \beta_2]\!] = [\![\beta_1]\!] \sqcap [\![\beta_2]\!]$
4. $[\![\overline{\beta}]\!] = [\![\beta]\!]^{-}$
5. $[\![\mathbf{skip}]\!] = \{[skip]\}$
6. $[\![\mathbf{fail}]\!] = \{[\delta]\}$
7. $[\![\mathbf{any}]\!] = \mathcal{S} \cup \{[skip]\}$
8. $[\![\mathbf{change}]\!] = \mathcal{S}$

Remark The meaning of action expression $\underline{a}$ is expressed by $[\![\underline{a}]\!]$: we specify the performance of elementary action a (simultaneous with some package of actions). Thus, only the performance of a is determined. Clause (7) expresses that in the denotation of action expression **any** the execution of *one* arbitrary s-set in $\mathcal{S} \cup \{[skip]\}$ is specified.
Example Let $A = \{a_1, a_2, a_3\}$. Then

- $[\![\underline{a_1}]\!] = \{\begin{bmatrix} a_1 \end{bmatrix}, \begin{bmatrix} a_1 \\ a_2 \end{bmatrix}, \begin{bmatrix} a_1 \\ a_3 \end{bmatrix}, \begin{bmatrix} a_1 \\ a_2 \\ a_3 \end{bmatrix}\}$

- $[\![\overline{\underline{a_1}}]\!] = \{\begin{bmatrix} a_2 \end{bmatrix}, \begin{bmatrix} a_3 \end{bmatrix}, \begin{bmatrix} a_2 \\ a_3 \end{bmatrix}, [skip]\}$

- $[\![\underline{a_1} \& \underline{a_2}]\!] = \{\begin{bmatrix} a_1 \\ a_2 \end{bmatrix}, \begin{bmatrix} a_1 \\ a_2 \\ a_3 \end{bmatrix}\}$

- $[\![\underline{a_1} \cup \underline{a_2}]\!] = \{[a_1], [a_2], \begin{bmatrix} a_1 \\ a_2 \end{bmatrix}, \begin{bmatrix} a_1 \\ a_3 \end{bmatrix}, \begin{bmatrix} a_2 \\ a_3 \end{bmatrix}, \begin{bmatrix} a_1 \\ a_2 \\ a_3 \end{bmatrix}\}$

- $[\![\mathbf{any}]\!] = \{[skip], [a_1], [a_2], [a_3], \begin{bmatrix} a_1 \\ a_2 \end{bmatrix}, \begin{bmatrix} a_1 \\ a_3 \end{bmatrix}, \begin{bmatrix} a_2 \\ a_3 \end{bmatrix}, \begin{bmatrix} a_1 \\ a_2 \\ a_3 \end{bmatrix}\}$

In this section, we also introduce an auxiliary notion to refer to the (in)equality of action expressions in terms of their semantics.

Definition 3.2.8 *We put* $\beta_1 =_A \beta_2$ *iff* $[\![\beta_1]\!] = [\![\beta_2]\!]$.

We can now state the following proposition concerning actions and their relations:

Proposition 3.2.9

- *For* A, *the following properties concerning* $\cup$ *and* & *operator hold:*
  1. $\beta \cup \beta =_A \beta$
  2. $\beta \& \beta =_A \beta$
  3. $\beta_1 \& \beta_2 =_A \beta_2 \& \beta_1$
  4. $\beta_1 \cup \beta_2 =_A \beta_2 \cup \beta_1$
  5. $\beta_1 \& (\beta_2 \cup \beta_3) =_A (\beta_1 \& \beta_2) \cup (\beta_1 \& \beta_3)$
  6. $\beta_1 \cup (\beta_2 \& \beta_3) =_A (\beta_1 \cup \beta_2) \& (\beta_1 \cup \beta_3)$
- A *satisfies the following properties regarding* '$\overline{\ }$':
  1. $\overline{\beta} \cup \beta =_A \textbf{any}$ *if* $l(\beta) = 1$
  2. $\overline{\beta} \& \beta =_A \textbf{fail}$
  3. $\overline{\beta_1 \cup \beta_2} =_A \overline{\beta_1} \& \overline{\beta_2}$
  4. $\overline{\beta_1 \& \beta_2} =_A \overline{\beta_1} \cup \overline{\beta_2}$
  5. $\overline{\overline{\beta}} =_A \beta$
- *For* A, *the following properties concerning the special action expressions hold:*
  1. $\beta \cup \textbf{fail} =_A \beta$
  2. $\overline{\textbf{any}} =_A \textbf{fail}$
  3. $\beta \cup \textbf{any} =_A \textbf{any}$
  4. $\textbf{any} =_A \textbf{change} \cup \textbf{skip}$
  5. $\overline{\textbf{skip}} =_A \textbf{change}$

Proof Can directly derived from the definitions. [See also Meyer, 1988; Dignum, 1989].

Below, we define a normal form for action expressions. This form is needed for some axioms on the postconditions of actions. These axioms only hold if the action expressions are in normal form [cf. Dignum and Meyer, 1990].

Definition 3.2.10 *An action expression $\beta \in Act$ is said to be in normal form (or to be a normal action) if the following holds.*
Every subexpression of β of the form $\beta_1 \cup \beta_2$ or $\beta_1 \& \beta_2$ has the property that $\bigcup\{S_1 \sqcap S_2 | S_1 \in [\![\beta_1]\!], S_2 \in [\![\beta_2]\!]$ and $S_1 \neq S_2\} = \emptyset$, i.e. $[\![\beta_1]\!]$ and $[\![\beta_2]\!]$ have no intersection consisting of s-sets that do not occur in both sets.
The subclass of Act consisting of action expressions in normal form will be denoted by Act_0.

Fortunately, the following theorem holds for A:

Proposition 3.2.11 *For any action expression $\beta \in Act$, an action expression $\beta_1 \in Act_0$ exists such that $\beta =_A \beta_1$.*

Proof This is clear from proposition 3.2.9.

Note that if $\beta_1 \cup \beta_2$ is in normal form, then $[\![\beta_1 \cup \beta_2]\!] = [\![\beta_1]\!] \cup [\![\beta_2]\!]$. And also, if $\beta_1 \& \beta_2$ is in normal form, then $[\![\beta_1 \& \beta_2]\!] = [\![\beta_1]\!] \cap [\![\beta_2]\!]$.

3.2.4 Positive and negative action expressions

In this subsection, we discuss some special actions: the *positive* and *negative* actions. We will use these special actions in chapter 3. There we will see that it makes a difference whether a group of actors performs a positive or a negative action. A positive action is an action that involves a certain kind of physical activity: a bodily movement and muscular activity, whereas a negative action refers to refraining from a physical activity: an omission [cf. Brouwer, 1990, p. 205]. For instance, 'to move the table', 'to close the window', 'to walk', 'to overtake', etc., are all positive actions and 'not move the table', 'to be silent', 'not walk', etc., all constitute negative actions. However, the difference between positive and negative actions is not clear cut, because (1) in several cases it is difficult to decide whether an action is positive or negative, and (2) a negative action is a non-action and, at the same time, a 'mode of action or conduct'.

Omissions are imputed to actors, and have to be taken into account in the dynamic variant of the deontic logic that treats omission as different from merely *not* performing some action. In DDL, we define omissions (negative actions) in terms of non-performance and in terms of the notions of *ability* and *opportunity* [cf. Linden, Hoek, and Meyer, 1996]. In this view, someone omits (neglects) doing something if he can do it, but does not do it.

Definition 3.2.12 *We define*

1. *the set Act_p of positive action expressions by the following BNF for its elements (γ):*

$$\gamma ::= \underline{a} | \gamma_1 \cup \gamma_2 | \gamma_1 \& \gamma_2 | \textbf{any} | \textbf{change},$$

with $\gamma_1, \gamma_2 \in Act_p$, and

2. *the set Act_n of negative action expressions by the following BNF for its elements (γ):*

$$\gamma ::= \underline{\overline{a}} | \gamma_1 \cup \gamma_2 | \gamma_1 \& \gamma_2 | \mathbf{fail} | \mathbf{skip},$$

with $\gamma_1, \gamma_2 \in Act_n$.

Note that

- $Act_p \cup Act_n \subset Act$. The converse ($Act_p \cup Act_n \supset Act$) does not hold because, for instance, $\underline{a_1}\&\underline{\overline{a_2}} \in Act$, but is not an element of $Act_p \cup Act_n$.
- $Act_p \cap Act_n = \emptyset$
- $\gamma \in Act_n$ iff $\overline{\gamma} \in Act_p$. This follows immediately from the definition.

3.2.5 Actions and worlds

We have to relate the action expressions in Act to worlds in which they are performed. Intuitively, the performance of an action in a world yields (a collection of) world(s) in which one arrives after having performed the action. The semantics of action expressions in a certain world can be given informally as follows.

Imagine a world w in which certain assertions hold. Then, by performing an elementary action a one moves into a next world w'. In world w', other assertions may hold than in w, since a may have changed something. For instance, if in w the proposition

$$\phi = \text{'the window is open'}$$

is true and a is the action 'close the window', then proposition ϕ clearly does not hold any longer in w', but

$$\phi' = \text{'the window is closed'}$$

does. We can present this as follows:

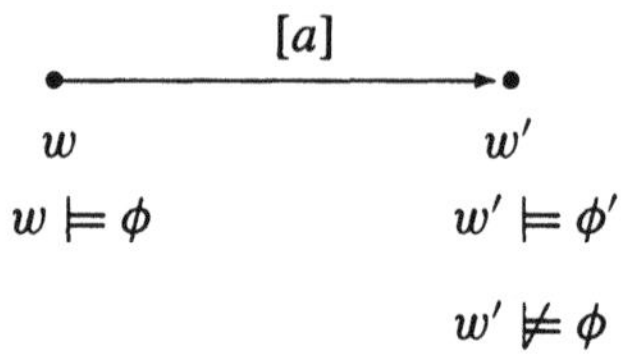

If one moves into a next world, other assertions may hold, except if one performs the action *skip*, because in that case nothing changes. (The action *skip* does not change any assertions in a world.)

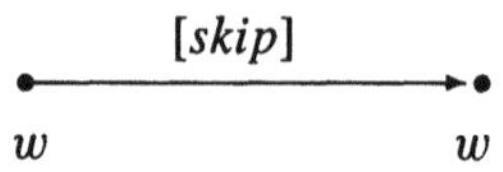

In general, $[\![\beta]\!]$ may lead one into one of several, possible worlds, due to the fact that we have a choice operator $\cup$ in our language. Thus, $[\![\beta]\!]$ may map w into a set $W_{\beta,w}$ of worlds. Schematically:

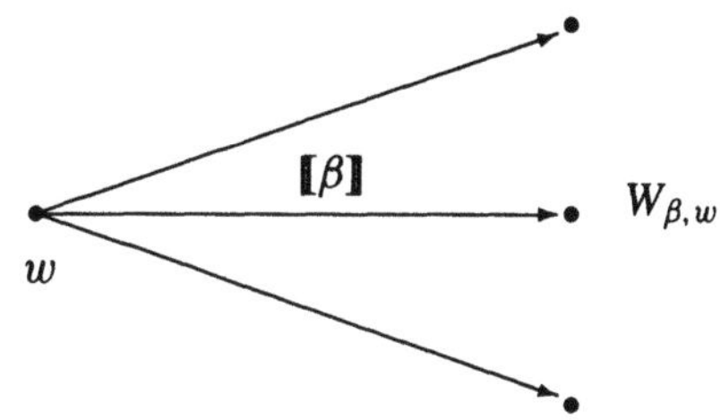

Now we can give the semantics of the various operators regarding *Act*:

- $\beta_1\&\beta_2$: the performance of β_1 and β_2 simultaneously. For elementary actions a_1 and a_2:

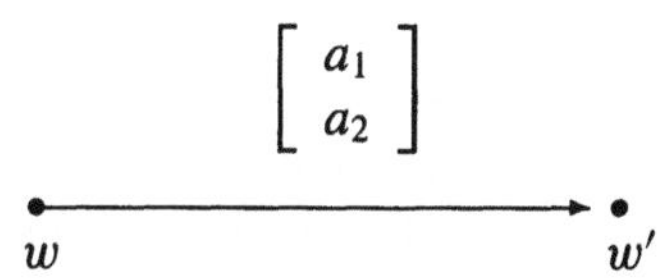

In general:

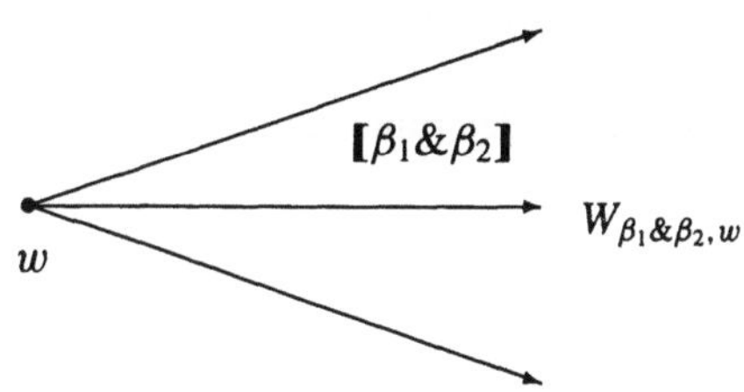

- $\beta_1 \cup \beta_2$: the performance of β_1 or β_2 (or both). For elementary actions a_1 and a_2 we get:

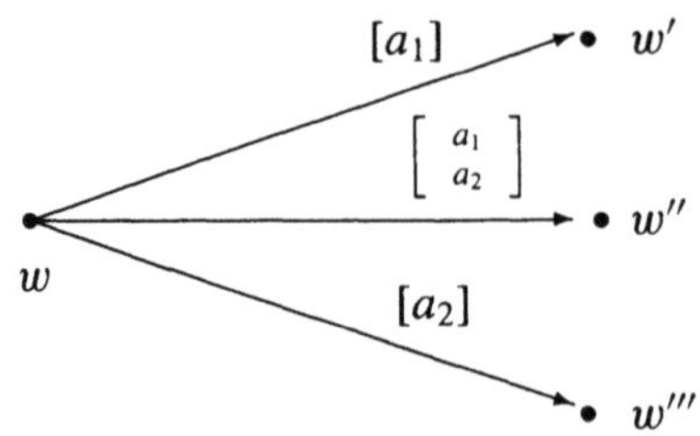

In general:

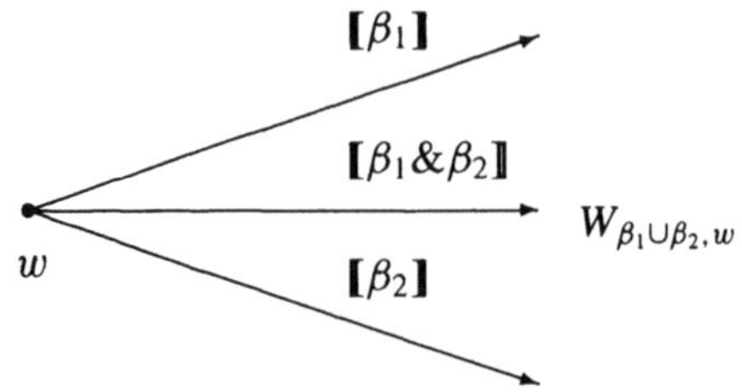

The semantics are based upon world transformations owing to action expressions β in Act: given a state w, $[\![\beta]\!](w)$ yields a collection of worlds which one obtains after having performed the action expression β. Formally, we stipulate that a set W of worlds assigns values to propositional variables and a given function $\rho : \mathcal{S} \cup \{[\delta]\} \cup \{[skip]\} \to (W \to W^*)$. W^* stands for the sets of elements of W that consists of at most one element. The function yields for each s-set its behaviour in terms of world transitions. Thus, $\rho(S)(w)$ gives the next world, performing all elementary actions in S jointly in world w. Function ρ is not further specified here, except for the s-sets $[\delta]$ and $[skip]$. For these, it stipulates that the failing s-set $[\delta]$ has no successor world and that the s-set $[skip]$ does not change the successor world.

We choose the s-sets to be deterministic.

Definition 3.2.13

- $\rho([\delta])w = \emptyset$
- $\rho([skip])w = w$
- *Function* $R(T) \in P^+(W) \to P^+(W)$ *is defined inductively by*[3]
  - $R(S)(W_0) = \cup_{w \in W_0} \rho(S)(w)$ *for* $S \in \mathcal{S} \cup \{[\delta]\} \cup \{[skip]\}$ *and* $W_0 \subseteq W$

[3] $P^+(W)$ stands for the powerset of sets of worlds, where the '+' indicates that the sets of worlds are non-empty.

- $R(T)(W_0) = \cup_{S \in T} R(S)(W_0)$

Definition 3.2.14 *The semantics of action expressions in a certain world can now be given by the function* $[\![\ ]\!]_R : Act \rightarrow (W \rightarrow P(W))$*:*

$$[\![\beta]\!]_R(w) = R([\![\beta]\!])(w).$$

This function is extended to $Act \rightarrow (P(W) \rightarrow P(W))$ *by*

$$[\![\beta]\!]_R(W') = \cup_{w \in W'} [\![\beta]\!]_R(w),$$

with $W' \subseteq W$.

3.3 Deontic assertions

Having given the semantics of action expressions, we can now discuss the language *Ass* of *DDL*. The language *Ass* of *DDL* consists of assertions concerning action expressions in *Act*, and is given by the BNF:

$$\Phi ::= \phi | \Phi_1 \wedge \Phi_2 | \Phi_1 \vee \Phi_2 | \Phi_1 \rightarrow \Phi_2 | \neg\Phi | [\beta]\Phi,$$

where ϕ denotes a propositional variable in W_s, being the set of wfs of the propositional calculus. Further, we define V as the propositional variable with liability to sanction as intended meaning. Expression $[\beta]\Phi$ means that Φ will hold after β has been performed. $[\beta]\Phi$ is a refined version of $\beta \rightarrow \Phi$ in traditional deontic logic, the difference being that now actions and assertions are strictly separated, and a notion of time-lag is built in.[4]

With the language *Ass*, we can formally express when an action is forbidden, permitted or obliged. To express these notions, we use the following abbreviations:

- $F(\beta)$ is an abbreviation of $[\beta]V$
- $P(\beta)$ is an abbreviation of $\neg[\beta]V$
- $O(\beta)$ is an abbreviation of $[\overline{\beta}]V$

These three abbreviations justify our claim that we are concerned with *deontic logic*. Thus, deontic logic can be reduced to a system of dynamic logic.

Definition 3.3.1 *A model M for DDL is given by*

$$M = (A, W, [\![\,]\!]_R, \pi),$$

where A is the set of actions, W a set of possible worlds, $[\![\,]\!]_R$ *a function that associates with action* $\beta \in Act$ *and world* w*, the set of possible worlds to which the performance of* β *leads, and* π *the usual truth relation between worlds and sentences:* $\pi : W \times W_s \rightarrow \{true, false\}$.

[4] $[\beta]\Phi$ is known in the realm of programming as the 'weakest precondition' of action expression β with respect to postcondition Φ.

For the semantics of assertions, we employ the semantics $[\![\ ]\!]_R$ of action expressions:

Definition 3.3.2 *For $w \in W$, $\Phi_1, \Phi_2 \in Ass_1$, $w \models \Phi_1 \vee \Phi_2, \ldots, w \models \neg\Phi_1$ are defined as usual.*
For the dynamic part, we define[5]

$$w \models [\beta]\Phi \textit{ iff} \forall_{w' \in [\![\beta]\!]_R(w)} w' \models \Phi.$$

We write $\models \Phi$ *iff* $\forall_{w \in W} w \models \Phi$.

This can be represented as:

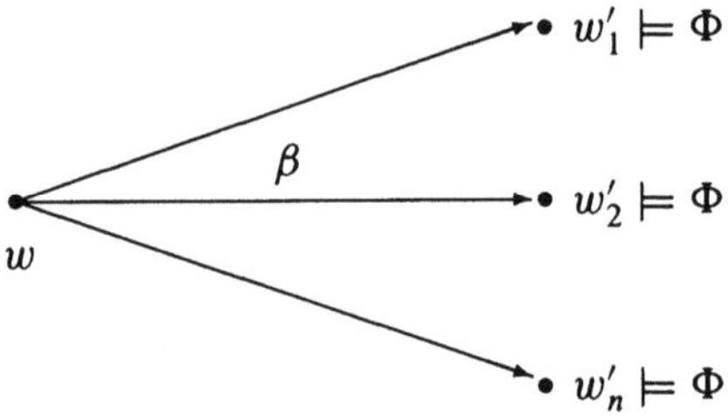

$< \beta >$ is the dual of $[\beta]\Phi$: $w \models < \beta > \Phi$ iff $w \models \neg[\beta]\neg\Phi$, i.e. $\exists_{w' \in [\![\beta]\!]_R(w)} w' \models \Phi$:

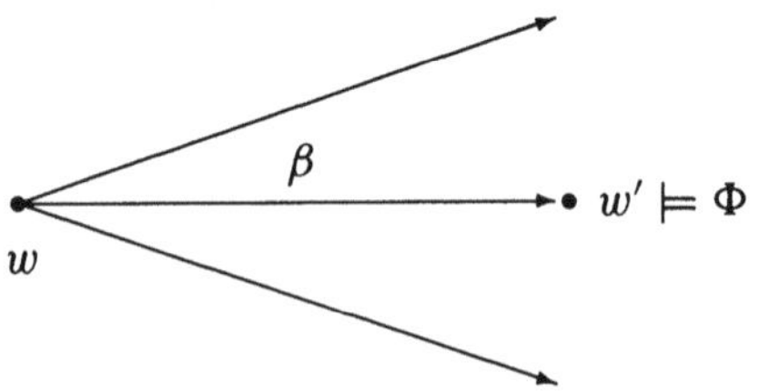

To be able to reason with language DDL, we introduce the following derivation rules:
Rules

(N)	if $\vdash \Phi$, then $\vdash [\beta]\Phi$
(S)	if $\beta_1 =_A \beta_2$ then $\vdash [\beta_1]\Phi \equiv [\beta_2]\Phi$
(MP)	if $\vdash \Phi_1$ and $\vdash \Phi_1 \rightarrow \Phi_2$, then $\vdash \Phi_2$

Note that the antecedent of rule (S) is not really an expression used in DDL. It would, however, not be difficult to axiomatise the equations given on the action expressions and to incorporate them into our logic. Without formally performing so, we consider this to be

[5] In words: performing action β in a world w necessarily renders proposition Φ true iff the proposition Φ holds for all worlds w' after w and performing β.

done and will not give all the axioms and derivation rules that are involved in this axiomatisation. We also have the derivation rule modus ponens.

The following axioms hold for *DDL*:

Axioms

1. all tautologies of the propositional calculus
2. $[\beta](\Phi_1 \rightarrow \Phi_2) \rightarrow ([\beta]\Phi_1 \rightarrow [\beta]\Phi_2)$
3. $[\beta_1 \cup \beta_2]\Phi \equiv [\beta_1]\Phi \wedge [\beta_2]\Phi$
4. $[\beta_1]\Phi \vee [\beta_2]\Phi \rightarrow [\beta_1 \& \beta_2]\Phi$
5. $[\mathbf{fail}]\Phi$
6. $[\mathbf{skip}]\Phi \equiv \Phi$

Some remarks

1. *DDL* is sound. The natural question arises whether *DDL* is complete with respect to the semantics we have defined. The problem of completeness of the system was discussed by Meyer [1989].
2. Axiom 5 states that if one is asked to perform an impossible action, e.g. $\beta_1 \& \overline{\beta_1}$, then there are no successor worlds and, consequently, assertion Φ is true in all successor worlds (since there are none). With this axiom, it is possible to prove, for example, $\vdash O(\mathbf{any})$ $([\mathbf{fail}]\Phi \rightarrow [\mathbf{fail}]V$ and $[\mathbf{fail}]V \rightarrow O(\mathbf{any}))$: 'Existence of an empty normative system'. This theorem is part of the idea of viewing deontic logic as a normal modal logic, which Von Wright rejected by his principle of deontic contingency.
3. Rule (N) states that a norm Φ cannot be remitted by any action if Φ can be derived from the system.

Now we give some theorems of *DDL* [cf. Meyer, 1988]:

1. $[\beta]true$
2. $[\beta](\Phi_1 \wedge \Phi_2) \equiv [\beta]\Phi_1 \wedge [\beta]\Phi_2$
3. $[\beta]\Phi_1 \vee [\beta]\Phi_2 \rightarrow [\beta](\Phi_1 \vee \Phi_2)$
4. $[\beta_1]\Phi_1 \wedge [\beta_2]\Phi_2 \rightarrow [\beta_1 \& \beta_2](\Phi_1 \wedge \Phi_2)$
5. $[\beta_1]\Phi_1 \wedge [\beta_2]\Phi_2 \rightarrow [\beta_1 \cup \beta_2](\Phi_1 \vee \Phi_2)$
6. $[\beta_1 \cup \beta_2 \cup (\beta_1 \& \beta_2)]\Phi \equiv [\beta_1 \cup \beta_2]\Phi$
7. $F(\beta_1 \cup \beta_2) \equiv F(\beta_1) \wedge F(\beta_2)$
8. $F(\beta_1) \vee F(\beta_2) \rightarrow F(\beta_1 \& \beta_2)$

9. $O(\beta_1) \vee O(\beta_2) \rightarrow O(\beta_1 \cup \beta_2)$

10. $O(\beta_1 \& \beta_2) \rightarrow O(\beta_1) \wedge O(\beta_2)$

11. $O(\beta_1) \wedge O(\beta_2) \rightarrow O(\beta_1 \& \beta_2)$

12. $P(\beta_1 \cup \beta_2) \equiv P(\beta_1) \vee P(\beta_2)$

13. $P(\beta_1 \& \beta_2) \rightarrow P(\beta_1) \wedge P(\beta_2)$

14. $P(\beta) \equiv < \beta > \neg V$

15. $P(\beta) \equiv \neg O(\overline{\beta})$

16. $F(\beta_1) \rightarrow F(\beta_1 \& \beta_2)$

17. $O(\beta_1 \& \beta_2) \rightarrow O(\beta_1)$

18. $O(\beta_1) \rightarrow O(\beta_1 \cup \beta_2)$

19. $O(\beta_1 \cup \beta_2) \wedge F(\beta_1) \rightarrow O(\beta_2)$

20. $F(\beta_1 \& \beta_2) \wedge O(\beta_1) \equiv F(\beta_2) \wedge O(\beta_1)$

21. $F(\beta_1 \cup (\overline{\beta_1} \& \beta_2)) \equiv F(\beta_1) \wedge F(\beta_2)$

22. $O(\beta_1 \cup \beta_1) \equiv O(\beta_1)$

23. $O(\beta_1 \cup \overline{\beta_1})$

24. $[\mathbf{fail}]V$

The theorems 7 up to 24 correspond with the theorems 1 up to 18 of SDL in subsection 2.4.1, since the properties regarding choice $\cup$ and simultaneous performance & are natural counterparts of those regarding $\vee$ and $\wedge$, respectively. So, most theorems of SDL with respect to the deontic operators correspond to a theorem of DDL.

Principle

$$\neg[\mathbf{any}]V,$$

corresponding with the schema (OD) of SDL, cannot be derived from the rules and axioms of DDL. To add this principle to DDL, we have to introduce the following constraint into the semantics:

$$\exists_{w' \in [\![\mathbf{any}]\!]_R(w)} w' \not\models V \text{ for all } w \in W.$$

This can be proven as follows. Suppose we have that $w \models \neg[\mathbf{any}]V$, i.e.

$$\neg\forall_{w' \in [\![\mathbf{any}]\!]_R(w)} w' \models V,$$

which is equivalent to $\exists_{w' \in [\![\mathbf{any}]\!]_R(w)} w' \not\models V$ for all $w \in W$.

Using this extra principle, we are able to derive some more theorems such as

1. $\vdash \neg O(\beta \& \overline{\beta})$
2. $\vdash O(\beta) \rightarrow P(\beta)$
3. $\vdash F(\beta) \rightarrow \neg O(\beta)$
4. $\vdash \neg(O(\beta) \wedge O(\overline{\beta}))$

At first, the axiom does not seem to be controversial, since it merely denies the existence of impossible obligations, however, this is controversial as we already mentioned in chapter 2.

It will be obvious that the system *DDL* expresses Ought-to-do sentences. We think that a system expressing Ought-to-do sentences fits better with the common-sense interpretation of legal rules, since norms are essentially related to individuals: it is somebody's obligation, permission or prohibition (cf. chapters 4 and 5). Furthermore, Meyer [1988]; Meyer, Dignum, and Wieringa [1994] showed that *DDL* avoids some of the very nasty paradoxes that often appear in other systems, especially where the connection between actions and assertions is concerned.

3.4 Conclusions

The system *DDL* presented in this chapter (together with its semantics) provides a workable framework for Ought-to-do reasoning, in contrast to *SDL*, which provides Ought-to-be reasoning. Both systems have their value, since sometimes we need to formalise Ought-to-do statements and sometimes Ought-to-be statements (cf. chapters 2 and 5). We stress again, though, that a comparison between *SDL* and *DDL* is *not* a topic of this book.

Chapter 4

Relativised deontic modalities in *SDL*

4.1 Introduction

We can distinguish three types of participants who play a very important role in a normative system: the *authorities*, who enact the norms, the *addressees*, to whom the norms are directed, and the *counterparties*, who have a 'right' against the addressees. In law, the word 'right' is often used to designate '*legal power*', '*legal claim*' and '*immunity* granted by an authority' [cf. Hohfeld, 1964].

The authorities are responsible for setting the norms and for supervising the enactment of the norms. In this chapter, we do not discuss the role of the authorities (this will be done in chapter 6). The role of the counterparties will not be discussed. The major topic of this chapter and the next one is the notion of addressees. In the remainder, we will call the addressees *(groups of) actors* or *(groups of) individuals.*

Most deontic logicians seem to concentrate their interest on *one* specific actor, and then discuss what his obligations are, whether one obligation follows from another, what is meant when it is said that obligations are consistent, and so on. Thus, the obligatory acts in these deontic logics are 'impersonal'. We cannot say that:

- Acts are obligatory for a particular individual or group of individuals.

- Some acts are obligatory for some, but not all, (groups of) individuals.

Thus, conventional approaches to deontic logic employ impersonal deontic operators. These approaches implicitly refer to one and the same individual all the time, explicit reference being unnecessary [Hintikka, 1970]. Sentences like 'it is obligatory for John that the window is closed and it is obligatory for Paul that the light is on' and 'it is obligatory for John that the window is closed and it is obligatory for Paul that the window is open' cannot be expressed within these approaches. They are limited, since they are not able to deal with problems related to (groups of) individuals.

Some researchers tried to include relativised deontic modalities in standard deontic logic (SDL) and to define 'personal' obligations and permissions in terms of the 'impersonal' ones. Relativised deontic modalities are concerned with what is obligatory or permitted for an actor or group of actors, as contrasted with what is only impersonally obligatory or permitted. Deontic operators are relativised to sets of one or more actors. However, we show that all these extensions have some shortcomings. For instance, in the proposals made by Bailhache [1991] and Hilpinen [1973], it is not possible to consistently express normative conflicts of the type 'it is obligatory for i_1 that p' and 'it is obligatory for i_2 that $\neg p$' and Hansson [1970] was forced to give up certain basic deontic principles, such as $O(p) \equiv \neg P(\neg p)$, to construct a model for relativised deontic modalities.

If some form of relativised obligation is introduced, then the impersonal obligation can be interpreted in several ways:

1. It is an obligation for all individuals (*general* obligation).

2. It is an obligation for some unspecific individual (*unspecific* obligation).

3. It is an obligation that implies the general obligation (*strong* obligation).

4. It is an obligation that is implied by the unspecific obligation (*weak* obligation).

However, Herrestad and Krogh [1995] showed that all these interpretations have to deal with one of the following two problems:[1]

- The problem of interdefinability of non-relativised obligation and permission (i.e. $O(p) \equiv \neg P(\neg p)$).

- The problem of asymmetry (e.g. the general obligation is coupled with the unspecific permission).

We do not think that these two problems are problems of interpretation, but features of these interpretations. Relativised deontic logic is an *extension* of SDL; thus, with the new expressive power and the new definitions of the O-operator, the formulas acquire some new meanings that cannot be expressed in SDL and are, therefore, subject to new intuitions. In this chapter, we investigate these new intuitions for the interpretations mentioned: we formalise some realistic, intuitive notions of these interpretations of non-relativised deontic operators and analyse the properties that hold for these new interpretations, and how these interpretations relate to the notions of the deontic operators *relativised to (groups of) actors*.

Thus, in this chapter we add actors and groups of actors to SDL. The concept of collective obligation - an obligation for a group of actors - is difficult [cf. Rescher, 1966],

[1] We will see that these two problems are related.

and can be seen as an extension to the relativised deontic modalities concerning what is obligatory or permitted for an actor. The motivation for this extension is that:

- There are situations that only can be accomplished by a group.
- We can express group liability (e.g. liability for a trading partnership).

In chapter 2, we saw that in SDL norms are expressed by applying sentential operator O to sentence letters p, meaning that $O(p)$ must be read as an Ought-to-be statement. We cannot express Ought-to-do statements in SDL, since in SDL we cannot talk about actions. This means that the relativised obligation $O_i(p)$ will be read as 'it is obligatory for i that p' or 'it is obligatory for i to accomplish p'. In the following chapter, we will add actors and groups of actors to DDL, so that we can express Ought-to-do statements such as $O(\beta)$, 'it is obligatory to do β' and the related relativised obligation $O(i : \beta)$, 'it is obligatory for i to do β'.

This chapter is structured along the following lines. In section 4.2, some formalisations of relativised deontic modalities are discussed. These formalisations concern connections between impersonal deontic operators and deontic operators relativised to individuals. Section 4.3 introduces the notion of collective obligation. Here, the deontic operators are relativised for groups of actors. Furthermore, the strong and weak obligations are introduced, and we formalise and analyse the properties that hold for these notions. Section 4.4 presents a recapitulation of the relations of all the notions of obligation and permission that are discussed in this chapter. We finish with some conclusions.

4.2 Formalisations of relativised deontic modalities

In this section, some existing formalisations of relativised deontic modalities are discussed. In these formalisations, the deontic operators are relativised to individuals: relativised deontic modalities are concerned with what is forbidden, obligatory or permitted for an individual, as contrasted with what is only *impersonally* obligatory. Such an extension of deontic logic is concerned with connections between obligations that bind particular individuals, on the one hand, and impersonal obligations, on the other hand. We can distinguish several obligations that bind particular individuals:

- a *personal* obligation: an obligation for a specific individual[2]
- a *general* obligation: an obligation for all individuals
- an *unspecific* obligation: an obligation for some individual

In order to make a comparison between the approaches, we translate the semantics of the approaches into one and the same semantics. We use the following model structure $M = (W, I, R, V)$ for system SDL_i consisting of four elements:

[2]We can also define the personal obligation as an obligation for a person that does not apply to another person. This definition is much stronger. Therefore, we call this interpretation of the personal obligation the *strict* personal obligation.

1. The set of possible worlds $W = \{w_1, w_2, \ldots\}$

2. The non-empty set of individuals $I = \{i_1, i_2, \ldots, i_n\}$

3. The set $\mathcal{R}$ of functions: $\{R_{i_1}, \ldots, R_{i_n}\}$ for each individual $i_1, i_2, \ldots, i_n \in I$. Thus, $\mathcal{R} = \{R_i \mid i \in I\}$. The function $R_i \in \mathcal{R}$ on W returns the deontically ideal worlds for individual i given a world: $R_i : W \to 2^W$.

4. A valuation function V, which assigns the value 'true' or 'false' to a proposition at a world in W.

The truth conditions for O_i and P_i are defined as follows

$$\mathcal{M}, w \models O_i(p) \text{ iff } R_i(w) \subseteq [\![p]\!] \tag{4.1}$$

and

$$\mathcal{M}, w \models P_i(p) \text{ iff } R_i(w) \cap [\![p]\!] \neq \emptyset, \tag{4.2}$$

with the following constraint (which gives schema (OD) for O_i: $\neg O_i(p \wedge \neg p)$)

$$R_i(w) \neq \emptyset, \text{ for all } R_i \in \mathcal{R} \text{ and for all } w \in W \tag{4.3}$$

From the semantics of O_i and P_i it follows that the rule and all axioms for O of the system SDL are also valid for O_i. This is intuitively correct, since the impersonal obligation $O(p)$ is read as an obligation related to one and the same individual all the time, which corresponds with $O_i(p)$, i.e. an obligation related to a single individual i. As we already mentioned in chapter 2, schema (OD) is controversial, because this schema states that there is no conflict of personal duties, which manifestly deviates from daily life situations, where we often find conflicts between legal rules, moral codes, promises, etc. However, in this chapter we do not remove this schema for O_i, since the proposals discussed in this chapter conventionally follow SDL - with its schema (OD). Although, we indicate which theorems expire if we do not enforce this schema.

The question arises whether there is a relation between the individuals. According to Hilpinen [1973] and Bailhache [1981, 1991], there is such a relation since they want a coherent system without conflicting obligations, such as $O_i(p) \wedge O_j(\neg p)$.[3] Hilpinen expressed this in the following condition:

> If a set of propositions A is consistent and
> $\{O_{i_1}(p_1^1), O_{i_1}(p_2^1), \ldots O_{i_1}(p_{n_1}^1), \ldots,$
> $O_{i_j}(p_1^j), \ldots O_{i_j}(p_{n_j}^j), \ldots, P_{i_j}(q)\} \subseteq A,$
> then $\{p_1^1, p_2^1, \ldots, p_{n_1}^1, \ldots, p_1^j, \ldots, p_{n_j}^j, \ldots\}$
> and $\{p_1^j, \ldots, p_{n_j}^j, q\}$ are consistent. [Hilpinen, 1973, p. 143]

[3] A conflict between two obligations means that it is impossible to fulfil both obligations simultaneously.

This means that all obligations for all individuals can jointly be realised and that a permission for some individual should not be in conflict with his obligations. Thus, it is not the case that an individual has an obligation that p and that there is an individual for whom $\neg p$ is obligatory. This can be formalised as

$$\neg(O_i(p) \wedge \exists_{j \in I} O_j(\neg p)),$$

which is equivalent to

$$O_i(p) \rightarrow \forall_{j \in I} P_j(p).$$

Bailhache described this as follows:

> It is advisable to note that this formula $[O_y(p) \rightarrow P_z(p)]$ appears paradoxical only if the normative addressee is unduly identified with the subject of proposition p. The formula does not say for example that 'if y is obliged to go into that house, then z is also permitted to go in'. The formula only corresponds to the following: as soon as an addressee is obliged that such a thing is accomplished, normative coherence makes it necessary that all other individuals are not obliged that this thing is not accomplished (in other words, that they are permitted that it is accomplished). [Bailhache, 1981, p. 76]

To accomplish this *normative coherence*, we have to add the following schema to system SDL_i:

$$\neg(O_i(p) \wedge O_j(\neg p)), \tag{4.4}$$

which is equivalent to

$$O_i(p) \rightarrow P_j(p). \tag{4.5}$$

However, Bailhache [1991] wanted to obtain a complete, coherent deontic system, i.e. what is obligatory, is permitted for all individuals. Yet, from $O_x(p)$ and $O_y(p)$, we can derive $P_z(p)$ and $P_z(q)$, hence $P_z(p) \wedge P_z(q)$, but not $P_z(p \wedge q)$, as required in a complete, coherent deontic system. Therefore, he added a stronger schema to system D_i^*:

$$O_{i_1}(p) \wedge O_{i_2}(q) \wedge \ldots \wedge O_{i_k}(v) \rightarrow \forall_{i \in I} P_i(p \wedge q \wedge \ldots \wedge v), \tag{4.6}$$

which is validated by adding the following constraint

$$\cap_{i \in I} R_i(w) \neq \emptyset, \text{ for all } w \in W. \tag{4.7}$$

This can be proven as follows. Let $O_{i_1}(p) \wedge O_{i_2}(q) \wedge \ldots \wedge O_{i_k}(v)$, then $R_{i_1}(w) \subseteq [\![p]\!] \wedge R_{i_2}(w) \subseteq [\![q]\!] \wedge \ldots \wedge R_{i_k}(w) \subseteq [\![v]\!]$ and thus $\cap_{i \in I} R_i(w) \subseteq \cap_{l=1,2,\ldots,k} R_{i_l}(w) \subseteq [\![p \wedge q \wedge \ldots \wedge v]\!]$. And since $\cap_{i \in I} R_i(w) \neq \emptyset$, it follows that $\cap_{i \in I} R_i(w) \cap [\![p \wedge q \wedge \ldots \wedge v]\!] \neq \emptyset$. Hence, $R_i(w) \cap [\![p \wedge q \wedge \ldots \wedge v]\!] \neq \emptyset$, for all $i \in I$ and for all $w \in W$. Thus, $\forall_{i \in I} P_i(p \wedge q \wedge \ldots \wedge v)$.

Although, we cannot express conflicts between special obligations for the same individual, we want to have the possibility to express conflicts between special (personal) obligations of different individuals, since 'they are prone to conflict because different individuals may acquire different special obligations without knowledge of the other's, i.e. there appears to be a *coordination problem* when special obligations are assigned' [Herrestad and Krogh, 1995, p. 486]. For example, a co-supervisor promises to a member of the reading committee that something will be changed in the thesis of a PhD student, and this PhD student promises his girl-friend not to overwork himself by not changing his thesis. The problem of conflicting obligations also arises when two authorities promulgate (enact) two conflicting norms. In chapter 7, we develop a theory to overcome these conflicts. That is why we do not enforce the principles (4.4) and (4.6), since it removes the possiblitity to express conflicting obligations of different individuals, with the result that the systems of norms need not be normatively consistent (i.e. may contain conflicting obligations).

With the semantics of personal obligation and personal permission, we can formalise the general and unspecific obligations and permissions:

- the *general* obligation and permission: $\forall_{i\in I} O_i(p)$ and $\forall_{i\in I} P_i(p)$;
- the *unspecific* obligation and permission: $\exists_{i\in I} O_i(p)$ and $\exists_{i\in I} P_i(p)$.

4.2.1 $O(p)$ as the general or unspecific obligations

In this subsection, we investigate the consequences of some possible definitions for the O-operator and the P-operator in terms of the O_i-operator and the P_i-operator. We will formalise some realistic, intuitive notions and analyse the properties that hold for some different proposals. Using the above semantics, the following possibilities are most obvious:

1. $O(p) \equiv \forall_{i\in I} O_i(p)$[4] and $P(p) \equiv \forall_{i\in I} P_i(p)$
2. $O(p) \equiv \exists_{i\in I} O_i(p)$ and $P(p) \equiv \exists_{i\in I} P_i(p)$
3. $O(p) \equiv \exists_{i\in I} O_i(p)$ and $P(p) \equiv \forall_{i\in I} P_i(p)$
4. $O(p) \equiv \forall_{i\in I} O_i(p)$ and $P(p) \equiv \exists_{i\in I} P_i(p)$

We will now discuss these four possibilities separately.

1. $O(p) \equiv \forall_{i\in I} O_i(p)$ and $P(p) \equiv \forall_{i\in I} P_i(p)$

This proposal for the interpretations of $O(p)$ and $P(p)$ corresponds with Hansson's proposal. Hansson suggested to interpret $O(p)$ as a general obligation, because

[4] $\forall_{i\in I} O_i(p)$ is an abbreviation of $\forall_i(I(i) \rightarrow O_i(p))$, with I the predicate symbol for indicating whether its argument is an element of the set of individuals. Note that $O(p)$ is equivalent to $O_{i_1}(p) \wedge O_{i_2}(p) \wedge \ldots \wedge O_{i_n}$.

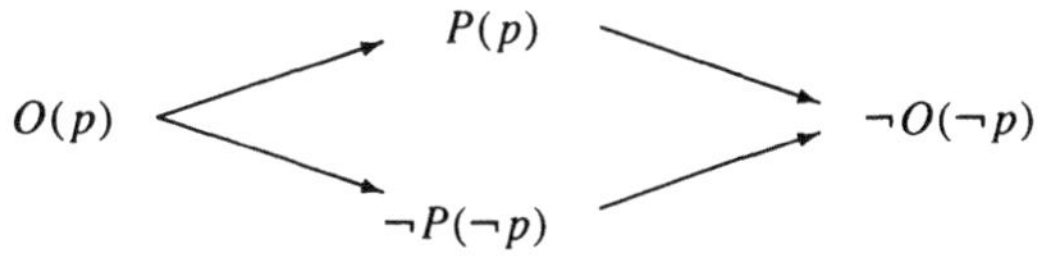

Figure 4.1: Hansson's arrangement of the different operators

> if we say 'it is obligatory to do p' in a context where there is no tacit reference to a special individual, we often mean 'it is obligatory *for everyone* to do p'. [Hansson, 1970, p. 246]

Thus, according to Hansson, $O(p)$ means 'it is obligatory for everyone to do p':

$$O(p) \equiv \forall_{i \in I} O_i(p).$$

Surprising is Hansson's definition of $P(p)$, 'it is permitted for everyone to do p':

$$P(p) \equiv \forall_{i \in I} P_i(p),$$

since he gave up the basic deontic principal that P is the dual of O, thus $P(p)$ is not definable as $\neg O(\neg p)$. Thus

$$P(p) \not\equiv \neg O(\neg p) \text{ and also } \neg P(\neg p) \not\equiv O(p).$$

$\neg P(\neg p)$ means that 'there is an individual i for whom p is obligatory' and $\neg O(\neg p)$ means 'there is an individual i for whom p is permitted'. Thus, $\neg P(\neg p)$ stands for the *unspecific obligation* and $\neg O(\neg p)$ for the *unspecific permission*.[5] In figure 4.1 the arrows indicate provable consequences of Hansson's proposal. It is easy to see that the following principles, which are valid in *SDL*, are also valid for this proposal:

1. $O(p) \wedge O(q) \equiv O(p \wedge q)$
2. $\neg O(p \wedge \neg p)$
3. $O(p \vee \neg p)$
4. $O(p) \rightarrow P(p)$

In relation to individual obligation and permission, the following principles hold:

1. $O(p) \rightarrow O_i(p)$
2. $P(p) \rightarrow P_i(p)$

[5] $\neg P(\neg p) \equiv \neg\forall_{i \in I} P_i(\neg p) \equiv \neg\forall_{i \in I} \neg O_i(p) \equiv \exists_{i \in I} O_i(p)$ and $\neg O(\neg p) \equiv \neg\forall_{i \in I} O_i(\neg p) \equiv \neg\forall_{i \in I} \neg P_i(p) \equiv \exists_{i \in I} P_i(p)$.

In the opinion of Kordig [1975], non-relativised deontic logic lacks a theoretical niche for the distinction between general obligations and obligations for a person. There is no way of saying that p is obligatory for an individual, and not for everyone. The following formula is not expressible in a non-relativised deontic logic

$$O_i(p) \wedge \neg O(p),$$

but it is expressible within this proposal. This illuminates *supererogation*. Supererogation means that there are duties 'far beyond' the 'basic' or 'rock-bottom duties for all': heroic and saintly deeds provide the most noteworthy examples of morally significant actions that lie outside the usual trichotomy, i.e. for everyone it is obligatory; for everyone it is permitted, but not obligatory; for everyone it is forbidden.[6] So, a hero and a saint, who perform supererogatory acts, can have obligations, which do not hold for all. However, there are - less exalted - examples. All motorvehicle drivers have obligations that are a condition of being a motorvehicle driver. But a lorry driver (who is also a motorvehicle driver) also has other obligations not applicable to other motorvehicle drivers. Such a lorry driver is to the set of motorvehicle drivers just as the saint or hero to mankind.

2. $O(p) \equiv \exists_{i\in I} O_i(p)$ **and** $P(p) \equiv \exists_{i\in I} P_i(p)$
Now, $O(p)$ means 'it is obligatory for someone that p' and $P(p)$ 'it is permitted for someone that p'. Just like the previous choice, permission $P(p)$ is not definable as $\neg O(\neg p)$. Thus, $P(p) \not\equiv \neg O(\neg p)$. $\neg O(\neg p)$ means that 'it is permitted for everyone that p' and $\neg P(\neg p)$ means that 'it is obligatory for everyone that p'. Thus, $\neg O(\neg p)$ now stands for the general permission and $\neg P(\neg p)$ for the general obligation.

The proposal of $O(p)$ as an unspecific obligation leads to an additional consequence regardless of the definition of $P(p)$: principle $O(p) \wedge O(q) \rightarrow O(p \wedge q)$ (OC) does not hold. This principle, which is equivalent to

$$\exists_{i\in I} O_i(p) \wedge \exists_{i\in I} O_i(q) \rightarrow \exists_{i\in I} O_i(p \wedge q),$$

> is clearly counter-intuitive: A janitor might be obliged that the floor in a building is swept clean every morning, and a financial minister might be obliged that the rate of inflation is as low as possible. That there is a person for whom it is obligatory that both the floor is swept and that the inflation rate is as low as possible, we find strange. [Herrestad and Krogh, 1995, p. 462]

Consequently, we cannot derive principle

$$\neg(O(p) \wedge O(\neg p)),$$

since it follows from (OC) and (OD). We will denote this principle as (OD^*).

However, Hilpinen [1973] and Bailhache [1981, 1991] want principle (OD^*) to obtain normative coherence, i.e. if an actor is obliged that p, then all actors are permitted that p. From (OD^*), which is equivalent to

$$\neg(\exists_{i\in I} O_i(p) \wedge \exists_{i\in I} O_i(\neg p)),$$

[6][Cf. Urmson, 1969, pp. 62, 64-65, 73.]

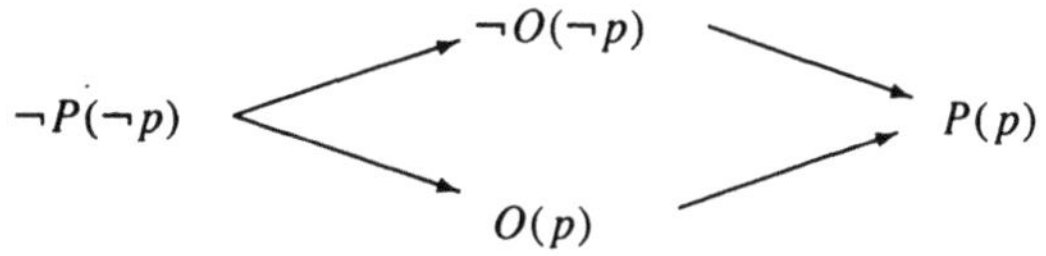

Figure 4.2: Arrangement of the different operators according to the second proposal

it follows that formula $O_i(p) \wedge O_j(\neg p)$ is contradictory. The principle is validated by adding the constraint

$$\bigcap_{i \in I} R_i(w) \neq \emptyset, \text{ for all } w \in W.$$

This can be proven as follows. Let $O(p)$ and $O(\neg p)$ hold. Then $\exists_{i \in I}(R_i(w) \subseteq [\![p]\!])$, say i_1, and $\exists_{i \in I}(R_i(w) \subseteq [\![\neg p]\!])$, say i_2. Hence, $R_{i_1}(w) \cap R_{i_2}(w) \subseteq [\![p]\!] \cap [\![\neg p]\!] = \emptyset$, and this contradicts that $\bigcap_{i \in I} R_i(w) \neq \emptyset$, thus $\neg(O(p) \wedge O(\neg p))$.

This is not what we want, as we already discussed in this section, since it removes the possibility of expressing conflicts between the personal obligations of different individuals.

It is easy to see that the following principles, which are valid in *SDL*, are also valid for this proposal:

1. $\neg O(p \wedge \neg p)$

2. $O(p \vee \neg p)$

3. $O(p) \rightarrow P(p)$

In relation to individual obligation and permission, the following principles hold:

1. $O_i(p) \rightarrow O(p)$

2. $P_i(p) \rightarrow P(p)$

3. $O(p) \equiv \forall_{i \in I} O_i(p)$ **and** $P(p) \equiv \exists_{i \in I} P_i(p)$
In contrast to the previous two proposals, schema $(Df.P)$ holds for this proposal:

$$P(p) \equiv \neg O(\neg p).$$

However, a consequence of this proposal is that we cannot express unspecific obligation and general permission with the help of $O(p)$ and $P(p)$. In the two previous proposals, we were able to express the two notions of obligation, i.e. general and unspecific obligation, and their duals, i.e, unspecific and general permission, from non-relativised obligation $O(p)$ and permission $P(p)$. Now, we can only express the notion of general obligation, and its dual the unspecific permission.

The following principles, which are valid in *SDL*, are also valid for this proposal:

1. $O(p) \wedge O(q) \equiv O(p \wedge q)$

2. $\neg O(p \wedge \neg p)$

3. $O(p \vee \neg p)$

4. $O(p) \rightarrow P(p)$

In relation to the individual obligation and permission, the following principles hold:

1. $O(p) \rightarrow O_i(p)$

2. $P_i(p) \rightarrow P(p)$

4. $O(p) \equiv \exists_{i \in I} O_i(p)$ **and** $P(p) \equiv \forall_{i \in I} P_i(p)$
For this proposal, schema ($Df.P$) also holds. However, just like in the previous proposal, we cannot express the two different notions of obligation with non-relativised obligation $O(p)$. In this case, we can only express the notions of unspecific obligation and general permission.

For the same reasons as in the second proposal, schemata (OC) and (OD^*) do not hold. Note that now the principle

$$O(p) \rightarrow P(p)$$

does not hold, since it is equivalent to (OD^*), meaning that 'if there is someone for whom it is obligatory that p, then it is permitted for everyone that p'.

The following principles, which are valid in SDL, are also valid for this proposal:

1. $\neg O(p \wedge \neg p)$

2. $O(p \vee \neg p)$

In relation to the individual obligation and permission, the following principles hold:

1. $O_i(p) \rightarrow O(p)$

2. $P(p) \rightarrow P_i(p)$

4.2.2 Evaluation of the four proposals

According to Herrestad and Krogh [1995], these four proposals suffer from one of the following two problems:

- the problem of interdefinability
- the problem of asymmetry

	Proposal 1	Proposal 2	Proposal 3	Proposal 4
$O(p) \wedge O(q) \rightarrow O(p \wedge q)$	+	−	+	−
$\neg(O(p) \wedge O(\neg p))$	+	−	+	−
$P(p) \equiv \neg O(\neg p)$	−	−	+	+
$O(p) \rightarrow P(p)$	+	+	+	−

+: the principle is valid. -: the principle is not valid.

Table 4.1: The basic principles in SDL and the four proposals

In the former two proposals, permission $P(p)$ is not definable as $\neg O(\neg p)$. In [Herrestad and Krogh, 1995, p. 461] this is called the *problem of interdefinability*. This is why they rejected these two proposals, for $(Df.P)$ is one of the fundamental elements of deontic logic concerning the relation between obligation and permission. In deontic logic, permission is treated as the dual of obligation, in the same way as possibility and necessity are in modal logic [cf. Wright, 1951].

In the latter two proposals, we cannot express the four notions with non-relativised obligation and permission. That is why Herrestad and Krogh rejected these proposals. About the third proposal they stated:

> This suggestion suffers from what we call the *problem of asymmetry*. It seems like the notion of non-relativised obligation is a strong notion, while the notion of non-relativised permission is a weak notion. (...) These notions are thus impersonal in two different ways. [Herrestad and Krogh, 1995, p. 463]

In the four proposals given, these two problems are related to each other. Since, if we choose for schema $(Df.P)$, i.e. $O(p) \equiv \neg P(\neg p)$, then we meet the problem of asymmetry, and if we choose to give up schema $(Df.P)$, we meet the problem of interdefinability. The problems of asymmetry and interdefinability can be solved by accepting two notions of non-relativised obligation and permission in a system which we will discuss in the next subsection.

We do not view these two problems as real problems. The proposals, with new definitions for the O- and P-operators and their new expressive power, are *extensions* of SDL with new meanings, not expressible in SDL, and are subject to new intuitions. It is, therefore, a mistake to read the formulas in these proposals as they are read in SDL, and it is methodologically strange to reject a proposal just because it does not satisfy some axiom. For instance, for the general obligation and permission it is obvious that they are not interdefinable. However, that is not a problem of the formalisation: it is a *feature* of these notions.

Finally, we summarise the basic principles in SDL that also hold for the four proposals in a table.

4.2.3 The combined approach

To solve the 'problem' of interdefinability and the 'problem' of asymmetry simultaneously, we allow two notions of obligation into the system: general obligation $O^+(p)$ with its dual, unspecific permission $P^+(p)$, and unspecific obligation $O^-(p)$ with its dual, general permission $P^-(p)$:

$$O^+(p) \equiv \forall_{i \in I} O_i(p) \tag{4.8}$$

$$P^+(p) \equiv \exists_{i \in I} P_i(p) \tag{4.9}$$

$$O^-(p) \equiv \exists_{i \in I} O_i(p) \tag{4.10}$$

$$P^-(p) \equiv \forall_{i \in I} P_i(p) \tag{4.11}$$

We do not enforce principle (OD^*) for O^-, as we stated in subsection 4.2.1. Further, the following four principles, which correspond with the principles in figure 4.1, are valid:

$$O^+(p) \rightarrow O^-(p) \tag{4.12}$$

$$P^-(p) \rightarrow P^+(p) \tag{4.13}$$

$$O^+(p) \rightarrow P^-(p) \tag{4.14}$$

$$O^-(p) \rightarrow P^+(p) \tag{4.15}$$

Figure 4.3 depicts the logical relations between operators O^+, O^-, P^+, P^-, O_i and P_i. In contrast to this approach, Bailhache [1991] wanted to keep principle (OD^*) for O^- to obtain a coherent normative system. This is validated by adding constraint (4.7). Now we can derive some extra principles, such as

$$O^-(p) \rightarrow P^-(p)$$

and, therefore,

$$O^-(p) \rightarrow P_i(p)$$

and

$$O_i(p) \rightarrow P^-(p).$$

The valid properties are summarised in figure 4.4.

Since the proposals - discussed in this section - consider (OD) as an axiom for O_i, we obtain the principles $O_i(p) \rightarrow P_i(p)$, $O^+(p) \rightarrow P^-(p)$ and $O^-(p) \rightarrow P^+(p)$. If we remove schema (OD) for O_i, so that we can express personal conflicts, these principles are not valid anymore. Then we get the properties summarised in figure 4.5.

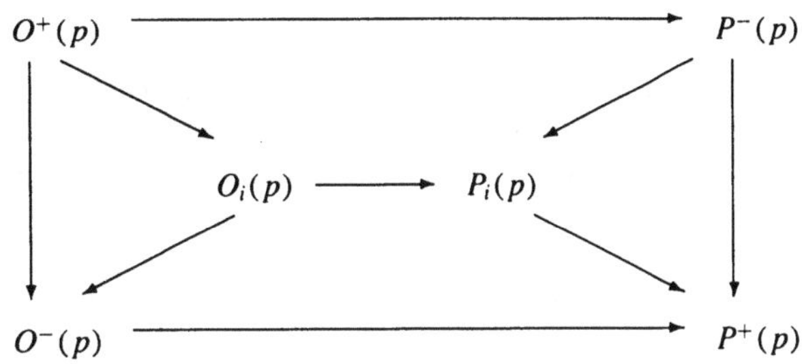

Figure 4.3: The logical relations between operators O^+, O^-, P^+, P^-, O_i and P_i

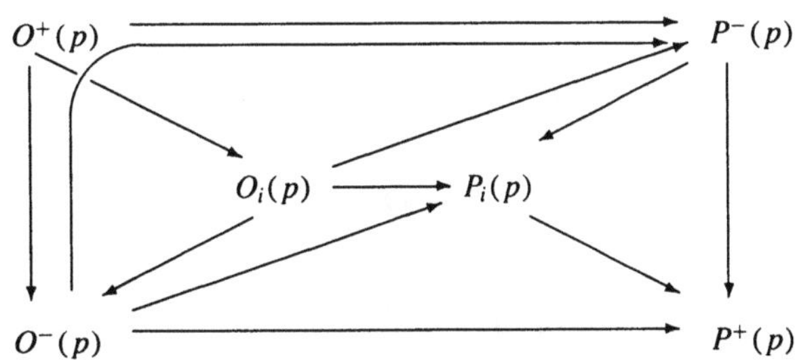

Figure 4.4: The logical relations with (OD^*) for O^-

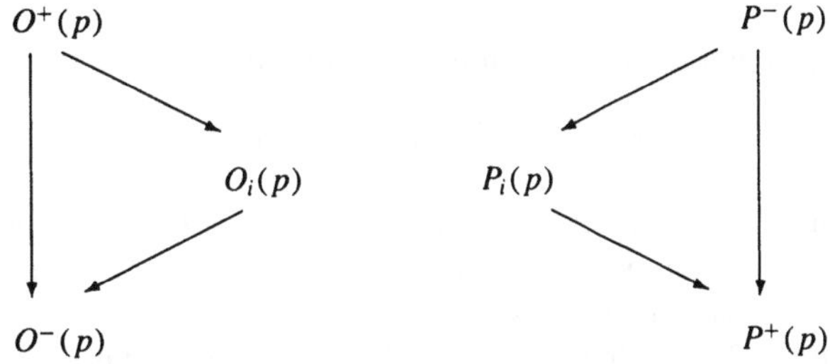

Figure 4.5: The logical relations without (OD) for O_i

4.2.4 Herrestad and Krogh

Herrestad and Krogh [1995] combined the approaches of Kordig and Hilpinen. Kordig [1975] introduced a stronger notion ($O_k^{\oplus}$) of general obligation $O^+(p)$ and its dual, a weaker notion ($P_k^{\oplus}$) of unspecific permission $P^+(p)$. Hilpinen [1973] introduced a weaker notion ($O_h^{\ominus}$) of unspecific obligation $O^-(p)$ and its dual, a stronger notion ($P_h^{\ominus}$) of general permission $P^-(p)$. With the general and unspecific obligations, we can only express obligations for any or some particular individual in a group. Neither Kordig nor Hilpinen exactly defined the stronger ($O_k^{\oplus}$) and the weaker ($O_h^{\ominus}$) notions of obligation, respectively. However, Herrestad and Krogh suggested that these notions are *collective* notions: a collective obligation as an obligation that rests on the group, and not on any single individual. They did not offer a (semantic) definition of these collective notions, however. A drawback of this is that the notions of $O_k^{\oplus}$ and $O_h^{\ominus}$ are vague and, as a consequence difficult to apply.

The following properties hold for these new notions:

$$O_k^{\oplus}(p) \rightarrow O^+(p) \tag{4.16}$$

$$P^+(p) \rightarrow P_k^{\oplus}(p) \tag{4.17}$$

$$O^-(p) \rightarrow O_h^{\ominus}(p) \tag{4.18}$$

$$P_h^{\ominus}(p) \rightarrow P^-(p) \tag{4.19}$$

The truth conditions for $O_k^{\oplus}$ and $P_k^{\oplus}$ are defined as follows:

$$M, w \models O_k^{\oplus}(p) \text{ iff } R_k^{\oplus}(w) \subseteq [\![p]\!] \tag{4.20}$$

and

$$M, w \models P_k^{\oplus}(p) \text{ iff } R_k^{\oplus}(w) \cap [\![p]\!] \neq \emptyset, \tag{4.21}$$

with the following condition for accessibility function $R_k^{\oplus}$:

$$\cup_{i \in I} R_i(w) \subseteq R_k^{\oplus}(w) \text{ for all } w \in W. \tag{4.22}$$

The intuition behind function $R_k^{\oplus}$ is that it returns at least the *union* of all ideal worlds of all individuals. This corresponds with Kordig's proposal. Note that we do not have $\cup_{i \in I} R_i(w) = R_k^{\oplus}(w)$, since in that case $O_k^{\oplus}(p) \equiv O^+(p)$.[7]

From (4.3) and (4.22) it follows that the following constraint is valid:

$$R_k^{\oplus}(w) \neq \emptyset \text{ for all } w \in W. \tag{4.23}$$

[7] Suppose $\cup_{i \in I} R_i(w) = R_k^{\oplus}(w)$ and $O^+(p)$ holds, then it follows that $\forall_{i \in I} R_i(w) \subseteq [\![p]\!]$, which is equivalent to $\cup_{i \in I} R_i(w) \subseteq [\![p]\!]$, that $O_k^{\oplus}(p)$ holds. The proof of the converse is analogous.

Thus, schema (OD^*) holds for $O_k^{\oplus}$:

$$\neg(O_k^{\oplus}(p) \wedge O_k^{\oplus}(\neg p)), \tag{4.24}$$

which is equivalent to

$$O_k^{\oplus}(p) \rightarrow P_k^{\oplus}(p). \tag{4.25}$$

The truth conditions for $O_h^{\ominus}$ and $P_h^{\ominus}$ are defined as follows:

$$M, w \models O_h^{\ominus}(p) \text{ iff } R_h^{\ominus}(w) \subseteq [\![p]\!] \tag{4.26}$$

and

$$M, w \models P_h^{\ominus}(p) \text{ iff } R_h^{\ominus}(w) \cap [\![p]\!] \neq \emptyset, \tag{4.27}$$

with accessibility function $R_h^{\ominus}$:

$$R_h^{\ominus}(w) = \cap_{i \in I} R_i(w) \text{ for all } w \in W. \tag{4.28}$$

The intuition behind function $R_h^{\ominus}$ is that it returns the *shared* ideal worlds of all individuals, i.e. the ideal worlds that all individuals have in common. This corresponds with Hilpinen's proposal.

The difference between Kordig's theory and Hilpinen's theory is that Kordig argued that if something is deontically relevant for one individual, it is also considered non-relativised deontically relevant $(R_i(w) \subseteq R_k^{\oplus}(w))$, whereas Hilpinen claimed that something is deontically relevant for everybody if and only if it is also considered non-relativised deontically relevant $(\cap_{i \in I} R_i(w) = R_h^{\ominus}(w))$.

Herrestad and Krogh rejected the principle (OD^*) for $O_h^{\ominus}$:

$$\neg(O_h^{\ominus}(p) \wedge O_h^{\ominus}(\neg p)), \tag{4.29}$$

since this would make principle (OD^*) for O^- derivable: principle (4.29) is equivalent to $O_h^{\ominus}(p) \rightarrow P_h^{\ominus}(p)$, and from (4.18) and (4.19) it follows that $O^-(p) \rightarrow P^-(p)$. For rejecting this principle, they did not add the constraint

$$R_h^{\ominus}(w) \neq \emptyset \text{ for all } w \in W. \tag{4.30}$$

Consequently, schema (OD) for $O_h^{\ominus}(p)$ is not valid:[8]

$$\neg O_h^{\ominus}(p \wedge \neg p). \tag{4.31}$$

However, schema (OC) is valid: let $O_h^{\ominus}(p) \wedge O_h^{\ominus}(q)$ hold, then $R_h^{\ominus}(w) \subseteq [\![p]\!]$ and $R_h^{\ominus}(w) \subseteq [\![q]\!]$, hence $R_h^{\ominus}(w) \subseteq [\![p]\!] \cap [\![q]\!] = [\![p \wedge q]\!]$. Thus, $O_h^{\ominus}(p \wedge q)$. In subsection 4.2.1, we saw that schema (OC) for O^- was counter-intuitive and does not hold. The fact that (OC)

[8] Note that schema (OD) is valid for O^-, however.

is not valid for O^- does not imply that (OC) is necessarily counter-intuitive for $O_h^\ominus$. In subsection 4.3.2, we shall see that it depends on the interpretation of $O_h^\ominus$ whether schema (OC) is intuitive or counter-intuitive.

From (4.22) and (4.28) we can derive the constraint

$$R_h^\ominus(w) \subseteq R_k^\oplus(w) \text{ for all } w \in W, \tag{4.32}$$

which provides us with the principle

$$O_k^\oplus(p) \rightarrow O_h^\ominus(p). \tag{4.33}$$

This can be proven as follows. Suppose that $O_k^\oplus(p)$ holds, then $R_k^\oplus(w) \subseteq [\![p]\!]$. Since $R_h^\ominus(w) \subseteq R_k^\oplus(w)$, it follows that $R_h^\ominus(w) \subseteq [\![p]\!]$. Thus, $O_h^\ominus(p)$.

Consequently, we can derive

$$P_h^\ominus(p) \rightarrow P_k^\oplus(p). \tag{4.34}$$

The problem of accepting $O_k^\oplus(p) \rightarrow P_h^\ominus(p)$

Just as where the general obligation implies the general permission (4.14) and the unspecific obligation implies the unspecific permission (4.15), Herrestad and Krogh aimed at holding these principles for $O_k^\oplus$ and $O_h^\ominus$:

$$O_k^\oplus(p) \rightarrow P_h^\ominus(p) \tag{4.35}$$

$$O_h^\ominus(p) \rightarrow P_k^\oplus(p) \tag{4.36}$$

However, this does not follow from the semantics given so far. That is why Herrestad and Krogh tried to add the constraint:

$$\text{if } R_k^\oplus(w) \subseteq [\![p]\!], \text{ then } R_h^\ominus(w) \cap [\![p]\!] \neq \emptyset \text{ for all } w \in W. \tag{4.37}$$

Now principle (4.35) is valid, and by contraposing (4.35) and substituting $\neg p$ for p, we obtain principle (4.36). However, now it also holds that constraint (4.30) is valid.[9] This provides principle (OD^*) for $O_h^\ominus$, which implies principle (OD^*) for O^-, which Herrestad and Krogh did not want.

According to Herrestad and Krogh, the problem is due to the validity of (ON) for $O_k^\oplus$, i.e. $O_k^\oplus(p \vee \neg p)$. The solution they provided is to block the inference of $P_h^\ominus(p)$ from $O_k^\oplus(p)$ when p is a tautology. Instead of (4.37), they offered the principle[10]

$$(\Diamond p \wedge \Diamond \neg p) \rightarrow (O_k^\oplus(p) \rightarrow P_h^\ominus(p)). \tag{4.38}$$

[9]Since $R_k^\oplus(w) \subseteq [\![p \vee \neg p]\!]$ is true for all $w \in W$, then by means of (4.37) and modus ponens $R_h^\ominus(w) \cap [\![p \vee \neg p]\!] \neq \emptyset$ is also true for all $w \in W$, which is equivalent to $R_h^\ominus(w) \neq \emptyset$ for all $w \in W$.

[10]$\Diamond$ is the possibility sign. $\Diamond p$ is true only in case p is true in some possible world.

However, the solution is not quite satisfactory, for the reason that we can derive the following formulas

$$P_h^{\ominus}(p) \rightarrow (O_h^{\ominus}(q) \rightarrow P_h^{\ominus}(q)), \tag{4.39}$$

because $R_h^{\ominus}(w) \neq \emptyset$, if $R_h^{\ominus}(w) \cap [\![p]\!] \neq \emptyset$, and by (4.38) also

$$O_k^{\oplus}(p) \rightarrow (O_h^{\ominus}(q) \rightarrow P_h^{\ominus}(q)), \tag{4.40}$$

if p is no tautology. Thus, if there is a proposition p (and p is no tautology) for which $P_h^{\ominus}(p)$ or $O_k^{\oplus}(p)$ is true, schema (OD^*) is valid for $O_h^{\ominus}$. We can solve this problem by stating that $P_h^{\ominus}(p)$ and $O_k^{\oplus}(p)$ are always false for every p which is no tautology. But the question then arises why one introduces, for example, a stronger notion of the obligation where this obligation actually has the value 'false'.

We do not think that the problem appears to be the validity of (ON) for $O_k^{\oplus}$. In subsection 4.3.3, we will provide a much simpler solution, based upon the interpretation of $O_k^{\oplus}$ and $O_h^{\ominus}$ as collective notions. The collective notions are formalised on the basis of the collective obligation, which we discuss in the following section.

4.3 The collective obligation

Usually, an actor is either an individual such as for example Paul, or a so-called collective agent such as for example the Dutch government, John and Paul, a firm, etc. Obligations can also be aimed at a collective agent, since there are cases in which the 'addressee' is not a single individual, but a group.[11] For instance, a mother may tell her sons:

'Boys, the table has to be set.'

This command is given to a group of boys, and it requires that the group accomplish something (i.e. that the table is set). This can be expressed as follows:

$$O_X(p),$$

where 'X' does not refer to an individual, but to a set of individuals, in this case the boys, and 'p' to the statement 'the table is set'. $O_X(p)$ can be read as 'it is obligatory for X that p'. 'X' is used for the expression of a *collective agency*. We call these obligations *collective obligations*. Relativised obligation $O_X(p)$ does not mean that this is a restricted general obligation, i.e. that for every actor in X it is obligatory that p, but that X *as a group* has to accomplish that p. It is an obligation for two or more individuals cooperating together to achieve some result, i.e. to bring about some situation.

Consider the following example, taken from [Rescher, 1966, p. 69]:

[11] The necessity to use groups of actors is stated as follows by [Bailhache, 1991, p. 80]: 'For imagine, for example, that such masons ought to build the foundation of the house, such roofers to assemble its roof, such electricians to set its electrical network, and so on: the firm, as the set of all these workers will have the duty of building the whole house. More generally, if it is obligatory for y that $p \rightarrow q$ and obligatory for z that p, which addressee will be touched by the resulting obligation (that q)? It will be at least the *set* of y and z - without being able to say which individual is concerned.'

'John and Paul are obliged that the table is moved across the room.'

This obligation is fulfilled if John alone accomplishes that the table is moved across the room, or that Paul alone accomplishes that the table is moved across the room, or that John and Paul together accomplish that the table is moved across the room. This obligation cannot be expressed in terms of individual obligations and that the obligation does not require that everyone (in this case, John and Paul) in the group takes part in the act to accomplish that p.

In the approach of Lindahl [1977] based on the theory of Kanger and Kanger [1966] for *atomic types of right*, the collective (two-agent) types are defined as legal relations between the parties: certain regulations of the coordination of the two parties' behaviour with respect to a state of affairs. For example, if John and Paul are obliged to move the table, then John and Paul may decide for themselves how the tasks are to be distributed between them. Thus, the collective obligation implicitly expresses a certain regulation of the coordination of the individual acts to accomplish the fulfillment of the obligation. In this section, we do not discuss the relations between the individuals in accomplishing a collective obligation, but we are interested in the formalisation of collective agents (groups of actors) in SDL and the relations between the collective obligations. In chapter 5 (section 5.7), we give a first step to make the legal relations meant by Lindahl in a collective obligation explicit through the notion of commitment.

So, in this section we add groups of actors to the system SDL, which can be seen as an extension of the relativised deontic modalities concerning what is obligatory or permitted for an actor. Further, we formalise some realistic, intuitive notions and analyse what properties hold for the relativised deontic modalities concerning groups of actors.

4.3.1 The semantics of the collective obligation

In order to discuss the relativised deontic modalities concerning groups of actors in SDL, we will use the following semantics. We will use model $M = (W, P^+(I), R_I, V)$ for system SDL_X consisting of four elements:

1. The set of possible worlds $W = \{w_1, w_2, \ldots\}$
2. The non-empty powerset $P^+(I)$ of the set of individuals $I = \{i_1, i_2, \ldots\}$.
3. The set of functions $R_I = \{R_X \mid X \in P^+(I)\}$. The function $R_X \in R_I$ on W returns the deontically ideal worlds for group X given a world: $R_X : W \to 2^W$.
4. A valuation function V, which assigns the value 'true' or 'false' to a proposition at a world in W.

We assume that $R_i(w) = R_{\{i\}}(w)$ for all $w \in W$ and $i \in I$.

The truth conditions for collective obligation O_X and collective permission P_X are now defined as follows:

$$M, w \models O_X(p) \text{ iff } R_X(w) \subseteq [\![p]\!] \tag{4.41}$$

and

$$M, w \models P_X(p) \text{ iff } R_X(w) \cap [\![p]\!] \neq \emptyset. \tag{4.42}$$

Schema (OD) holds by adding the following constraint:

$$R_X(w) \neq \emptyset, \text{ for all } R_X \in R_I \text{ and for all } w \in W. \tag{4.43}$$

Truth conditions (4.41) and (4.42) are sufficient to validate the rule and all axioms of system SDL for the collective obligation and permission. At first glance, this seems to be correct, since the impersonal obligation in SDL is read as an obligation related to one and the same individual or group all the time, which corresponds with $O_i(p)$ or $O_X(p)$: an obligation related to a single individual i or a single group X. However, we shall see that the validity of schema (OD) for O_X depends on the interpretation of collective obligation $O_X(p)$.

4.3.2 The interpretation of $O_X(p)$

We discuss two possible interpretations of $O_X(p)$:

1. The *strict collective obligation*: an obligation aimed strictly at group X.
2. The *weak collective obligation*: an obligation for some subgroup of X, i.e.[12]

$$O_X(p) \equiv \exists_{Y \in P^+(X)} O_Y(p) \tag{4.44}$$

The strict collective obligation

If we interpret $O_X(p)$ as a strict collective obligation, we can discuss the theory of the relativised deontic modalities concerning groups of actors analogously with the theory concerning actors, since now every group stands on its own, like the actors. In this interpretation of $O_X(p)$, we consider the groups to be single 'addressees'. The only difference with the theory concerning actors is the number of addressees. Let $I = \{i_1, \ldots, i_n\}$, then we have n addressees for the theory concerning individuals and $2^n - 1$ addressees for the theory concerning groups of individuals.

A consequence of this interpretation is that there is no relation between the different groups if we accept conflicts between collective obligations for different groups, such as

$$O_X(p) \wedge O_Y(\neg p).$$

If we want to obtain a coherent normative system, i.e. every group is permitted what is obligatory, with the formal counterpart

$$O_{X_1}(p) \wedge O_{X_2}(q) \wedge \ldots \wedge O_{X_k}(v) \rightarrow \forall_{X \in P^+(I)} P_X(p \wedge q \wedge \ldots \wedge v), \tag{4.45}$$

[12] $P^+(X)$ stands for the non-empty powerset of set X.

then there is a relation between the groups, expressed by the following constraint

$$\cap_{X \in P^+(I)} R_X(w) \neq \emptyset, \text{ for all } w \in W. \tag{4.46}$$

As we have seen in section 4.2, this removes the possibility of expressing conflicts between collective obligations for different groups of individuals. That is why we do not enforce principle (4.45).

The weak collective obligation

Bailhache [1991] stated that if there is a group for which it is obligatory to accomplish p, say X, and there is a group for which it is obligatory to accomplish q, say Y, then it is obligatory for *at least* group $X \cup Y$ to accomplish $p \wedge q$. This can be formalised as follows

$$O_X(p) \wedge O_Y(q) \rightarrow O_{X \cup Y}(p \wedge q), \tag{4.47}$$

but this does not follow from the semantics given so far.

To validate principle (4.47), we add an extra condition for accessibility function R_X:

$$R_X(w) \subseteq R_Y(w) \text{ if } Y \in P^+(X) \text{ for all } w \in W. \tag{4.48}$$

Thus, if something is deontically relevant to a group X, it is also considered deontically relevant to every subgroup of X. Note that

$$R_I(w) = \cap_{X \in P^+(I)} R_X(w). \tag{4.49}$$

It is easy to show that principle (4.47) is now valid: let $O_X(p) \wedge O_Y(q)$, then $R_X(w) \subseteq [\![p]\!]$ and $R_Y(w) \subseteq [\![q]\!]$. Since $R_{X \cup Y}(w) \subseteq R_X(w)$ and $R_{X \cup Y}(w) \subseteq R_Y(w)$, it holds that $R_{X \cup Y}(w) \subseteq R_X(w) \cap R_Y(w) \subseteq [\![p]\!] \cap [\![q]\!] = [\![p \wedge q]\!]$. Hence, $O_{X \cup Y}(p \wedge q)$.

Further, we can derive the formula following immediately from (4.48)

$$O_X(p) \rightarrow O_{X \cup Y}(p). \tag{4.50}$$

Thus, if it is obligatory for a group to accomplish something, then it is also obligatory for every superset of that group. And, consequently,

$$P_{X \cup Y}(p) \rightarrow P_X(p). \tag{4.51}$$

At first glance, this may seem paradoxical, since it is normally incorrect to say, for instance, that if X is obliged that p, then X and Y are obliged that p. However, we interpret $O_X(p)$ as an obligation for group X without being able to say to which subgroup of X this obligation applies. Thus, if ‘it is obligatory for John to accomplish that the window is closed’, then ‘it is also obligatory for John and Paul to accomplish that the window is closed’, meaning that John has to accomplish this, or Paul, or Paul and John together. We can formalise this *weak collective obligation* as follows:[13]

$$O_X(p) \equiv \exists_{Y \in P^+(X)} O_Y(p), \tag{4.52}$$

which is valid by constraint (4.48). Suppose that $O_X(p)$ holds, then $R_X(w) \subseteq [\![p]\!]$. Hence, $\exists_{Y \in P^+(X)}(R_Y(w) \subseteq [\![p]\!])$, namely X, thus $\exists_{Y \in P^+(X)} O_Y(p)$. Suppose that $\exists_{Y \in P^+(X)} O_Y(p)$, then $\exists_{Y \in P^+(X)}(R_Y(w) \subseteq [\![p]\!])$, say Z. Since $Z \in P^+(X)$, it follows that $R_X(w) \subseteq R_Z(w)$. Hence, $R_X(w) \subseteq [\![p]\!]$ and thus $O_X(p)$.

Consequently, by schema $(Df.P)$, it holds that

$$P_X(p) \equiv \forall_{Y \in P^+(X)} P_Y(p). \tag{4.53}$$

The 'paradox' involved in (4.50), since it is misleading to say that i and j have an obligation to accomplish p, if i has an obligation to accomplish p, bears resemblance to the Ross paradox - $O(p) \rightarrow O(p \vee q)$ - which is a valid principle in SDL: 'it is obligatory that the letter is mailed' implies that 'it is obligatory that the letter is mailed or burnt'. These paradoxes are associated with weakening and so with the meaning of the implication: a formula $A \rightarrow B$ is valid if the consequent is weaker than the antecedent. Therefore, these paradoxes do not form real problems.

If we want to express that i and j are 'essential' group-components to fulfill an obligation, then we can formalise this as follows:

$$O_{\{i,j\}}(p) \wedge \neg O_i(p) \wedge \neg O_j(p) \tag{4.54}$$

We can regard (4.54) as a definition of genuine group obligation or *cooperative obligation* [cf. Hilpinen, 1973].

With this interpretation of $O_X(p)$, we have to give up schema (OD) for O_X if we want to express conflicts between the collective obligations of different groups, such as

$$O_X(p) \wedge O_Y(\neg p).$$

This formula does not hold in the semantics so far given, because $(O_X(p) \wedge O_Y(\neg p)) \rightarrow (O_{X \cup Y}(p) \wedge O_{X \cup Y}(\neg p))$ and $(O_{X \cup Y}(p) \wedge O_{X \cup Y}(\neg p))$ contradicts principle (OD^*). Principle (OD^*) is derived from axioms (OC) and (OD), thus we have to reject one of these axioms. We cannot reject (OC), since this follows immediately from the truth condition for O_X. Furthermore, it would be counter-intuitive to reject this schema. Thus, we reject schema (OD) by giving up constraint (4.43).[14] Now, we are able to express conflicts between collective obligations of groups. Since (OD) does not hold, we can also express

[13] There is another possible interpretation of $O_X(p)$:

$$O_X(p) \equiv \exists_{Y \in P^+(X)} O^*_Y(p),$$

with O^*_Y a strict collective obligation. This interpretation of $O_X(p)$ corresponds to the interpretation of the weak collective obligation, in the sense that all principles which are valid for the weak collective obligation also are valid for this third interpretation.

[14] By giving up constraint (4.43), we also have to give up constraint (4.3). Hence, (OD) and (OD^*) for O_i are not valid any more.

conflicts between collective obligations for the same group, such as

$$O_X(p) \wedge O_X(\neg p).$$

At first glance, this seems to be a drawback since, if we have a conflict, such as $O_X(p) \wedge O_Y(\neg p)$, we can derive anything for the group $X \cup Y$, for instance $O_{X \cup Y}(q)$, since $O_X(p) \wedge O_Y(\neg p) \rightarrow O_{X \cup Y}(p) \wedge O_{X \cup Y}(\neg p)$, and from schema (OC) it follows that $O_{X \cup Y}(p \wedge \neg p)$. From rule (ROM) it follows that $O_{X \cup Y}(q \wedge \neg q))$ and hence, by using once again the rule (ROM), it follows that $O_{X \cup Y}(q)$. However, this is not a real drawback since, if a group has to accomplish something that is impossible, it is hard to say anything meaningful about that group, so that we can derive anything about the obligations for that group.

4.3.3 The strong and weak obligations

With the semantics of the collective obligation and collective permission, we can also formalise the unspecific and general collective obligations and collective permissions. We claim that the general collective obligation and permission are the strongest notions of obligation and permission, and the unspecific collective obligation and permission the weakest notions of obligation and permission. We call the general collective obligation the *strong obligation*, the unspecific collective obligation the *weak obligation*, the general collective permission the *strong permission* and the unspecific collective permission the *weak permission*. We can formalise these notions as follows:

$$O^{\oplus}(p) \equiv \forall_{X \in P^{+}(I)} O_X(p) \tag{4.55}$$

$$O^{\ominus}(p) \equiv \exists_{X \in P^{+}(I)} O_X(p) \tag{4.56}$$

$$P^{\ominus}(p) \equiv \forall_{X \in P^{+}(I)} P_X(p) \tag{4.57}$$

$$P^{\oplus}(p) \equiv \exists_{X \in P^{+}(I)} P_X(p) \tag{4.58}$$

We define the truth conditions for $O^{\oplus}$ and $P^{\oplus}$ as follows

$$M, w \models O^{\oplus}(p) \text{ iff } R^{\oplus}(w) \subseteq [\![p]\!] \tag{4.59}$$

and

$$M, w \models P^{\oplus}(p) \text{ iff } R^{\oplus}(w) \cap [\![p]\!] \neq \emptyset. \tag{4.60}$$

To accomplish that these notions are the notions of the strong obligation and the weak permission, we have to restrict accessibility function $R^{\oplus}$ as follows:[15]

$$R^{\oplus}(w) = \cup_{X \in P^{+}(I)} R_X(w) \text{ for all } w \in W. \tag{4.61}$$

[15]Suppose $O^{\oplus}(p)$. This holds iff $R^{\oplus}(w) \subseteq [\![p]\!]$ iff $\cup_{X \in P^{+}(I)} R_X(w) \subseteq [\![p]\!]$ iff $\forall_{X \in P^{+}(I)}(R_X(w) \subseteq [\![p]\!])$ iff $\forall_{X \in P^{+}(I)} O_X(p)$.

With this restriction of $R^{\oplus}$, we accomplish that $O^{\oplus}(p) \equiv \forall_{X \in P^{+}(I)} O_X(p)$ and, consequently, $P^{\oplus}(p) \equiv \exists_{X \in P^{+}(I)} P_X(p)$.

Note that the following constraint holds[16]

$$\cup_{i \in I} R_i(w) \subseteq R^{\oplus}(w) \text{ for all } w \in W, \tag{4.62}$$

and that truth conditions (4.59) and (4.60) are equivalent to

$$M, w \models O^{\oplus}(p) \text{ iff } \forall_{X \in P^{+}(I)} (R_X(w) \subseteq [\![p]\!]) \tag{4.63}$$

and

$$M, w \models P^{\oplus}(p) \text{ iff } \exists_{X \in P^{+}(I)} (R_X(w) \cap [\![p]\!] \neq \emptyset). \tag{4.64}$$

Schema (OD) becomes valid by adding the following constraint:

$$R^{\oplus}(w) \neq \emptyset \text{ for all } w \in W, \tag{4.65}$$

which corresponds with $\exists_{X \in P^{+}(I)} (R_X(w) \neq \emptyset)$.

It is easy to see that the following principles are valid:

1. $O^{\oplus}(p) \wedge O^{\oplus}(q) \rightarrow O^{\oplus}(p \wedge q)$
2. $O^{\oplus}(p \vee \neg p)$
3. $\neg O^{\oplus}(p \wedge \neg p)$
4. $P^{\oplus}(p) \equiv \neg O^{\oplus}(\neg p)$
5. $\neg(O^{\oplus}(p) \wedge O^{\oplus}(\neg p))$
6. $O^{\oplus}(p) \rightarrow P^{\oplus}(p)$

The rule and all axioms of *SDL* are valid for the strong obligation $O^{\oplus}$. Note that it does not matter whether we interpret $O_X(p)$ as the strict collective obligation or as the weak collective obligation, since the strong obligation is an obligation aimed at all groups. Note that the general obligation corresponds with the strong obligation, in the sense that the principles that hold for O^{+} also hold for $O^{\oplus}$.

We can define the truth conditions for $O^{\ominus}$ and $P^{\ominus}$ as follows

$$M, w \models O^{\ominus}(p) \text{ iff } R^{\ominus}(w) \subseteq [\![p]\!] \tag{4.66}$$

and

$$M, w \models P^{\ominus}(p) \text{ iff } R^{\ominus}(w) \cap [\![p]\!] \neq \emptyset. \tag{4.67}$$

---

[16] We mark again that $R_i(w) = R_{\{i\}}(w)$ for all $i \in I$ and for all $w \in W$.

To accomplish that these notions are the notions of the weak obligation and the strong permission, we restrict accessibility function $R^{\ominus}$ as follows

$$R^{\ominus}(w) \subseteq \cap_{X \in P^{+}(I)} R_X(w) \text{ for all } w \in W. \tag{4.68}$$

However, this is not an accurate definition for the weak obligation as the unspecific collective obligation. Now, we can only derive that $\exists_{X \in P^{+}(I)} O_X(p) \rightarrow O^{\ominus}(p)$: suppose that $\exists_{X \in P^{+}(I)} O_X(p)$. This holds iff $\exists_{X \in P^{+}(I)}(R_X(p) \subseteq [\![p]\!])$, hence $\cap_{X \in P^{+}(I)} R_X(w) \subseteq [\![p]\!]$ and since $R^{\ominus}(w) \subseteq \cap_{X \in P^{+}(I)} R_X(w)$, it follows that $R^{\ominus}(w) \subseteq [\![p]\!]$. Thus, $O^{\ominus}(p)$. That is why we define the truth conditions for $O^{\ominus}$ and $P^{\ominus}$ as follows:

$$M, w \models O^{\ominus}(p) \text{ iff } \exists_{X \in P^{+}(I)}(R_X(w) \subseteq [\![p]\!]) \tag{4.69}$$

and

$$M, w \models P^{\ominus}(p) \text{ iff } \forall_{X \in P^{+}(I)}(R_X(w) \cap [\![p]\!] \neq \emptyset). \tag{4.70}$$

For the weak obligation, it does matter how we interpret $O_X(p)$.[17] As we have seen, there are two possible interpretations for the collective obligation:

1. the strict collective obligation
2. the weak collective obligation

The strict collective obligation
Suppose that we interpret $O_X(p)$ as the strict collective obligation. Then schema (OD) for $O^{\ominus}$ is validated by adding the constraint

$$\forall_{X \in P^{+}(I)}(R_X(w) \neq \emptyset) \text{ for all } w \in W. \tag{4.71}$$

$\neg O^{\ominus}(p \wedge \neg p)$ holds iff $\neg\exists_{X \in P^{+}(I)}(R_X(w) \subseteq [\![p \wedge \neg p]\!])$ iff $\forall_{X \in P^{+}(I)} \neg(R_X(w) \subseteq \emptyset)$ iff $\forall_{X \in P^{+}(I)}(R_X(w) \neq \emptyset)$.

We do not want schema (OD^{*}) for $O^{\ominus}$, since it removes the possibility of expressing conflicting collective obligations of different groups. According to the semantics given, this schema does not hold.[18] Thus, principle $O^{\ominus}(p) \rightarrow P^{\ominus}(p)$ does not hold either, which is equivalent to principle (OD^{*}) for $O^{\ominus}$.

Since we do not have principle (OD^{*}) for the weak obligation $O^{\ominus}$, schema (OC) does not hold for $O^{\ominus}$ either. In subsection 4.2.1, we saw that the formula

$$(\exists_{i \in I} O_i(p) \wedge \exists_{i \in I} O_i(q)) \rightarrow \exists_{i \in I} O_i(p \wedge q) \tag{4.72}$$

[17] The strong obligation is an obligation for all groups in $P^{+}(I)$. Hence, it does not matter how we interpret the collective obligation in a strong obligation, since for every set of individuals the same obligation holds.

[18] Schema (OD^{*}) would be valid by adding the constraint $\cap_{X \in P^{+}(I)} R_X(w) \neq \emptyset$ for all $w \in W$.

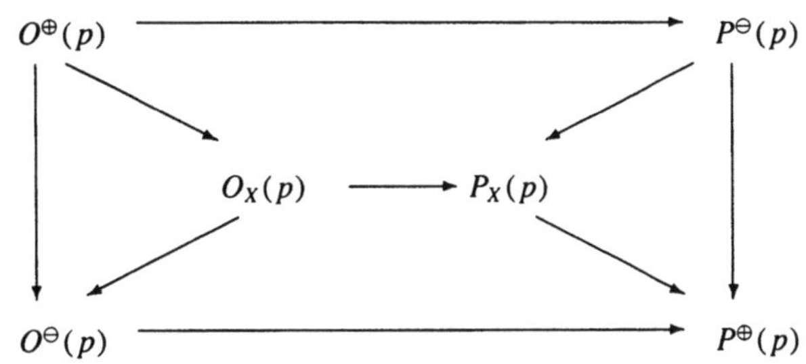

Figure 4.6: Logical relations with O_X as the strict collective obligation

was clearly counter-intuitive. That was the reason why we gave up schema (OC) for the unspecific obligation $O^-(p)$. Analogously, we will reject (OC) for the weak obligation $O^{\ominus}(p)$:

$$(\exists_{X\in P^+(I)} O_X(p) \wedge \exists_{X\in P^+(I)} O_X(q)) \rightarrow \exists_{X\in P^+(I)} O_X(p \wedge q), \tag{4.73}$$

since this is also counter-intuitive. Suppose that (OC) would be valid and suppose further that only $O_X(p)$ and $O_Y(q)$ hold. Then $\exists_{X\in P^+(I)} O_X(p \wedge q)$, say Z, thus $O_Z(p \wedge q)$. Hence, it follows that $O_Z(p)$ and $O_Z(q)$ hold. Thus, the obligation to accomplish p and q, respectively, is not strictly aimed at group X and Y, respectively, but also at group Z and this is in contradiction with the interpretation of $O_X(p)$ as the strict collective obligation.

Note that the weak obligation corresponds with the unspecific obligation in the sense that the principles that hold for O^- also hold for $O^{\ominus}$.

Further, the following four principles are valid if we interpret $O_X(p)$ as the strict collective obligation:

1. $O^{\oplus}(p) \rightarrow P^{\ominus}(p)$
2. $O^{\ominus}(p) \rightarrow P^{\oplus}(p)$
3. $O^{\oplus}(p) \rightarrow O^{\ominus}(p)$
4. $P^{\ominus}(p) \rightarrow P^{\oplus}(p)$

The former two principles are valid, because of constraint (4.71). The latter two principles are obvious. Figure 4.6 summarises the logical relations between the operators $O^{\oplus}$, $O^{\ominus}$, $P^{\oplus}$, $P^{\ominus}$, O_X and P_X.[19]

As we have seen in subsection 4.2.4, the theory developed by Herrestad and Krogh suffers from the problem that principle (OD^*) creeps back in for $O_h^{\ominus}$ if we accept the principle $O_k^{\oplus}(p) \rightarrow P_h^{\ominus}(p)$. The solution they provide - to block the inference of $P_h^{\ominus}(p)$ from

[19]Note that this figure corresponds with figure 4.3

$O_k^{\oplus}(p)$ when p is a tautology - was not satisfactory, since we were able to derive the undesirable principles $P_h^{\ominus}(p) \to (O_h^{\ominus}(q) \to P_h^{\ominus}(q))$ and $O_k^{\oplus}(p) \to (O_h^{\ominus}(q) \to P_h^{\ominus}(q))$, if p is no tautology.

The above consideration is a solution to this problem, since the principle $O^{\oplus}(p) \to P^{\ominus}(p)$ is valid and principle (OD^*) does not creep back in for $O^{\ominus}$. Further, the undesirable principles $P^{\ominus}(p) \to (O^{\ominus}(q) \to P^{\ominus}(q))$ and $O^{\oplus}(p) \to (O^{\ominus}(q) \to P^{\ominus}(q))$ are not valid, which is easy to see from truth conditions (4.69) and (4.70).

This solution consists of substituting the truth condition for $O_k^{\oplus}$, $P_k^{\oplus}$, $O_h^{\ominus}$ and $P_h^{\ominus}$ given by Herrestad and Krogh by the truth conditions given in this section, with the consequence that $O^{\oplus}$ is defined as the strong obligation and $O^{\ominus}$ as the weak obligation. The justification for these definitions is that we claim that the strong obligation is the strongest notion of the obligation and the weak obligation is the weakest notion of the obligation. An advantage of this consideration is that $O^{\oplus}$ and $O^{\ominus}$ are defined exactly in contrast to Herrestad and Krogh's theory, where the notions of $O_k^{\oplus}$ and $O_h^{\ominus}$ are vague and, as a consequence, difficult to apply.

The interpretation of $O_X(p)$ as a strict collective obligation is necessary for this solution, as we shall see in the consideration of the weak collective obligation below.

The weak collective obligation

If we interpret $O_X(p)$ as the weak collective obligation, then schema (OC) for $O^{\ominus}$ is valid, since for this interpretation the following principle is valid (which we saw in the previous subsection):

$$O_X(p) \wedge O_Y(q) \to O_{X \cup Y}(p \wedge q),$$

because constraint (4.48) holds. Thus, $O^{\ominus}(p) \wedge O^{\ominus}(q) \to O^{\ominus}(p \wedge q)$ is also valid.

Schema (OD) does not hold for $O^{\ominus}$, since (OD) does not hold for the weak collective obligation either (see previous subsection). Suppose (OD) holds for $O^{\ominus}$, then $\neg O^{\ominus}(p \wedge p)$ holds and this is equivalent to $\forall_{X \in P^{+}(I)} \neg O_X(p \wedge \neg p)$. Hence, this implies that schema (OD) is valid for $O_X(p)$. Thus, since we do not have schema (OD) for the weak collective obligation, we do not have this schema for the weak obligation either. Consequently, schema (OD^*) does not hold, since it follows from schemata (OD) and (OC).

From (4.52) and (4.56) we can derive the following principles

$$O_I(p) \equiv O^{\ominus}(p) \tag{4.74}$$

and, consequently,

$$P_I(p) \equiv P^{\ominus}(p). \tag{4.75}$$

Thus, $O_I(p)$ coincides with the weak obligation and $P_I(p)$ with the strong permission.

Now, we only need two different notions to distinguish the weak, collective and strong obligations, since collective obligation $O_I(p)$ collapses in the weak obligation $O^{\ominus}(p)$.

Further, the following two principles are valid

1. $O^{\oplus}(p) \to O^{\ominus}(p)$

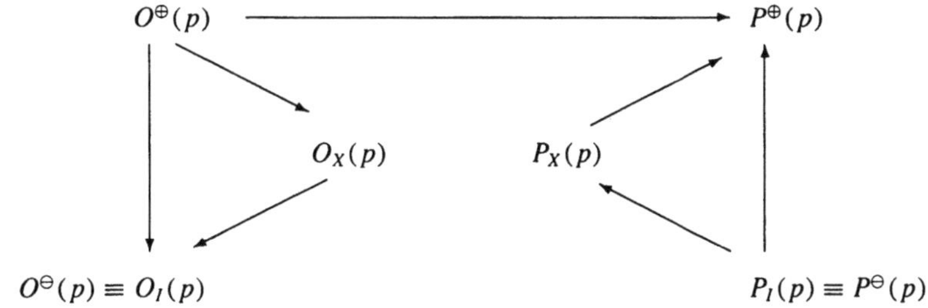

Figure 4.7: Logical relations with O_X as the weak collective obligation

2. $P^{\ominus}(p) \rightarrow P^{\oplus}(p)$

Principles $O^{\oplus}(p) \rightarrow P^{\ominus}(p)$ and $O^{\ominus}(p) \rightarrow P^{\oplus}(p)$ do not hold, since we do not have constraint (4.43), otherwise (OD^*) creeps back in for the weak obligation and, in addition for the unspecific obligation, thus also $O^{\ominus}(p) \rightarrow P^{\ominus}(p)$. This can easily be shown.[20]

This corresponds with the problem of accepting $O^{\oplus}(p) \rightarrow P^{\ominus}(p)$ discussed in subsection 4.2.4 and above.

Note that the principle

$$O^{\oplus}(p) \rightarrow P^{\oplus}(p)$$

is valid: 'if it is obligatory for all sets of actors that p, then it is permitted for some sets of actors that p.' Thus, schema (OD^*) holds for $O^{\oplus}$, because of constraint (4.65) and the truth conditions (4.59) and (4.60), but not for the weak collective obligation O_X, since we do not have constraint (4.43). Figure 4.7 summarises the logical relations between the operators $O^{\oplus}$, $O^{\ominus}$, $P^{\oplus}$, $P^{\ominus}$, O_X and P_X.

4.4 The notions of obligation

In this chapter, we distinguished six notions of obligations:

1. the personal obligation: $O_i(p)$
2. the general obligation: $O^{+}(p)$
3. the unspecific obligation: $O^{-}(p)$
4. the collective obligation: $O_X(p)$
5. the strong obligation: $O^{\oplus}(p)$

[20]Suppose $O^{\oplus}(p) \rightarrow P^{\ominus}(p)$. This holds iff $\forall_{X \in P^+(I)}(R_X(w) \subseteq [\![p]\!]) \rightarrow \forall_{X \in P^+(I)}(R_X(w) \cap [\![p]\!] \neq \emptyset)$ iff $\forall_{X \in P^+(I)}(R_X(w) \neq \emptyset)$ iff $R_I(w) \neq \emptyset$ iff $\bigcap_{X \in P^+(I)} R_X(w) \neq \emptyset$. The constraint $\bigcap_{X \in P^+(I)} R_X(w) \neq \emptyset$ validates the constraint $\exists_{X \in P^+(I)}(R_X(w) \subseteq [\![p]\!]) \rightarrow \forall_{X \in P^+(I)}(R_X(w) \cap [\![p]\!] \neq \emptyset)$. Thus, $O^{\ominus}(p) \rightarrow P^{\ominus}(p)$, which is equivalent to principle (OD^*), creeps back in for the weak obligation.

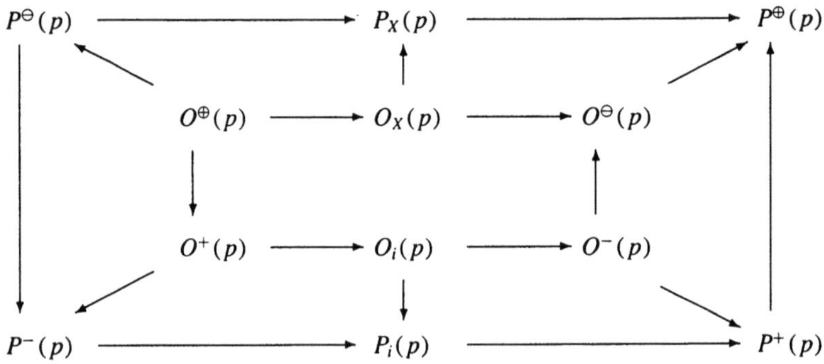

Figure 4.8: The logical relations with $O_X(p)$ as the strict collective obligation

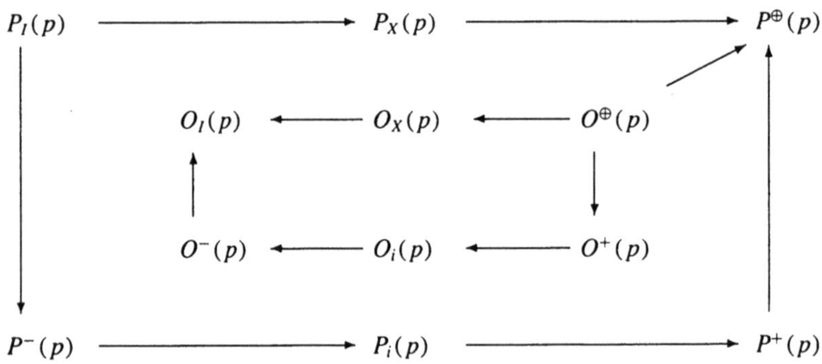

Figure 4.9: The logical relations with $O_X(p)$ as the weak collective obligation

6. the weak obligation: $O^{\ominus}(p)$

with the corresponding notions of permission. In this section, we summarise the relations between these notions, with $O_X(p)$ as the strict collective obligation. In the previous subsection, we saw that the validity of some relations, such as $O^{\oplus}(p) \rightarrow P^{\ominus}(p)$, depends on the interpretation of $O_X(p)$. In figure 4.8, the relations between the different notions are given, if we interpret $O_X(p)$ as the strict collective obligation. If we consider $O_X(p)$ to be the weak obligation, we do not need six but five different notions of obligation, since the weak collective obligation $O_I(p)$ collapses in the weak obligation $O^{\ominus}(p)$. Further, the principles $O^{\oplus}(p) \rightarrow P^{\ominus}(p)$ and $O^{\ominus}(p) \rightarrow P^{\oplus}(p)$ do not hold in this case, as we already discussed in the previous subsection. The valid properties of the notions, with $O_X(p)$ as the weak collective obligation, are summarised in figure 4.9.

4.5 Evaluation and conclusions

In this section we discussed and modified formalisations of relativised deontic modalities in *SDL*. A disadvantage to relativise the O-operator is that we cannot make a distinction between 'it is obligatory that i brings it about that not p' and 'it is obligatory that i does not bring it about that p'. In the formalisations presented in this chapter only the first sentence is represented: $O_i(\neg p)$. The distinction between the above sentences can be made by constructing the class of (individual agent) *act-positions* to express a new class of normative positions developed by Kanger [1971] and Lindahl [1977]. The treatment of act descriptions employs a relativised monadic operator E_i. The expression $E_i p$ is read as 'actor i brings it about that p' or 'actor i sees to it that p'.

The sentence $O(E_i p)$ is read as 'it is obligatory that i brings it about that p', just as $O_i(p)$. However, now we have four atomic types of obligations [cf. Makinson, 1986] instead of two atomic types $O_i(p)$ and $O_i(\neg p)$:

1. $O(E_i p)$: 'it is obligatory that i brings it about that p'.
2. $O(E_i \neg p)$: 'it is obligatory that i brings it about that not p'.
3. $O(\neg E_i p)$: 'it is obligatory that i does not bring it about that p'.
4. $O(\neg E_i \neg p)$: 'it is obligatory that i does not bring it about that not p'.

The first two expressions correspond with what is meant in this chapter with $O_i(p)$ or $O_i(\neg p)$. It is obvious that with this relativised monadic operator E_i, deontic logic becomes more powerful than the relativising of the O-operator.

However, in this chapter our aim was to discuss the possible interpretations of non-relativised deontic operators, and how these interpretations relate to the notions of the deontic operators *relativised to (groups of) actors*. The result of the presentations of formalisations of relativised deontic modalities is a distinction between several levels of notions of obligation and permission. The first level is the level of the personal notions: O_i and P_i. The second level is the level of the general and unspecific notions: O^+ and P^-, and O^- and P^+, respectively. The third level is the level of the collective notions: $O_X(p)$ and $P_X(p)$, and the last level we discussed is the level of strong and weak notions: $O^\oplus$ and $P^\ominus$, and $O^\ominus$ and $P^\oplus$, respectively. The relations between these four levels are summarised in figures 4.8 and 4.9.

The extension by including relativised deontic modalities in *SDL* provides us with the possibility of expressing, for example, that an act is obligatory for an individual, but not for everyone:

$$O_i(p) \wedge \neg\forall_{j\in I} O_j(p),$$

which is not expressible within a non-relativised deontic logic.

A problem arose in Herrestad and Krogh's theory when they added the principle $O_k^\oplus(p) \rightarrow P_h^\ominus(p)$ to their system, since this gave principle (OD^*) for $O_h^\ominus$ and for O^-. They proposed a restricted bridge principle. However, this solution is not quite satisfactory. Instead, we suggest defining $O^{\oplus}(p)$ as the strong obligation and $O^{\ominus}(p)$ as the weak obligation, based on the collective obligation $O_X(p)$ interpreted as the strict collective obligation. We have shown that this smoothly solves the problem without undesirable consequences. The interpretation of $O_X(p)$ as the strict collective obligation is essential since the problem is not solved if we interpret $O_X(p)$ as the weak collective obligation. This distinction between the interpretations of $O_X(p)$ is important, since it acquires different meanings of and intuitions about collective obligations.

The extension of counterparties to the system SDL_X has not been discussed. The counterparty is an individual or a group of individuals that has a 'right' against the addressee, that has a 'duty' (an obligation). 'Right' and 'duty' are correlative terms, i.e. when a right is invaded, a duty is violated.

Several authors [Kanger, 1971, 1985; Lindahl, 1977; Makinson, 1986; Herrestad and Krogh, 1995] analysed or described the types of rights relationships between the addressees (or bearers) and counterparties from the classic work by Hohfeld [1964] to express directed obligation for example. An example of a directed obligation is that John is obliged towards Paul that he shall stay away from Paul's land. In other words, Paul has a *right* against John that the latter will stay away from Paul's land, the correlative (and equivalent) being that John is under a *duty* toward Paul to stay away from the place [cf. Hohfeld, 1964]. Just like the bearer, the counterparty can be a group of individuals, so that we may distinguish two interpretations of the directed obligation:

1. The *strict directed obligation*: an obligation for X strictly towards group Y.

2. The *weak directed obligation*: an obligation for X towards some subgroup of Y.

The authors mentioned above analysed and described the strict directed obligation. The formalisation of the weak directed obligation is an interesting extension of the counterparty relativised deontic modalities. We will leave this for further research.

In the next chapter, we will give a description of relativised deontic operators pertaining to Ought-to-do statements.

Chapter 5

Relativised deontic modalities in *DDL*

5.1 Introduction

A normative rule is aimed at actors, who are expected to follow the norms specified by the (relevant) authority. The addition of actors to DDL allows us to express who has the responsibility for performing an action. For instance, the applicability of the norm 'it is obligatory to perform action β ($O(\beta)$)' depends on the individual for whom the norm is meant. According to the Dutch Traffic Regulation 1990, the speed limit for mopeds is 30 km/h within built-up areas and 50 km/h for motor vehicles. Therefore, the norm $O(\beta)$, where β is the action 'to drive slower than 30 km/h' is aimed at moped riders and not at motor-vehicle drivers. Thus, moped riders can be fined for speeding with respect to this norm, but on the strength of this norm motor-vehicle drivers cannot.

It is obvious that an action cannot be performed by itself; it has to be performed by an actor or a group of actors. We will take an event to be an action initiated by an actor or a group of actors. We distinguish two kinds of events [cf. Royakkers and Dignum, 1995]:

1. The *individual events*, i.e. actions initiated by individuals.

2. The *collective events*, i.e. actions initiated by groups of actors.

With the help of these events, we extend DDL with actors and groups of actors. The concept of collective events is new, and can be seen as a modification and an extension of the actor logic $L(Sig_{Dyn})$ developed by Wieringa and Meyer [1993].

This chapter mainly deals with a semantic and an axiomatic study of extensions of DDL, taking into consideration actors and groups of actors on the basis of dynamic logic. These extensions of DDL enable us to distinguish between strong, general, personal, unspecific, weak and group obligations (the same types of obligations as in chapter 4), and to formalise and analyse the relations between these different notions of obligation.

The organisation of this chapter is as follows. Section 5.2 deals with the semantics of individual events and the extension of DDL concerning the addition of actors on the basis of individual events. In section 5.3, we discuss the semantics of collective events and the extension of DDL adding of groups of actors on the basis of collective events. Section 5.4 presents the distinction between the different notions of obligation and their relations and analyses the properties of some notions of obligation. In section 5.5, we discuss the satisfaction of norms by groups. Section 5.6 reconsiders the relation between Ought-to-be and Ought-to-do. The notion of commitment to determine the relation between individuals is discussed in sectionp.comm. In the final section, we provide some conclusions.

5.2 The extension of DDL with actors

In this section, we discuss the extension of DDL with actors on the basis of individual event expressions. First, we discuss the semantics of individual event expressions.

5.2.1 The semantics of individual event expressions

The set of actors who initiate the actions is denoted by I. An atomic individual event is an action initiated by an actor. (For short, we will write 'events' instead of 'individual events' in this section.) An atomic event is denoted by an actor $i \in I$ and an action β as follows: $i : \beta$. We define $\underline{Evt}$ as the set of atomic events.[1]

The set of all event expressions Evt can now be determined by the following BNF for its elements (α):

$$\alpha ::= \quad i : \beta | \alpha_1 \cup^\star \alpha_2 | \alpha_1 \&^\star \alpha_2 | \overline{\alpha},$$

where $i \in I$, $\alpha_1, \alpha_2 \in Evt$ and $\beta \in Act$.

The meaning of $\alpha_1 \cup^\star \alpha_2$ is a choice between α_1 and α_2. Furthermore, $\alpha_1 \&^\star \alpha_2$ stands for the simultaneous performance of α_1 and α_2, and $\overline{\alpha}$ stands for the negation of event expression α. The event expression i : **any** means that i performs a universal ('do not care which') action. The i : **change** can then be characterised as the performance of a 'do not care which, but not the *skip*' action by i. The event expression i : **skip** stands for i 'performing' the empty action, i.e. the event that has no effect ('does nothing'). Finally, the event expression i : **fail** means that i performs an action that always fails. After this event, the system stops and nothing can be done any more. Note that the meanings of these event expressions correspond with the meanings of the action expressions discussed in chapter 3, except that actors are added here.

Remarks

1. Wieringa and Meyer [1993] make a distinction between two kinds of choices:
   - The active choice: the choice labelled by an actor who *makes* the choice. They write $i : (\beta_1 \oplus \beta_2)$ for the active choice made by actor i.

[1]Note that an action β in an atomic event is not necessarily an atomic action.

- The passive choice: the choice between β_1 and β_2 is an underspecification, because it is either action β_1 or action β_2, but it is not specified which. They write $+$ for passive choice.

They show that active and passive choices differ. For example, the passive choice is associative ($i : ((\beta_1 + \beta_2) + \beta_3) = i : (\beta_1 + (\beta_2 + \beta_3))$) and the active choice is not. In our language of Evt, the choice $i : \beta_1 \cup^* \beta_2$ stands for the passive choice.

2. The performance of an atomic event, e.g. $i : \underline{a_1} \& \underline{a_2}$ (e.g. to walk & to whistle) involves the performance of the (semantical) elementary actions a_1 (to walk) and a_2 (to whistle), possibly together with other elementary actions (e.g. to look, to cross the street, etc.). The meaning of $i : \underline{a_1} \& \underline{a_2}$ only stipulates the performance of actions a_1 and a_2 (corresponding semantical $\underline{a_1}$ and a_2), but i is free to perform any other set of elementary actions simultaneous with a_1 and a_2.

Formally, we give the semantics of event expressions by means of *synchronicity* sets, similar to the ones defined in chapter 3. These synchronicity sets denote performances of 'packages' of (semantical) elementary actions that have to be performed simultaneously by the same actor.

Definition 5.2.1

1. *Set* $\{\delta\}$ *is a synchronicity set (s-set).*
2. *Set* $\{i : skip\}$ *is an s-set.*
3. *Every pair of a non-empty subset of A and an individual in I is an s-set.*

We use $S, S_1, S_2, \ldots$ for s-sets. The set of all s-sets, except $\{\delta\}$, will be denoted by $\mathcal{S}^*$. In concrete cases, we write an s-set using brackets. For instance, let $A = \{a_1, a_2, a_3\}$ and $I = \{i_1, i_2\}$, then s-set S consisting of the atomic actions a_1 and a_2 performed by i_1 is written as

$$S = [i_1 : A'], \text{ or } S = \begin{bmatrix} i_1 : & \begin{matrix} a_1 \\ a_2 \end{matrix} \end{bmatrix},$$

with $A' = \{a_1, a_2\}$.

The s-set consisting of event $i_1 : skip$ is written as $[i_1 : skip]$. Thus, $\mathcal{S}^* = \{[i : A'] \mid i \in I, A' \subseteq A, A' \neq \emptyset\} \cup \{[i : skip] \mid i \in I\}$. For the above example, $\mathcal{S}^* =$

$$\{[i_1 : skip], [i_1 : a_1], [i_1 : a_2], [i_1 : a_3], \begin{bmatrix} i_1 : & \begin{matrix} a_1 \\ a_2 \end{matrix} \end{bmatrix}, \begin{bmatrix} i_1 : & \begin{matrix} a_1 \\ a_3 \end{matrix} \end{bmatrix}, \begin{bmatrix} i_1 : & \begin{matrix} a_2 \\ a_3 \end{matrix} \end{bmatrix}, \begin{bmatrix} i_1 : & \begin{matrix} a_1 \\ a_2 \\ a_3 \end{matrix} \end{bmatrix},$$

$$[i_2 : skip], [i_2 : a_1], [i_2 : a_2], [i_2 : a_3], \begin{bmatrix} i_2 : & \begin{matrix} a_1 \\ a_2 \end{matrix} \end{bmatrix}, \begin{bmatrix} i_2 : & \begin{matrix} a_1 \\ a_3 \end{matrix} \end{bmatrix}, \begin{bmatrix} i_2 : & \begin{matrix} a_2 \\ a_3 \end{matrix} \end{bmatrix}, \begin{bmatrix} i_2 : & \begin{matrix} a_1 \\ a_2 \\ a_3 \end{matrix} \end{bmatrix}\}.$$

We use $\mathcal{S}_i^*$ to denote the set of all s-sets, except s-set $[\delta]$, with i as the individual, thus $\mathcal{S}_i^* = \{[i : A'] \mid A' \subseteq A, A' \neq \emptyset\} \cup \{[i : skip]\}$.

Definition 5.2.2 *Let $I = \{i_1, i_2, \ldots, i_n\}$, then T is defined as the set of the elements of the indirect product of $S^*_{i_1}, S^*_{i_2}, \ldots, S^*_{i_{n-1}}$ and $S^*_{i_n}$. We denote this as $T =_{def} \times_{i \in I} S^*_i$. An element of T is called a step. We use the letter 't' with possible marks for steps. We use t_i for the set of actions in A in the s-set of t which has i as the actor.*

Thus, a step t of T is an n-tuple. The order of the s-sets in a step is irrelevant. For instance, let $A = \{a_1, a_2, a_3\}$ and $I = \{i_1, i_2, i_3\}$, then the triple t consisting of s-sets $[i_1 : a_1]$, $\left[i_2 : \begin{array}{c} a_1 \\ a_3 \end{array}\right]$ and $\left[i_3 : \begin{array}{c} a_1 \\ a_2 \\ a_3 \end{array}\right]$ is written as

$$\left([i_1 : a_1], \left[i_2 : \begin{array}{c} a_1 \\ a_3 \end{array}\right], \left[i_3 : \begin{array}{c} a_1 \\ a_2 \\ a_3 \end{array}\right] \right)$$

and this is equal to the step

$$\left(\left[i_3 : \begin{array}{c} a_1 \\ a_2 \\ a_3 \end{array}\right], [i_1 : a_1], \left[i_2 : \begin{array}{c} a_1 \\ a_3 \end{array}\right] \right),$$

with, e.g. $t_{i_2} = \{a_1, a_3\}$. Note that the equality can be formally realised by defining an equivalence relation between steps. Here, it suffices to give this informal account.

A step denotes a deterministic sets of actions for all actors simultaneously. It shows for each actor what he will do next. The usefulness of the *skip* operator is that we can now say that in a certain situation some actors do nothing or do not affect the situation. Without the *skip* operator, we would have to indicate for each moment what actions are performed by each actor, even though some actors do not affect the situation. This leads to a very artificial and counter-intuitive specification, because it is unlikely that every actor does something all the time. We will use *skip* to indicate that actions performed by some actor have no influence on the situation.

Since our language of events contains a non-deterministic (choice) operator $\cup^\star$, we have to consider sets of steps $t \in T$. We use $T, T_1, T_2, \ldots$ to denote sets of steps.

Our event domain M_T is now given by:

Definition 5.2.3 *M_T is the collection of sets T consisting of steps.*

Note that M_T is the powerset of T, normally denoted by 2^T or $P(T)$. We will use the operations $\Cup$, $\Cap$ and $\tilde{}$ (operator for the set-theoretic complement) on the domain M_T as semantical counterparts of the syntactical operators $\cup^\star$, $\&^\star$ and $\bar{}$, respectively, in our language *Evt* of event expressions. Before we give these definitions, we define a handy operator on sets of steps:

Definition 5.2.4 *Let T be a set of steps, then*

$$T^\delta = \begin{cases} T \setminus \{[\delta]\} & \text{if } \exists_{t \in T} t \neq [\delta] \\ \{[\delta]\} & \text{otherwise.} \end{cases}$$

Now we can give the semantical operators on M_T. For the simultaneous operator $\&^*$, we use a set intersection $\dot{\cap}$, which is almost the same as the normal set intersection.

Definition 5.2.5 *For* $T_1, T_2 \in M_T$

$$T_1 \dot{\cap} T_2 = \begin{cases} T_1 \cap T_2 & \text{if } T_1 \cap T_2 \neq \emptyset \\ \{[\delta]\} & \text{otherwise.} \end{cases}$$

Operator $\dot{\cup}$ on sets of steps is defined as follows:

Definition 5.2.6 *For* $T_1, T_2 \in M_T$*:*

$$T_1 \dot{\cup} T_2 = (T_1 \cup T_2)^{\delta}.$$

Thus, the choice between two sets of steps is the union of those two sets minus $\{[\delta]\}$, unless the union does not contain anything else.

The definition of '$^{-}$' is given as follows:

Definition 5.2.7

1. *For a step t,*

$$t^{-} = T \setminus \{t\}.$$

2. *For a non-empty set* $T \in M_T$*,*

$$T^{-} = \dot{\cap}\{t^{-} | t \in T\}.$$

Thus, for a step t the negation just yields the set-theoretic complement of $\{t\}$ with respect to T. For the negation of a set of steps T, we take the intersection of the sets of the negation of all the steps contained in T. Note that $T \subseteq T$ and that $T \in M_T$. Now we can define the semantics of event expressions:

Definition 5.2.8 *The semantic function* $[\![\ ]\!] \in Evt \to M_T$*, with* $\underline{a}, \beta_1, \beta_2 \in Act, i \in I$ *and* $\alpha, \alpha_1, \alpha_2 \in Evt$*, is given by:*

1. $[\![i : \underline{a}]\!] = \{t \in T \mid a \in t_i\}$
2. $[\![i : \beta_1 \cup \beta_2]\!] = [\![i : \beta_1]\!] \dot{\cup} [\![i : \beta_2]\!]$
3. $[\![i : \beta_1 \& \beta_2]\!] = [\![i : \beta_1]\!] \dot{\cap} [\![i : \beta_2]\!]$
4. $[\![i : \overline{\beta_1}]\!] = [\![i : \beta_1]\!]^{-}$
5. $[\![\alpha_1 \cup^* \alpha_2]\!] = [\![\alpha_1]\!] \dot{\cup} [\![\alpha_2]\!]$
6. $[\![\alpha_1 \&^* \alpha_2]\!] = [\![\alpha_1]\!] \dot{\cap} [\![\alpha_2]\!]$
7. $[\![\overline{\alpha}]\!] = [\![\alpha]\!]^{-}$

8. $[\![i : \mathbf{fail}]\!] = \{[\delta]\}$

9. $[\![i : \mathbf{any}]\!] = T$

10. $[\![i : \mathbf{skip}]\!] = \{t \in T \mid t_i = \{skip\}\}$

11. $[\![i : \mathbf{change}]\!] = T \setminus [\![i : \mathbf{skip}]\!]$

Remarks

1. $[\![i : \underline{a}]\!]$ expresses the meaning of event expression $i : \underline{a}$: we specify the performance of the elementary action a (simultaneous with some package of actions) by i and simultaneous with the performance of undetermined actions by the other individuals. Thus, only the performance of a by i is determined. $[\![i : \mathbf{any}]\!]$ stands for the set of all steps in T.
Suppose α is event expression $i_1 : \underline{a} \cup^\star i_2 : \underline{b}$, then $[\![\alpha]\!]$ is the set of all steps containing an s-sets with elementary action a performed by i_1 or b performed by i_2. In the same way, $[\![i_1 : \underline{a} \&^\star i_2 : \underline{b}]\!]$ is the set of all steps consisting of elementary action a performed by i_1 and b performed by i_2.

2. Definition 5.2.8.7 defines negation as a complement operator. $\overline{\alpha}$ means: 'α does not occur, and it is not specified what does occur.' This is similar to the meaning of negation in propositional logic. Wieringa and Meyer [1993] call this interpretation of event negation *passive event negation.*

3. From definitions 5.2.8.4 and 5.2.8.7 it now follows that $[\![i : \overline{\beta}]\!] = \overline{[\![i : \beta]\!]}$. Thus, the negation of event expression $i : \beta$ stands for not-performing action expression β by actor i. Wieringa and Meyer [1993] call this interpretation of event negation *active event negation.*[2] They make a distinction between active event negation in a *local* way and in a *global* way. In a local way, it can be interpreted as the statement that i does something other than β, and in a global way it can be interpreted as the statement that another actor performs β. We use the local active event negation, because we can derive $\overline{[\![i : \mathbf{fail}]\!]} = [\![i : \mathbf{any}]\!]$, and this is only reasonable if we assume local active event negation.[3]

4. Above we noted that event expression $i : \beta_1 \cup \beta_2$ stands for the passive choice. This is expressed formally in definition 5.2.8.2.

[2] Note that we do not make a distinction between active and passive event negation.

[3] 'The local interpretation of event negation is enforced by the axiom

$$[\![i : \alpha]\!] \cup \overline{[\![i : \alpha]\!]} = [\![i : \mathbf{any}]\!].$$

The global interpretation of event negation cannot be axiomatised in the example specification, for it requires a constant that denotes the process "any actor does something".' [Wieringa and Meyer, 1993, p. 305]

Example Let $A = \{a_1, a_2\}$ and $I = \{i_1, i_2\}$. Then,

- $\llbracket i_1 : \underline{a_1} \rrbracket =$

$$\{([i_1 : a_1], [i_2 : a_1]), ([i_1 : a_1], [i_2 : a_2]),$$

$$([i_1 : a_1], [i_2 : skip]), \left([i_1 : a_1], \left[i_2 : \begin{matrix} a_1 \\ a_2 \end{matrix}\right]\right),$$

$$\left(\left[i_1 : \begin{matrix} a_1 \\ a_2 \end{matrix}\right], [i_2 : a_1]\right), \left(\left[i_1 : \begin{matrix} a_1 \\ a_2 \end{matrix}\right], [i_2 : a_2]\right),$$

$$\left(\left[i_1 : \begin{matrix} a_1 \\ a_2 \end{matrix}\right], \left[i_2 : \begin{matrix} a_1 \\ a_2 \end{matrix}\right]\right), \left(\left[i_1 : \begin{matrix} a_1 \\ a_2 \end{matrix}\right], [i_2 : skip]\right)\}$$

- $\llbracket i_1 : \underline{\overline{a_1}} \rrbracket = \overline{\llbracket i_1 : \underline{a_1} \rrbracket} =$

$$\{([i_1 : a_2], [i_2 : a_1]), ([i_1 : a_2], [i_2 : a_2]),$$

$$([i_1 : a_2], [i_2 : skip]), ([i_1 : skip], [i_2 : a_1]),$$

$$([i_1 : skip], [i_2 : a_2]), ([i_1 : skip], [i_2 : skip]),$$

$$\left([i_1 : a_2], \left[i_2 : \begin{matrix} a_1 \\ a_2 \end{matrix}\right]\right), \left([i_1 : skip], \left[i_2 : \begin{matrix} a_1 \\ a_2 \end{matrix}\right]\right)\}$$

- $\llbracket i_1 : \underline{a_1} \&^\star i_1 : \underline{a_2} \rrbracket = \llbracket i_1 : \underline{a_1} \& \underline{a_2} \rrbracket =$

$$\{\left(\left[i_1 : \begin{matrix} a_1 \\ a_2 \end{matrix}\right], [i_2 : a_1]\right), \left(\left[i_1 : \begin{matrix} a_1 \\ a_2 \end{matrix}\right], [i_2 : a_2]\right),$$

$$\left(\left[i_1 : \begin{matrix} a_1 \\ a_2 \end{matrix}\right], \left[i_2 : \begin{matrix} a_1 \\ a_2 \end{matrix}\right]\right), \left(\left[i_1 : \begin{matrix} a_1 \\ a_2 \end{matrix}\right], [i_2 : skip]\right)\}$$

- $\llbracket i_1 : \underline{a_1} \cup^\star i_1 : \underline{a_2} \rrbracket = \llbracket i_1 : \underline{a_1} \rrbracket \uplus \llbracket i_1 : \underline{a_2} \rrbracket = \llbracket i_1 : \mathbf{change} \rrbracket$
- $\overline{\llbracket i_1 : \underline{a_1} \cup^\star i_2 : \underline{a_2} \rrbracket} = T \setminus \llbracket i_1 : \underline{a_1} \cup^\star i_2 : \underline{a_2} \rrbracket = \overline{\llbracket i_1 : \underline{a_1} \rrbracket} \Cap \overline{\llbracket i_2 : \underline{a_2} \rrbracket} =$

$$\{([i_1 : a_2], [i_2 : a_1]), ([i_1 : a_2], [i_2 : skip]),$$

$$([i_1 : skip], [i_2 : skip]), ([i_1 : skip], [i_2 : a_1])\}$$

- $\overline{\llbracket i_1 : \underline{a_1} \&^\star i_2 : \underline{a_2} \rrbracket} = T \setminus \llbracket i_1 : \underline{a_1} \&^\star i_2 : \underline{a_2} \rrbracket = \overline{\llbracket i_1 : \underline{a_1} \rrbracket} \uplus \overline{\llbracket i_2 : \underline{a_2} \rrbracket} =$ $\llbracket i_1 : \underline{\overline{a_1}} \rrbracket \uplus \llbracket i_2 : \underline{\overline{a_2}} \rrbracket$.

Note that $\llbracket i_1 : a_1 \&^\star i_1 : \overline{a_1} \rrbracket = \llbracket i_1 : \mathbf{fail} \rrbracket = \{[\delta]\}$ and that $\llbracket i_1 : a_1 \&^\star i_2 : \overline{a_1} \rrbracket \neq \{[\delta]\}$

In this section, we also introduce an auxiliary notion to be used in the sequel:

Definition 5.2.9 *We put* $\alpha_1 =_T \alpha_2$ *iff* $[\![\alpha_1]\!] = [\![\alpha_2]\!]$.

The following proposition can easily be derived from the semantic function:

Proposition 5.2.10

1. *For* M_T*, the following properties concerning operators* $\cup^\star$ *and* $\&^\star$ *hold:*
   (a) $\alpha \cup^\star \alpha =_T \alpha$
   (b) $\alpha \&^\star \alpha =_T \alpha$
   (c) $\alpha_1 \cup^\star \alpha_2 =_T \alpha_2 \cup^\star \alpha_1$
   (d) $\alpha_1 \&^\star \alpha_2 =_T \alpha_2 \&^\star \alpha_1$
   (e) $\alpha_1 \&^\star (\alpha_2 \cup^\star \alpha_3) =_T (\alpha_1 \&^\star \alpha_2) \cup^\star (\alpha_1 \&^\star \alpha_3)$
   (f) $\alpha_1 \cup^\star (\alpha_2 \&^\star \alpha_3) =_T (\alpha_1 \cup^\star \alpha_2) \&^\star (\alpha_1 \cup^\star \alpha_3)$
2. M_T *satisfies the following properties regarding* '$\overline{\ }$'*:*
   (a) $\alpha \&^\star \overline{\alpha} =_T i : \mathbf{fail}$
   (b) $\alpha \cup^\star \overline{\alpha} =_T i : \mathbf{any}$
   (c) $\overline{\alpha_1 \cup^\star \alpha_2} =_T \overline{\alpha_1} \&^\star \overline{\alpha_2}$
   (d) $\overline{\alpha_1 \&^\star \alpha_2} =_T \overline{\alpha_1} \cup^\star \overline{\alpha_2}$
   (e) $\overline{\overline{\alpha}} =_T \alpha$
3. M_T *satisfies the following properties regarding the actions performed by an actor* i*:*
   (a) $i : \beta_1 \cup^\star i : \beta_2 =_T i : \beta_1 \cup \beta_2$
   (b) $i : \beta_1 \&^\star i : \beta_2 =_T i : \beta_1 \& \beta_2$
   (c) $\overline{i : \beta} =_T i : \overline{\beta}$.
4. M_T *satisfies the following properties concerning the special events:*
   (a) $\alpha \cup^\star i : \mathbf{fail} =_T \alpha$
   (b) $\alpha \&^\star i : \mathbf{fail} =_T i : \mathbf{fail}$
   (c) $(i : \mathbf{change}) \cup^\star (i : \mathbf{skip}) =_T i : \mathbf{any}$
   (d) $(i : \mathbf{change}) \&^\star (i : \mathbf{skip}) =_T i : \mathbf{fail}$
   (e) $\overline{i : \mathbf{skip}} =_T i : \mathbf{change}$
   (f) $\overline{i : \mathbf{any}} =_T i : \mathbf{fail}$

Remarks

1. The choice has the usual properties of choice in process algebra: it is commutative, associative and idempotent. The simultaneous event also has these properties. It can easily be proven from the equations mentioned above.

2. In the models presented by Wieringa and Meyer [1993], the formulas $i : \beta \cup^{\star} i :$ **fail** $= i : \beta$ and $i : \beta \&^{\star} i :$ **fail** $= i :$ **fail** are omitted from the specification. In their models, these two formulas are not valid. They argue that $i : \beta \cup^{\star} i :$ **fail** $= i : \beta$ is only valid if $i : \beta$ is a choice over a set of options that includes $i :$ **fail**, which, according to Meyer and Wieringa, is highly questionable. The formula $i : \beta \&^{\star} i :$ **fail** $= i :$ **fail** is not valid, for the following reason: $i : \beta \&^{\star} i :$ **fail** does not denote anything at all, because it means that i performs β and does nothing at the same time, and is, therefore, not equal to $i :$ **fail**, which means that i fails but that other actors can still perform actions.

   In our semantics of event expressions, these formulas are valid. The event expression $i :$ **fail** is the event that always fails. After this event, the system stops and nothing can be done any more by anybody (there is no successor state). Thus, if i fails, then there are no actors that still perform actions. Thus, in our model it holds that $i_1 :$ **fail** $= i_2 :$ **fail**, which does not hold in the Wieringa and Meyer's models. In an analogous way, we can defend the validity of the formula $i : \beta \cup^{\star} i :$ **fail** $= i : \beta$.

   The interpretation of the action expression **fail** in Wieringa and Meyer [1993] corresponds more or less with the action **skip** used here. There, the action expression **fail** is interpreted as 'to do nothing' and the event expression $i :$ **fail** as 'i fails but the rest of the world can still continue performing events' [Wieringa and Meyer, 1993, p. 306], which can be interpreted as the event $i :$ **skip**: 'i does not affect the situation, but the rest of the world can still do so.' Also, in our system the formulas $i : \beta \cup^{\star} i :$ **skip** $\neq i : \beta$ and $i : \beta \&^{\star} i :$ **skip** $\neq i :$ **skip**. The different interpretation of the action expression **fail** is the reason why Wieringa and Meyer omitted the two formulas mentioned above from the specification; it is also the reason why we add these formulas to our model.

5.2.2 $DDL(Evt)$

Now we extend the system DDL with actors by changing the language Ass of DDL. The language Ass consists of assertions pertaining to actions (and actions that are composed sequentially). The expressions of $DDL(Evt)$ are assertions concerning events in Evt. An expression Φ of $DDL(Evt)$ is a norm formulation in the terminology of Ruiter [1989].

Definition 5.2.11 *The language Ass^* of $DDL(Evt)$ consists of assertions (Φ) concerning events in Evt:*

$$\Phi ::= \phi \mid \neg\Phi \mid \Phi_1 \vee \Phi_2 \mid \Phi_1 \wedge \Phi_2 \mid \Phi_1 \rightarrow \Phi_2 \mid [\alpha]\Phi,$$

with $\phi \in L$, $\Phi, \Phi_1, \Phi_2 \in Ass^*$ and $\alpha \in Evt$.

As in chapter 3, the deontic operators are defined as follows: $F(\alpha) \equiv [\alpha]V$, $O(\alpha) \equiv F(\overline{\alpha})$ and $P(\alpha) \equiv \neg F(\alpha)$, with the special propositional symbol V, which means that the situation is in contravention of the law. Thus, α is forbidden ($F(\alpha)$) is reduced to a dynamic expression as follows:

$$F(\alpha) \equiv [\alpha]V.$$

$[\alpha]$ is interpreted as a modal operator of the necessity ($\Box$) in a Kripke structure induced by the performance of events.

Definition 5.2.12 *A model M for DDL(Evt) is given by*

$$M = (I, A, W, [\![\,]\!]_R, \pi),$$

where I is the set of actors, A the set of actions, W a set of possible worlds, $[\![\,]\!]_R$ a function that associates with event $\alpha \in Evt$ and world w, the set of possible worlds to which the performance of α leads, and π the usual truth relation between worlds and propositions: $\pi : W \times L \to \{true, false\}$.

We stipulate that we have a set W of worlds assigning values to propositional variables and a given function $\rho : T \to (W \to W)$, which for each step yields its behaviour in terms of world transitions. Thus, $\rho(t)(w)$ gives the next world when each individual i performs all the semantical actions in t_i simultaneously in world w. (t_i is the set of actions in A in the s-set of t which has i as the actor.)

Definition 5.2.13

- $\rho([\delta])(w) = \emptyset$.
- *For a step t, the function $R(t) \in W \to W$ is defined by*

$$R(t)(w) = \rho(t)(w).$$

- *For a set T of steps,*

$$R(T)(w) = \{w' \mid w' = R(t)(w) \textit{ for } t \in T\}.$$

Definition 5.2.14 *Function $[\![\,]\!]_R : Evt \to (W \to 2^W)$ is defined as*

$$[\![\alpha]\!]_R(w) = R([\![\alpha]\!])(w).$$

The truth definitions are standard. For dynamic formulas they are as follows:

Definition 5.2.15

$$w \models [\alpha]\Phi \textit{ iff } \forall_{w' \in [\![\alpha]\!]_R(w)} w' \models \Phi,$$

i.e. sentence $[\alpha]\Phi$ is true in w iff Φ holds in every world accessible from w by the performance of α.

For assertions, we can now give the formal system $DDL(Evt)$ that is sound with respect to the given semantics:
Axioms

1. all tautologies of the propositional calculus
2. $[\alpha](\Phi_1 \rightarrow \Phi_2) \rightarrow ([\alpha]\Phi_1 \rightarrow [\alpha]\Phi_2)$
3. $[\alpha_1 \cup^\star \alpha_2]\Phi \equiv [\alpha_1]\Phi \wedge [\alpha_2]\Phi$
4. $[\alpha_1]\Phi \vee [\alpha_2]\Phi \rightarrow [\alpha_1 \&^\star \alpha_2]\Phi$
5. $[i : \mathbf{fail}]\Phi$
6. $[i : \mathbf{skip}]\Phi \equiv \Phi$

Rules
(MP)

$$\frac{\Phi_1 \rightarrow \Phi_2, \Phi_1}{\Phi_2}$$

(R)

$$\text{if } \alpha_1 =_T \alpha_2, \text{ then } [\alpha_1]\Phi \equiv [\alpha_2]\Phi$$

(N)

$$\frac{\Phi}{[\alpha]\Phi}$$

Note that we do not have the schema $\neg[i : \mathbf{any}]V$ corresponding with the schema (OD) of SDL_i[4], so that we can express conflicts between personal duties. Using the definitions of deontic operators, the following proposition can be derived immediately.

Proposition 5.2.16 *Let β, β_1 and β_2 be events, then all the theorems given in section 3.3 hold for $DDL(Evt)$.*

5.2.3 The general and unspecific obligations

In the previous subsection, we formalised the concept of actors in $DDL(Evt)$, which allows us to specify which actors are permitted or obliged to perform an action. In this subsection an analysis is made of the (restricted) general and (restricted) unspecific obligations and permissions, which gives us new expressible power, and their relations.

With the help of the personal obligation and permission, we can formalise the general and unspecific obligations and permissions analogous to the previous chapter:

[4]To add schema $\neg[i : \mathbf{any}]V$ to system $DDL(Evt)$, we have to introduce the following constraint on the semantics:

$$\exists_{w' \in [\![i:\mathbf{any}]\!]_R(w)} w' \not\models V \text{ for all } w \in W.$$

- the general obligation ($O^+(\beta)$) and permission ($P^-(\beta)$):

$$O^+(\beta) \equiv \forall_{i \in I} O(i : \beta)^5 \text{ and } P^-(\beta) \equiv \forall_{i \in I} P(i : \beta).$$

- the unspecific obligation ($O^-(\beta)$) and permission ($P^+(\beta)$):

$$O^-(\beta) \equiv \exists_{i \in I} O(i : \beta)^6 \text{ and } P^+(\beta) \equiv \exists_{i \in I} P(i : \beta).$$

The restricted general obligation ($O_X^+(\beta)$) is defined as

$$O_X^+(\beta) \equiv \forall_{i \in X} O(i : \beta),$$

where $X \subseteq I$, and the restricted unspecific obligation ($O_X^-(\beta)$) as

$$O_X^-(\beta) \equiv \exists_{i \in X} O(i : \beta),$$

where $X \subseteq I$. Analogously, we define the restricted general and unspecific permissions:

$$P_X^+(\beta) \equiv \exists_{i \in X} P(i : \beta)$$

and

$$P_X^-(\beta) \equiv \forall_{i \in X} P(i : \beta).$$

The general obligation
The best known norms are the legal norms. These norms are mostly aimed at individuals belonging to a particular group. Most of the normative rules are restricted general norms, because these rules are aimed *not* at all actors but at actors of a particular group. For instance, the various sections of the Dutch traffic regulations are aimed at specific groups of road users, such as the group of cyclists, motor-vehicle drivers, etc. For instance:

Article 20. Within built-up areas the following speed limits hold:
- for motor vehicles: 50 km/h
- for mopeds and motorised wheelchairs: 30 km/h

Thus, for every individual in the group of motor-vehicle drivers it is forbidden to drive faster than 50 km/h (within built-up areas). This prohibition is a *general* prohibition with respect to the group of motor-vehicle drivers: it is a prohibition in force for everybody in the group of the motor-vehicle drivers. This can be formalised as follows:

$$\forall_{i \in M} F(i : \beta),$$

where $M \subseteq I$ denotes the group of motor-vehicle drivers and β the action 'to drive faster than 50 km/h'. Thus, a motor-vehicle driver satisfies this norm if he does not perform action β. A restricted general obligation is aimed at individuals in a certain group and allows us to express that each individual in that group separately has the responsibility to satisfy the norm. Thus, a general obligation implies a personal obligation: let $i_1 \in I$ and $\beta \in Act$, then

$$O^+(\beta) \equiv \forall_{i \in I} O(i : \beta) \text{ en } \forall_{i \in I} O(i : \beta) \rightarrow O(i_1 : \beta).$$

The unspecific obligation

The opposite of the general obligation is the *unspecific* obligation. This is an obligation for a non-specified individual. It is an obligation in force for at least one of the actors in the group. We can denote this by the existential quantifier $\exists$. For instance, $\exists_{i \in U} F(i : \beta_1)$, where $U \subseteq I$ denotes the group of road users and β_1 the action 'to drive faster than 30 km/h', is a prohibition in force, e.g. for moped riders and not, e.g. for motor-vehicle drivers.

Note that the (restricted) general obligation implies the (restricted) unspecific obligation:

$$O_X^+(\beta) \rightarrow O_X^-(\beta),$$

where $X \subseteq I$.

A restricted unspecific obligation is aimed at individuals in a certain group, and allows us to express that some individual in that group has the responsibility to satisfy the norm, without specifying who, e.g. if the group leaves the room, the light has to been turned off. Thus, a personal obligation implies an impersonal obligation:

$$O(i_1 : \beta) \rightarrow O^-(\beta).$$

Now we are also able to express that an action β is obligatory for a particular person i_1, but not for all individuals:

$$O(i_1 : \beta) \wedge \neg \forall_{i \in I} O(i : \beta),$$

which is equivalent to

$$O(i_1 : \beta) \wedge P^+(\overline{\beta}).$$

The strict personal obligation

Finally, we define the *strict* personal obligation. This is an obligation only for a specific individual; thus, no other individual has that obligation. An example of a strict personal obligation can be a decision (an order which is not of a general nature, including refusal of an application for such an order),[7] or an obligation for the prime minister. A strict personal obligation for i_1 can be formalised as follows:

$$O(i_1 : \beta) \wedge \forall_{i \in I \setminus \{i_1\}} \neg O(i : \beta).$$

5.2.4 The relations between the notions of obligation and permission

In subsection 4.2.3, we gave the relations between the general, personal and unspecific notions of obligation and permission for *SDL*. The results were summarised in figures 4.3 and 4.4. The valid principles between the various notions of the obligation and permission for *DDL* are summarised in figure 5.1. In *DDL*, the following two principles are valid:

$$O^+(\beta) \rightarrow O^-(\beta) \qquad (5.1)$$

[7] See section 1:3 of the General Administrative Law Act ('Algemene Wet Bestuursrecht').

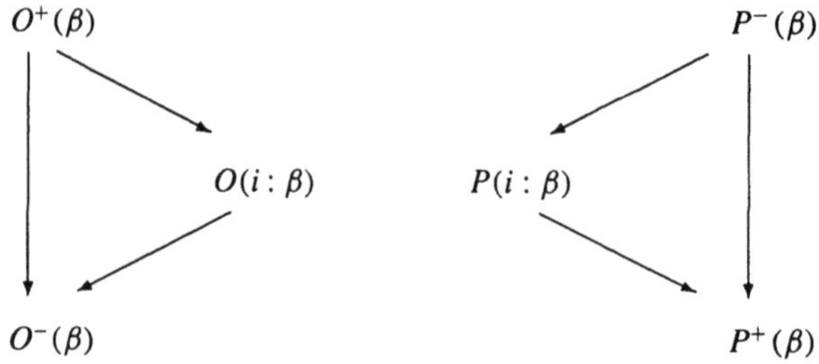

Figure 5.1: The principles between the notions of the obligation and permission

and

$$P^-(\beta) \to P^+(\beta). \tag{5.2}$$

The principles relating to a notion of obligation and a notion of permission are not valid, i.e. $O^+(\beta) \to P^-(\beta)$, $O^-(\beta) \to P^+(\beta)$, $O^+(\beta) \to P^+(\beta)$ and $O^-(\beta) \to P^-(\beta)$, since we do not have schema $\neg[i : \mathbf{any}]V$ corresponding with schema (OD) of SDL_i.

The obligations 'it is obligatory for the zoo caretaker to feed the monkeys' and 'it is obligatory for the visitors not to feed the monkeys', with β the action 'to feed the monkeys', are intuitively not in conflict. In general, obligations $O(i:\beta)$ and $O(j:\overline{\beta})$ are never in conflict (if $i \neq j$), in contrast to obligations $O_i(p)$ and $O_j(\neg p)$ in the extension of SDL concerning the addition of actors (see previous chapter). Obligations $O_i(p)$ and $O_j(\neg p)$ are always in conflict, since 'p' is a description of a state of affairs, for instance 'that the monkeys are fed'. Then, i has to accomplish that the monkeys are fed and j has to accomplish that the monkeys are not fed, i.e. the opposite of what i has to accomplish. Thus, principle $\neg(O_i(p) \wedge O_j(\neg p))$ and thus also principle $\neg(O^-(p) \wedge O^-(\neg p))$ are defensible, if one wants to obtain a coherent normative system, i.e. without conflicting obligations, as was considered desirable by Bailhache [1991] and Hilpinen [1973].

5.2.5 The directed obligation

Actions performed by an individual, can be directed towards another individual or group of individuals (*directed actions*) or can be independent of another individual or group of individuals (*undirected actions*). Some examples of directed actions are 'to give right of way', 'to overtake', 'to pay', etc. It matters greatly to whom such an action is directed. For instance, according to the Dutch traffic regulation it is obligatory for motor-vehicle drivers to give right of way to motor-vehicle drivers from the right, but they are not obliged to give right of way to cyclists from the right. Examples of undirected actions are 'to drive at a speed of 50 km/h', 'to turn left' and 'to park'.

In this subsection, we give a formalisation of directed actions in our semantics of actions. Let a_1 be a directed action (e.g. 'to give right of way') and $I = \{i_1, \ldots, i_n\}$, then a_1

will be defined as

$$a_1 := \underline{a_1(i_1)} \cup \underline{a_1(i_2)} \cup \ldots \cup \underline{a_1(i_n)}.$$

The domain of the action a_1 is I. $\underline{a_1(i_k)}$ will be read as 'to give right of way to i_k.' Note that $\underline{a_1(i_k)}$ is a directed *atomic* action and a_1 is not. With the help of these directed actions, we can express directed obligations. The directed obligation

$$O(i : \underline{a(j)})$$

is read as 'individual i is obliged to give right of way to j', with a the directed action 'to give right of way'. Thus, individual i (the bearer) has a *duty* and individual j (the counterparty) has a *right* [cf. Hohfeld, 1964].

5.3 The extension of *DDL* with groups of actors

In this section, we discuss the extension of *DDL* concerning the addition of groups of actors on the basis of collective event expressions. First, we discuss the semantics of collective event expressions.

5.3.1 The semantics of collective event expressions

It is important to note that collective event $X : \beta$ is not an event that is performed if and only if every actor in group X performs the action β. A group event $X : \beta$ can be performed if only a subgroup of X (maybe one person or the whole group together) has performed the action β. Thus, we can express, on the one hand, that group X as a whole has the responsibility to perform action β, even if the action is performed by a subgroup (the electricians) of X (the firm). On the other hand, we can model the fact that if the group as a whole performs an action, none of its members performs that action, for instance, when a construction company builds a house.

In the discussion of the semantics of collective event expressions, i.e. actions performed by a group of actors, we see that most definitions are extensions of the definitions of subsection 5.2.1.

The set of all event expressions Evt' can be determined by the following BNF for its elements (α):

$$\alpha ::= \quad X : \beta | \alpha_1 \cup' \alpha_2 | \alpha_1 \&' \alpha_2 | \overline{\alpha},$$

where $X \in P^+(I)$, with $P^+(I)$ the non-empty powerset of I, $\alpha_1, \alpha_2 \in Evt'$ and $\beta \in Act$.

Definition 5.3.1

1. *Set* $\{\delta\}$ *is a synchronicity set (s-set).*
2. *Set* $\{X : skip\}$ *is an s-set, with* X *a non-empty subset of* I.
3. *Every pair of a non-empty subset of* A *and a non-empty subset of* I *is an s-set.*

We use $S, S_1, S_2, \ldots$ for s-sets. The set of all s-sets, except $\{\delta\}$, will be denoted by S'.

Let $X \in P^+(I)$ and $A = \{a_1, a_2\}$, then s-set S consisting of elementary actions a_1 and a_2 performed by set X is written as

$$S = [X : A'], \text{ or } S = \left[X : \begin{array}{c} a_1 \\ a_2 \end{array} \right],$$

with $A' = \{a_1, a_2\}$. Thus, $S' = \{[X : A'] \mid A' \subseteq A, A' \neq \emptyset, X \in P^+(I)\} \cup \{[X : skip] \mid X \in P^+(I)\}$. Let X be the set $\{i_1, i_2\}$, then $S' =$

$$\{[\{i_1\} : a_1], [\{i_1\} : a_2], [\{i_1\} : skip], \left[\{i_1\} : \begin{array}{c} a_1 \\ a_2 \end{array} \right],$$

$$[\{i_1, i_2\} : a_1], [\{i_1, i_2\} : a_2], [\{i_1, i_2\} : skip], \left[\{i_1, i_2\} : \begin{array}{c} a_1 \\ a_2 \end{array} \right],$$

$$[\{i_2\} : a_1], [\{i_2\} : a_2], [\{i_2\} : skip], \left[\{i_2\} : \begin{array}{c} a_1 \\ a_2 \end{array} \right]\}.$$

Further, we use S'_X to denote the set of all s-sets with X in $P^+(I)$, thus $S'_{\{i_1, i_2\}} = \{[\{i_1, i_2\} : A'] \mid A' \subseteq A, A' \neq \emptyset\}$.
Note that $S^* \subseteq S'$, if we assume that $S^*_i = S'_{\{i\}}$.

It is clear that a group can only do something if some members of the group do something, and it is plausible to assume that the elementary actions of a group are constituted, in some way or other, by the elementary actions of the members of the group. For instance, if a member performs an elementary action a, the group also performs this action. However, the group is not restricted to performing the elementary actions that are performed by the individual members of the group, since a group can perform an elementary action that cannot be performed by a single individual. For instance, 'to lift a stone of 500 lbs'. This relationship between the group and the members of the group with respect to their performances of elementary actions manifests itself in the following definition.

Definition 5.3.2 *Let $I = \{i_1, i_2, \ldots, i_n\}$, then T' will be defined as*

$$T' =_{def} \{\times_{X \in P^+(I)} S'_X \mid \forall_{X,Y \in P^+(I)} Y \subseteq X \rightarrow t_Y \subseteq t_X,$$

$$\forall_{X,Y \in P^+(I)} t_Y = \{skip\} \rightarrow t_{X \cup Y} = t_X\},$$

with t_X the set of actions in s-set $[X : t_X]$, a coefficient of step t corresponding with X. An element of T' will be called a step. We use the letter 't' with possible marks for steps.

A step t of T' is a $2^n - 1$-tuple. The order of the s-sets in a step is again irrelevant. T' is not just the indirect product of all the sets S'_X, with $X \in P^+(I)$, but a subset of this indirect product. T' has been restricted for the following two reasons:

1. Let t be a step in T' containing s-set $[Y : t_Y]$ with $t_Y = \{a_1, \ldots, a_m\}$, a subset of A. Thus, group Y simultaneously performs the actions $a_1, \ldots, a_m$. Then all supersets of Y also perform these actions, possibly together with other actions in A, because of the fact that Y is a subgroup of X. (X performs the actions in t_Y if and only if some subset of X performs these actions.)

   Example Let $A = \{a_1, a_2\}$ and $I = \{i_1, i_2\}$, then

   $$([\{i_1\} : \ a_1 \ ], [\ \{i_2\} : a_2 \ ], [\{i_1, i_2\} : \ a_1 \ ]) \notin T'.$$

   For instance, if John posted the letter, then also the group John and Paul posted the letter, because John is a subgroup of the group consisting of John and Paul.

2. Let t be a step in T' containing the s-set $[Y : skip]$. This means that Y does not affect the situation. Thus, for every real superset X of Y it follows that the groups X and $X \setminus Y$ perform the same actions.

   Example Let $A = \{a_1, a_2\}$ and $I = \{i_1, i_2\}$, then

   $$\left([\{i_1\} : \ skip \ ], [\ \{i_2\} : a_1 \ ], \left[\{i_1, i_2\} : \ \begin{array}{c} a_1 \\ a_2 \end{array}\right]\right) \notin T'.$$

Example Let $A = \{a_1, a_2\}$ and $I = \{i_1, i_2\}$, then $T' =$

$$\begin{array}{c}
\{([\{i_1\} : \ skip \ ], [\ \{i_2\} : skip \ ], [\{i_1, i_2\} : \ skip \ ]), \\
([\{i_1\} : \ skip \ ], [\ \{i_2\} : a_1 \ ], [\{i_1, i_2\} : \ a_1 \ ]), \\
([\{i_1\} : \ skip \ ], [\ \{i_2\} : a_2 \ ], [\{i_1, i_2\} : \ a_2 \ ]), \\
\left([\{i_1\} : \ skip \ ], \left[\{i_2\} : \ \begin{array}{c} a_1 \\ a_2 \end{array}\right], \left[\{i_1, i_2\} : \ \begin{array}{c} a_1 \\ a_2 \end{array}\right]\right), \\
([\{i_1\} : \ a_1 \ ], [\ \{i_2\} : skip \ ], [\{i_1, i_2\} : \ a_1 \ ]), \\
([\{i_1\} : a_1], [\{i_2\} : a_1], [\{i_1, i_2\} : \ a_1 \ ]), \\
\left([\{i_1\} : a_1], [\{i_2\} : a_1], \left[\{i_1, i_2\} : \ \begin{array}{c} a_1 \\ a_2 \end{array}\right]\right), \\
\left([\{i_1\} : a_1], [\{i_2\} : a_2], \left[\{i_1, i_2\} : \ \begin{array}{c} a_1 \\ a_2 \end{array}\right]\right), \\
\left([\{i_1\} : \ a_1 \ ], \left[\{i_2\} : \ \begin{array}{c} a_1 \\ a_2 \end{array}\right], \left[\{i_1, i_2\} : \ \begin{array}{c} a_1 \\ a_2 \end{array}\right]\right),
\end{array}$$

$$([\{i_1\}:\ a_2\ ],[\ \{i_2\}:skip\ ],[\{i_1,i_2\}:\ a_2\ ]),$$

$$\left([\{i_1\}:\ a_2\ ],[\ \{i_2\}:a_1\ ],\left[\{i_1,i_2\}:\begin{array}{c}a_1\\a_2\end{array}\right]\right),$$

$$([\{i_1\}:a_2],[\{i_2\}:a_2],[\{i_1,i_2\}:\ a_2\ ]),$$

$$\left([\{i_1\}:a_2],[\{i_2\}:a_2],\left[\{i_1,i_2\}:\begin{array}{c}a_1\\a_2\end{array}\right]\right),$$

$$\left([\{i_1\}:\ a_2\ ],\left[\{i_2\}:\begin{array}{c}a_1\\a_2\end{array}\right],\left[\{i_1,i_2\}:\begin{array}{c}a_1\\a_2\end{array}\right]\right),$$

$$\left(\left[\{i_1\}:\begin{array}{c}a_1\\a_2\end{array}\right],[\{i_2\}:skip],\left[\{i_1,i_2\}:\begin{array}{c}a_1\\a_2\end{array}\right]\right),$$

$$\left(\left[\{i_1\}:\begin{array}{c}a_1\\a_2\end{array}\right],[\{i_2\}:a_2],\left[\{i_1,i_2\}:\begin{array}{c}a_1\\a_2\end{array}\right]\right),$$

$$\left(\left[\{i_1\}:\begin{array}{c}a_1\\a_2\end{array}\right],\left[\{i_2\}:\begin{array}{c}a_1\\a_2\end{array}\right],\left[\{i_1,i_2\}:\begin{array}{c}a_1\\a_2\end{array}\right]\right),$$

$$\left(\left[\{i_1\}:\begin{array}{c}a_1\\a_2\end{array}\right],[\{i_2\}:a_1],\left[\{i_1,i_2\}:\begin{array}{c}a_1\\a_2\end{array}\right]\right)\}.$$

Since our language of event expressions contains a non-deterministic (choice) operator $\cup'$, we have to consider sets of steps $t \in T'$. We use $T, T_1, T_2, \ldots$ to denote sets of steps.

Our event model $M_{T'}$ is now given by:

Definition 5.3.3 *$M_{T'}$ is the collection of sets T consisting of steps.*

Note that $M_{T'}$ is the powerset of T', normally denoted by $2^{T'}$ or $P(T')$. We shall use the operations $\sqcup$, $\sqcap$ and $\tilde{}$ (operator for the set-theoretic complement) on the domain $M_{T'}$ as semantical counterparts of the syntactical operators $\cup'$, &$'$ and $\bar{}$, respectively, in our language Evt' of event expressions. Before we give these definitions, we define a handy operator on the sets of steps:

Definition 5.3.4 *Let T be a set of steps, then*

$$T^\delta = \begin{cases} T\setminus\{[\delta]\} & \text{if } \exists_{t\in T} t \neq [\delta] \\ \{[\delta]\} & \text{otherwise.}\end{cases}$$

Now we can give the semantical operators on $M_{T'}$. For the simultaneous operator &$'$, we use a set intersection $\sqcap$, which is almost the same as the normal set intersection.

Definition 5.3.5 *For $T_1, T_2 \in M_{T'}$,*

$$T_1 \sqcap T_2 = \begin{cases} T_1 \cap T_2 & \text{if } T_1 \cap T_2 \neq \emptyset \\ \{[\delta]\} & \text{otherwise.}\end{cases}$$

Operator $\sqcup$ on sets of steps is defined as follows:

Definition 5.3.6 *For* $T_1, T_2 \in M_{T'}$,

$$T_1 \sqcup T_2 = (T_1 \cup T_2)^{\delta}.$$

Thus, the choice between two sets of steps is the union of those two sets minus $\{[\delta]\}$, unless the union does not contain anything else.

The definition of '$\bar{}$' is given as follows:

Definition 5.3.7

1. *For a step t,*

$$\bar{t} = T' \setminus \{t\}.$$

2. *For a non-empty set* $T \in M_{T'}$,

$$\bar{T} = \sqcap\{\bar{t} \mid t \in T\}.$$

Thus, for a step t the negation just yields the set-theoretic complement of $\{t\}$ with respect to T'. For the negation of a set of steps T, we take the intersection of the sets of the negation of all the steps contained in T. Note that $T \subseteq T'$ and that $T' \in M_{T'}$.

Now we can define the semantics of event expressions in Evt':

Definition 5.3.8 *The semantic function* $[\![\ ]\!] \in Evt' \to M_{T'}$, *with* $\beta, \beta_1, \beta_2 \in Act$, $X \in P^+(I)$ *and* $\alpha, \alpha_1, \alpha_2 \in Evt'$, *is given by:*

1. $[\![X : \underline{a}]\!] = \{t \in T' \mid a \in t_X\}$
2. $[\![X : \beta_1 \cup \beta_2]\!] = [\![X : \beta_1]\!] \sqcup [\![X : \beta_2]\!]$
3. $[\![X : \beta_1 \& \beta_2]\!] = [\![X : \beta_1]\!] \sqcap [\![X : \beta_2]\!]$
4. $[\![X : \overline{\beta}]\!] = \overline{[\![X : \beta]\!]}$
5. $[\![\alpha_1 \cup' \alpha_2]\!] = [\![\alpha_1]\!] \sqcup [\![\alpha_2]\!]$
6. $[\![\alpha_1 \&' \alpha_2]\!] = [\![\alpha_1]\!] \sqcap [\![\alpha_2]\!]$
7. $[\![\overline{\alpha}]\!] = \overline{[\![\alpha]\!]}$
8. $[\![X : \mathbf{fail}]\!] = \{[\delta]\}$
9. $[\![X : \mathbf{any}]\!] = T'$
10. $[\![X : \mathbf{skip}]\!] = \{t \in T' \mid \forall_{Y \in P^+(X)} t_Y = \{skip\}\}$
11. $[\![X : \mathbf{change}]\!] = T' \setminus [\![X : \mathbf{skip}]\!]$

Remarks

1. $[\![X : \underline{a}]\!]$ expresses the meaning of event expression $X : \underline{a}$: it is the set of all steps in T' which contains the s-set $[X : t_X]$ with $a \in t_X$: X performs the elementary action a possibly together with other elementary actions.

2. $[\![\alpha]\!]^-$ stands for the set-theoretic complement of $[\![\alpha]\!]$ with respect to T'. $[\![X : \overline{a}]\!]$ is the set of all steps in T' which contains the s-set $[X : t_X]$ with $a \notin t_X$. Thus, no subgroup of X performs action a.

3. $[\![X : \textbf{any}]\!]$ stands for the set of all steps in T'.

4. $[\![X : \textbf{skip}]\!]$ is the set of all steps, such that for every non-empty subset Y of X it follows that $[Y : skip]$ is an s-set in these steps. If a situation is not affected by group X, then it is also not affected by a subgroup of X.

To understand the semantical function, we provide some examples.

Example Let $A = \{a_1, a_2\}$ and $I = \{i_1, i_2\}$, then

- $[\![\{i_1\} : \underline{a_1}]\!] = \{t \mid t_{\{i_1\}} \in \{\{a_1\}, \{a_1, a_2\}\}, \forall_{X \in P^+(I), X \neq \{i_1\}} t_X \in P^+(A)\} \cap T'$

- $[\![\{i_1, i_2\} : \overline{a_1}]\!] = [\![\overline{\{i_1, i_2\} : \underline{a_1}}]\!] = T' \setminus [\![\{i_1, i_2\} : \underline{a_1}]\!] =$

$$\{t \mid t_{\{i_1, i_2\}} \in \{\{skip\}, \{a_2\}\}, \forall_{X \in P^+(I), X \neq \{i_1, i_2\}} t_X \in P^+(A)\} \cap T'$$

- $[\![\{i_1, i_2\} : skip]\!] = \{t \mid t_{\{i_1, i_2\}} = \{skip\}, \forall_{X \in P^+(I), X \neq \{i_1, i_2\}} t_X \in P^+(A)\} \cap T' =$

$$\{t \mid \forall_{X \in P^+(I)} t_X = \{skip\}\}$$

- $[\![\overline{\{i_1\} : \underline{a_1} \cup' \{i_2\} : \underline{a_2}}]\!] = T' \setminus [\![\{i_1\} : \underline{a_1} \cup' \{i_2\} : \underline{a_2}]\!] = [\![\overline{\{i_1\} : \underline{a_1}}]\!] \cap [\![\overline{\{i_2\} : \underline{a_2}}]\!] =$

$$\{t \mid t_{\{i_1\}} \in \{\{skip\}, \{a_2\}\}, \forall_{X \in P^+(I), X \neq \{i_1\}} t_X \in P^+(A)\} \cap$$

$$\{t \mid t_{\{i_2\}} \in \{\{skip\}, \{a_1\}\}, \forall_{X \in P^+(I), X \neq \{i_2\}} t_X \in P^+(A)\} \cap T' =$$

$$\{t \mid t_{\{i_1\}} \in \{\{skip\}, \{a_2\}\}, t_{\{i_2\}} \in \{\{skip\}, \{a_1\}\}, t_{\{i_1, i_2\}} \in P^+(A)\} \cap T'$$

Note that every time we take the intersection with T' to ensure that the constraints defined on steps are enforced.

Note that $[\![i_1 : \beta]\!]$ is not equal to $[\![\{i_1\} : \beta]\!]$. $i_1 : \beta$ is an individual event expression, and the semantic function for individual event expressions (definition 5.2.8) differs from the semantic function for group event expressions (definition 5.3.8).

Proposition 5.3.9 *Let I be the set of actors, $X, Y \in P^+(I)$ and $\beta_1, \beta_2 \in Act$. Then*

1. $[\![X : \beta_1 \& \beta_2]\!] \subseteq [\![X : \beta_1]\!]$
2. $[\![X : \beta_1]\!] \subseteq [\![X : \beta_1 \cup \beta_2]\!]$
3. $[\![X : \beta_1 \&' X : \overline{\beta_1}]\!] = \{[\delta]\}$
4. $\forall_{X,Y}\{[\![X : \mathbf{fail}]\!] = [\![Y : \mathbf{fail}]\!]\}$
5. $\forall_{X,Y}\{[\![X : \mathbf{any}]\!] = [\![Y : \mathbf{any}]\!]\}$

Proof

1. $[\![X : \beta_1 \&' \beta_2]\!] = [\![X : \beta_1]\!] \sqcap [\![X : \beta_2]\!] \subseteq [\![X : \beta_1]\!]$
2. $[\![X : \beta_1]\!] \subseteq [\![X : \beta_1]\!] \sqcup [\![X : \beta_2]\!] = [\![X : \beta_1 \cup \beta_2]\!]$
3. $[\![X : \beta_1 \&' X : \overline{\beta_1}]\!] = [\![X : \beta_1]\!] \sqcap [\![X : \overline{\beta_1}]\!] = [\![X : \beta_1]\!] \sqcap \overline{[\![X : \beta_1]\!]} = \{[\delta]\}$
4. Follows immediately from 5.3.8.8.
5. Follows immediately from 5.3.8.9.

If some actors in a group X perform action a, and other actors in X do not perform a, then this does not mean that X performs action $a \& \overline{a}$. X performs action a if and only if some subgroup of X performs a, and X does not perform a if and only if no subgroup of X (thus, also no actor of X) performs action a. Thus, a group X, just like individuals, cannot perform an impossible action $\beta \& \overline{\beta}$. Event $X : \beta \& \overline{\beta}$ means that the action $\beta \& \overline{\beta}$ performed by X always fails.

In this section, we also introduce an auxiliary notion that we will use in the sequel:

Definition 5.3.10 *We put $\alpha_1 =_{T'} \alpha_2$ iff $[\![\alpha_1]\!] = [\![\alpha_2]\!]$.*

Proposition 5.3.11 *All the equations of proposition 5.2.10 hold for $M_{T'}$ with $X : \beta$ instead of $i : \beta$, $\cup'$ instead of $\cup^\star$, $\&'$ instead of $\&^\star$, $X \in P^+(I)$ and $\alpha_1, \alpha_2 \in Evt'$.*

In chapter 3, we made a distinction between *positive* and *negative* action expressions. We saw that a positive action expression expresses an action that involves a certain form of physical activity, and a negative action means not carrying out that physical activity: an omission (see subsection 3.2.4). This distinction carries much weight with collective event expressions, since a group performs a positive action γ if and only if a subgroup of that group performs action γ and a group 'performs' a negative action $\overline{\gamma}$ if and only if every subgroup of that group does not perform γ.

The following principles are valid for a special kind of collective event expressions: positive or negative actions performed by groups of actors.

Proposition 5.3.12 *Let I be the set of actors, $X, Y \in P^{+}(I)$ and $\gamma \in Act_p$. Then*

1. $Y \in P^{+}(X) \rightarrow [\![Y : \gamma]\!] \subseteq [\![X : \gamma]\!]$
2. $Y \in P^{+}(X) \rightarrow [\![X : \overline{\gamma}]\!] \subseteq [\![Y : \overline{\gamma}]\!]$
3. $[\![X \cap Y : \gamma]\!] \subseteq [\![X : \gamma]\!] \sqcap [\![Y : \gamma]\!]$, *with* $X \cap Y \neq \emptyset$
4. $[\![X : \gamma]\!] \sqcup [\![Y : \gamma]\!] \subseteq [\![X \cup Y : \gamma]\!]$
5. $[\![X \cup Y : \overline{\gamma}]\!] \subseteq [\![X : \overline{\gamma} \&' Y : \overline{\gamma}]\!]$
6. *If* $Y \in P^{+}(X)$ *then* $[\![X : \overline{\gamma} \&' Y : \gamma]\!] = \{[\delta]\}$

Proof

1. Let $Y \in P^{+}(X)$ and $t \in [\![Y : \gamma]\!]$. Then t contains an s-set $[Y : t_Y]$, with $t_Y \subseteq A$. By definition 5.3.2, the s-set with group X also contains t_Y, possibly together with other actions in A, because γ does not contain negative actions. Thus, $t \in [\![X : \gamma]\!]$. Hence, $Y \in P^{+}(X) \rightarrow [\![Y : \gamma]\!] \subseteq [\![X : \gamma]\!]$.

2. Let $Y \in P^{+}(X)$. Then, by 5.3.12.1, $[\![Y : \gamma]\!] \subseteq [\![X : \gamma]\!]$. This is equivalent to $T' \setminus [\![X : \gamma]\!] \subseteq T' \setminus [\![Y : \gamma]\!]$. Hence, by definitions 5.3.8.4 and 5.3.8.7, $[\![X : \overline{\gamma}]\!] \subseteq [\![Y : \overline{\gamma}]\!]$.

3. Let $t \in [\![X \cap Y : \gamma]\!]$. Then, t contains an s-set $[X \cap Y : t_{X \cap Y}]$, with $t_{X \cap Y} \subseteq A$. By definition 5.3.2, the s-sets with group X and group Y also contain $t_{X \cap Y}$, possibly together with other actions in A, because γ does not contain negative actions. Thus, $t \in [\![X : \gamma]\!] \sqcap [\![Y : \gamma]\!]$. Hence, $[\![X \cap Y : \gamma]\!] \subseteq [\![X : \gamma]\!] \sqcap [\![Y : \gamma]\!]$. The converse does not hold. Suppose $I = \{i_1, i_2, i_3\}$ and $A = \{a_1, a_2\}$, then step t:

$$\left(\left[\{i_1\} : \; a_1 \right], \left[\{i_2\} : \; a_2 \right], \left[\{i_3\} : \; a_1 \right], \left[\{i_1, i_2\} : \; \begin{matrix} a_1 \\ a_2 \end{matrix} \right], \right.$$
$$\left. \left[\{i_1, i_3\} : \; a_1 \right], \left[\{i_2, i_3\} : \; \begin{matrix} a_1 \\ a_2 \end{matrix} \right], \left[\{i_1, i_2, i_3\} : \; \begin{matrix} a_1 \\ a_2 \end{matrix} \right] \right),$$

is an element of $[\![\{i_1, i_2\} : a_1]\!] \sqcap$
$[\![\{i_2, i_3\} : a_1]\!]$, but not an element of $[\![\{i_1, i_2\} \cap \{i_2, i_3\} : a_1]\!] = [\![\{i_2\} : a_1]\!]$, because $a_1 \notin t_{\{i_2\}}$.

4. Let $t \in [\![X : \gamma]\!] \sqcup [\![Y : \gamma]\!]$. Then t contains an s-set $[X : A']$ or $[Y : A']$, with $A' \subseteq A$. By definition 5.3.2, the s-sets with group $X \cup Y$ also contain A', possibly together with other actions in A, because γ does not contain negative actions. Thus, $t \in [\![X \cup Y : \gamma]\!]$. Hence, $[\![X : \gamma]\!] \sqcup [\![Y : \gamma]\!] \subseteq [\![X \cup Y : \gamma]\!]$.

5. By proposition 5.3.12.4 and definitions 5.3.8.4 and 5.3.8.7 it follows that $[\![X \cup Y : \overline{\gamma}]\!] = \overline{[\![X \cup Y : \gamma]\!]}$
$\subseteq \overline{[\![X : \gamma]\!] \sqcup [\![Y : \gamma]\!]}$. This is equal to $\overline{[\![X : \gamma]\!]} \sqcap \overline{[\![Y : \gamma]\!]} = [\![X : \overline{\gamma}]\!] \sqcap [\![Y : \overline{\gamma}]\!] = [\![X : \overline{\gamma} \&' Y : \overline{\gamma}]\!]$.

6. Let $Y \in P^+(X)$. Then $[\![X : \overline{\gamma} \&' Y : \gamma]\!] = [\![X : \overline{\gamma}]\!] \sqcap [\![Y : \gamma]\!] \subseteq [\![Y : \overline{\gamma}]\!] \sqcap [\![Y : \gamma]\!] = [\![\overline{Y : \gamma}]\!] \sqcap [\![Y : \gamma]\!] = \{[\delta]\}$.

5.3.2 $DDL(Evt')$

At this point, we are able to extend the system DDL with groups of actors, by changing the language Ass of DDL. The language Ass' consists of assertions concerning actions. The expressions of $DDL(Evt')$ are assertions concerning events in Evt'. An expression Φ of $DDL(Evt')$ is a norm formulation in the terminology of Ruiter [1989].

Definition 5.3.13 *The language Ass' of $DDL(Evt')$ consists of assertions (Φ) concerning events in Evt':*

$$\Phi ::= \phi \mid \neg\Phi \mid \Phi_1 \vee \Phi_2 \mid \Phi_1 \wedge \Phi_2 \mid \Phi_1 \rightarrow \Phi_2 \mid [\alpha]\Phi,$$

with $\Phi, \Phi_1, \Phi_2 \in Ass'$ and $\alpha \in Evt'$.

Definition 5.3.14 *A model M for $DDL(Evt')$ is given by*

$$M = (P^+(I), A, W, [\![\ ]\!]_R, \pi),$$

where $P^+(I)$ is the non-empty powerset of the set I of actors, A the set of actions, W a set of possible worlds, $[\![\ ]\!]_R$ a function that associates with event $\alpha \in Evt'$ and world w, the set of possible worlds to which the performance of α leads, and π the usual truth relation between worlds and propositions.

We stipulate that we have a set W of worlds assigning values to propositional variables and a given function $\rho : T' \rightarrow (W \rightarrow W)$, which for each step yields its behaviour in terms of world transitions. Thus, $\rho(t)(w)$ gives the next world when each group X performs all the semantical actions in t_X simultaneously in world w. (t_X is the set of actions in the coefficient of t which has X as its group.)

Definition 5.3.15

- $\rho([\delta])(w) = \emptyset$.
- *For a step t, the function $R(t) \in W \rightarrow W$ is defined by*

  $$R(t)(w) = \rho(t)(w).$$

- *For a set T of steps,*

  $$R(T)(w) = \{w' \mid w' = R(t)(w) \text{ for } t \in T\}.$$

Definition 5.3.16 *The function* $[\![\,]\!] : Evt' \to (W \to Pow(W))$ *is defined as*

$$[\![\alpha]\!]_R(w) = R([\![\alpha]\!])(w).$$

The truth definitions are standard. For dynamic formulas they are as follows:
Definition 5.3.17

$$w \models [\alpha]\Phi \text{ iff } \forall_{w' \in [\![\alpha]\!]_R(w)} w' \models \Phi,$$

i.e. sentence $[\alpha]\Phi$ *is true in* w *iff* Φ *holds in every world accessible from* w *by performing* α.

For assertions, we can give the formal system $DDL(Evt')$, which is sound with respect to the given semantics:
Axioms

1. all tautologies of the propositional calculus
2. $[\alpha](\Phi_1 \to \Phi_2) \to ([\alpha]\Phi_1 \to [\alpha_2]\Phi_2)$
3. $[\alpha_1 \cup' \alpha_2]\Phi \equiv [\alpha_1]\Phi \wedge [\alpha_2]\Phi$
4. $[\alpha_1]\Phi \vee [\alpha_2]\Phi \to [\alpha_1 \&' \alpha_2]\Phi$
5. $[X : \textbf{fail}]\Phi$
6. $[X : \textbf{skip}]\Phi \equiv \Phi$

Rules
(MP)

$$\frac{\Phi_1 \to \Phi_2, \Phi_1}{\Phi_2}$$

(R)

$$\text{if } \alpha_1 =_{T'} \alpha_2, \text{ then } [\alpha_1]\Phi \equiv [\alpha_2]\Phi$$

(N)

$$\frac{\Phi}{[\alpha]\Phi}$$

Using the definitions of the deontic operators, the following proposition follows immediately.

Proposition 5.3.18 *Let* $\beta, \beta_1, \beta_2 \in Evt'$, *then all the theorems given in section 3.3 hold for* $DDL(Evt')$.

Finally, we introduce the notion of involvement between events in Evt':

Definition 5.3.19 *Let* $\alpha_1, \alpha_2 \in Evt'$, *then we define '*$\alpha_1$ *involves* α_2*'* ($\alpha_1 \rhd \alpha_2$) *as follows:*

$$\alpha_1 \rhd \alpha_2 \text{ iff } [\![\alpha_1]\!] \subseteq [\![\alpha_2]\!].$$

Corollary 5.3.20 *Let* $\alpha_1, \alpha_2 \in Evt'$, *then we have*

$$\alpha_1 \rhd \alpha_2 \to ([\alpha_2]V \to [\alpha_1]V).$$

5.4 The strong and weak obligations

We take as a primitive notion the relativised obligation $O(X : \beta)$, which means that 'group X is obliged to perform β'. In this section, we show that it is possible to define all sorts of notions of collective and individual obligation in terms of $O(X : \beta)$, and discuss the relation between all these notions of obligation and permission. With the help of group obligation $O(X : \beta)$, we can distinguish three notions of obligations:

- The *strong* obligation ($O^{\oplus}(\beta)$): for every set in $P^{+}(I)$ it is obligatory to perform β: $\forall_{X \in P^{+}(I)} O(X : \beta)$,[8] with I the set of actors.
- The *weak* obligation ($O^{\ominus}(\beta)$): there is a set in $P^{+}(I)$ for which it is obligatory to perform β: $\exists_{X \in P^{+}(I)} O(X : \beta)$.[9]
- The *group* obligation: for the group X it is obligatory to perform β: $O(X : \beta)$.

It is clear that the strong obligation implies group obligation, and that group obligation in turn implies the weak obligation.

In comparison with the strong and the weak obligations, the *restricted* strong and weak obligations are restricted to a set in $P^{+}(I)$ instead of to I itself. Let $X \in P^{+}(I)$, then $O^{\oplus}_{X}(\beta)$ (equivalent to $\forall_{Y \in P^{+}(X)} O(Y : \beta)$) is an example of a restricted strong obligation.

5.4.1 The relations between group and individual norms

Most existing formalisations of relativised deontic modalities are relativised to *actors* and not to groups of actors. In section 5.2.3, we distinguished, analogous to the collective obligations, three notions of obligations:

- The *general* obligation ($O^{+}(\beta)$): for all actors it is obligatory to perform β.
- The *personal* obligation ($O(i : \beta)$): for i it is obligatory to perform β.
- The *unspecific* obligation ($O^{-}(\beta)$): for some person it is obligatory to perform β.

It is obvious that we have a distinction between the notions of obligation with the personal obligation as the primitive notion and the notions of obligation with the group obligation as the primitive notion. The notions of strong, weak and group obligations enable us to analyse obligations concerning *groups of actors*: collective obligations, and the notions of general, unspecific and personal obligations enable us to analyse obligations concerning *actors*: individual obligations.

However, we can formalise the general, personal and unspecific obligations in terms of group obligation $O(\{i\} : \beta)$. Group obligation $O(\{i\} : \beta)$ can be considered to be an individual obligation. Therefore, we can formalise

[8]Note that the following equivalence holds: $\forall_{X \in P^{+}(I)} O(X : \beta) \equiv \wedge_{X \in P^{+}(I)} O(X : \beta)$.
[9]Note that the following equivalence holds: $\exists_{X \in P^{+}(I)} O(X : \beta) \equiv \vee_{X \in P^{+}(I)} O(X : \beta)$.

- the general obligation ($O^{+'}(\beta)$) as

$$\forall_{i \in I} O(\{i\} : \beta)$$

- the personal obligation as

$$O(\{i\} : \beta)$$

- the unspecific obligation ($O^{-'}(\beta)$) as

$$\exists_{i \in I} O(\{i\} : \beta)$$

With the help of the two new notions $O^{+'}$ and $O^{-'}$ we can define the different notions of collective obligation (i.e. strong, weak and group obligations) and individual obligation (i.e. general, unspecific and personal obligations) in the same semantical model.

Note that $O(\{i\} : \beta)$ is not the same as $O(i : \beta)$, since they differ semantically. $O(i : \beta)$ is an assertion concerning an event in Evt and $O(\{i\} : \beta)$ is an assertion concerning an event in Evt'. However, both obligations express the same: 'An obligation for i to perform the action β.' The only difference in interpretation is that in $O(\{i\} : \beta)$ individual i is considered to be a group of one individual and in $O(i : \beta)$ to be just an individual.

Now, the following two relations hold:

- The strong obligation implies the general obligation:

$$O^{\oplus}(\beta) \rightarrow O^{+'}(\beta).$$

- The unspecific obligation implies the weak obligation:

$$O^{-'}(\beta) \rightarrow O^{\ominus}(\beta).$$

If something is obligatory for all groups of a set of actors (the strong obligation), then it is also obligatory for all groups consisting of one actor, i.e. the general obligation, and if something is obligatory for a group consisting of one actor, thus for an actor, then it is also obligatory for some group of actors (the unspecific obligation).

In contrast to the two relations mentioned above, the relation between the group obligation and the personal obligation is not fixed. However, in certain cases the relation is determined by the kind of action (i.e. a positive or negative action), which we will discuss in the next section.

Figure 5.2 represents all the notions of obligation mentioned above. In chapter 4, we discussed the problem of the interdefinability of obligation and permission. This problem does not pose itself for the group obligation and permission, since we have $O(X : \beta) \equiv \neg P(X : \overline{\beta})$. We call $P(X : \beta)$ the dual of $O(X : \beta)$: the principle of interdefinability [cf. Herrestad and Krogh, 1995]. Also, for the strong and weak obligations we do not have this problem; however, the (restricted) weak permission is coupled with the (restricted) strong obligation, and the (restricted) strong permission with the (restricted) weak obligation. This is called the *asymmetry* between permission and obligation:

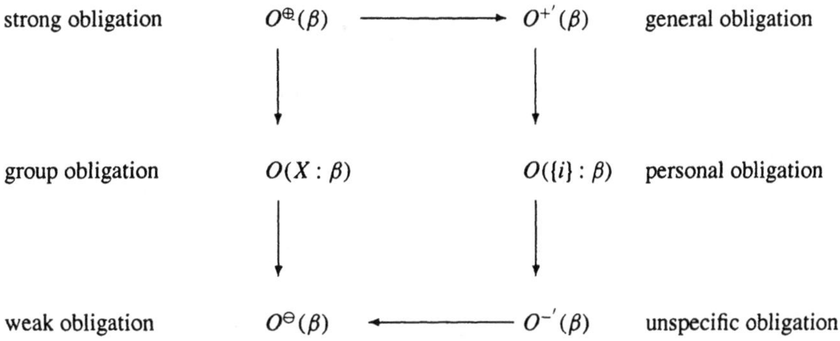

Figure 5.2: The notions of obligation

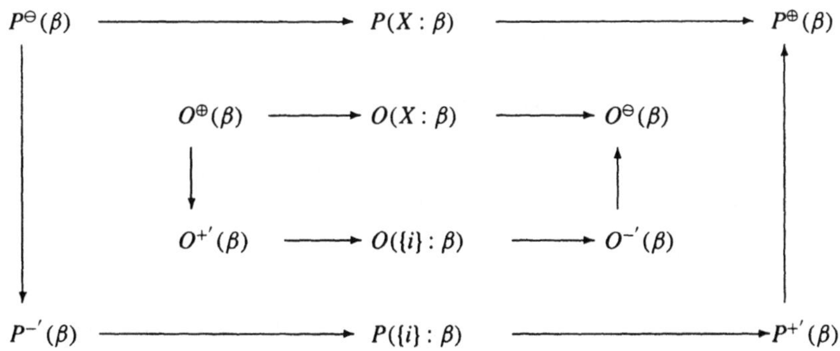

Figure 5.3: The valid relations between the different notions of obligation and permission

- $O^{\oplus}(\beta) \equiv \neg P^{\oplus}(\overline{\beta})$:[10] 'for every group it is obligatory to perform β' is equivalent to 'there is no group for which it is permitted not to perform β'.

- $O^{\ominus}(\beta) \equiv \neg P^{\ominus}(\overline{\beta})$:[11] 'there is a group for which it is obligatory to perform β' is equivalent to 'it is not permitted for all groups not to perform β'.

The valid relations between the different notions of obligation and permission are summarised in figure 5.3, which corresponds with figure 4.9.[12]

---

[10] $O^{\oplus}(\beta) \equiv \forall_{X \in P^{+}(I)} O(X:\beta) \equiv \forall_{X \in P^{+}(I)} \neg P(X:\overline{\beta}) \equiv \neg \exists_{X \in P^{+}(I)} P(X:\overline{\beta}) \equiv \neg P^{\oplus}(\overline{\beta})$.

[11] $O^{\ominus}(\beta) \equiv \exists_{X \in P^{+}(I)} O(X:\beta) \equiv \exists_{X \in P^{+}(I)} \neg P(X:\overline{\beta}) \equiv \neg \forall_{X \in P^{+}(I)} P(X:\overline{\beta}) \equiv \neg P^{\ominus}(\overline{\beta})$.

[12] Note that in figure 4.9 principle $O^{\oplus}(p) \to P^{\oplus}(p)$ is valid, and that the corresponding principle $O^{\oplus}(\beta) \to P^{\oplus}(\beta)$ is not valid in $DDL(Evt')$.

5.5 When does a group satisfy a norm?

In this chapter, we have formalised the concept of groups of actors ($DDL(Evt')$) in dynamic deontic logic, which allows us to specify that a group is obliged, prohibited or permitted to perform an action. The addition of groups of actors in a deontic system gives us the opportunity to express which group has the responsibility to perform an action. In this section, we investigate when a group of actors satisfies a norm.

We consider sets of actors. Suppose that four friends go to a restaurant, and after their meal they (for short, group X) have to pay 50 dollars. The norm '*it is obligatory for X to pay 50 dollars*' is fulfilled if and only if a subgroup of X pays 50 dollars. Not everyone has to pay 50 dollars, to satisfy that norm. Even if no one pays the 50 dollars, it is possible that the obligation will be fulfilled, for example, if everyone pays 12.50 dollars. Thus, $O(X : \beta)$ is *not* equivalent to $\forall_{i \in X} O(\{i\} : \beta)$ (the restricted general obligation), with β the action 'to pay 50 dollars'.

Suppose that for group X it is forbidden to steal 50 dollars. Group X satisfies this norm if the event is not performed. Thus, no subgroup of X may steal 50 dollars to satisfy the norm.

In this example, we have suggested that sometimes a group X fulfills obligation $O(X : \beta)$ if and only if every subgroup has to perform action β, and sometimes it is sufficient that some subgroup performs action β to fulfill the obligation. In the former case, it concerns a negative action, and in the latter, a positive action:

1. A group X 'performs' negative action $\overline{\gamma}$, i.e. does not perform action γ, if and only if every subgroup of X does not perform action γ. Thus, X is obliged not to perform γ if and only if every subgroup of X is obliged not to perform γ. The formal counterpart of this is:

$$O(X : \overline{\gamma}) \equiv \forall_{Y \in P^+(X)} O(Y : \overline{\gamma}).$$

   This can be proven as follows. Suppose that $\forall_{Y \in P^+(X)} O(Y : \overline{\gamma})$. X is a subset of X, hence $\forall_{Y \in P^+(X)} O(X : \overline{\gamma}) \rightarrow O(X : \overline{\gamma})$. Suppose now that $O(X : \overline{\gamma})$ and $Y \in P^+(X)$. Then, it follows by 5.3.12.1 that $[\![Y : \gamma]\!] \subseteq [\![X : \gamma]\!]$, and by 5.3.19 and 5.3.20 that $[X : \gamma]V \rightarrow [Y : \gamma]V$. This holds for every set Y in $P^+(X)$, thus $[X : \gamma]V \rightarrow \forall_{Y \in P^+(X)}[Y : \gamma]V$. Hence, $O(X : \overline{\gamma}) \rightarrow \forall_{Y \in P^+(X)} O(X : \overline{\gamma})$.

2. A group X performs positive action γ if and only if a subgroup of X performs action γ. Thus, X is obliged to perform action γ if and only if some subgroup of X is obliged to perform action γ.[13] The formal counterpart of this is:

$$O(X : \gamma) \equiv \exists_{Y \in P^+(X)} O(Y : \gamma).$$

   This can be proven analogously as above.

[13]Note that formula $O(X : \gamma) \rightarrow O(X \cup Y : \gamma)$ is valid, which seems paradoxical, more or less in the same way as the Ross paradox. See also section 4.3.2.

Now it is easy to see that the following proposition holds:

Proposition 5.5.1 *Let $X \in P^+(I)$ and $\gamma \in Act_p$, then*

1. $O(I : \overline{\gamma}) \equiv O^{\oplus}(\overline{\gamma})$
2. $O(I : \gamma) \equiv O^{\ominus}(\gamma)$

Thus, the strong obligation collapses in group obligation $O(I : \beta)$, if β is a negative action, and the weak obligation collapses in group obligation $O(I : \beta)$, if β is a positive action.

Further, the following two relations hold between group obligation $O(X : \beta)$ and personal obligation $O(\{i\} : \beta)$:

Proposition 5.5.2 *Let $i \in X \in P^+(I)$. Then,*

$$O(X : \beta) \rightarrow O(\{i\} : \beta) \textit{ iff } \beta \in Act_n \vee X = \{i\}$$

and

$$O(\{i\} : \beta) \rightarrow O(X : \beta) \textit{ iff } \beta \in Act_p \vee X = \{i\}.$$

If it is obligatory for X *not* to perform a positive action, then for every subgroup of X it is forbidden to perform that action, thus also for every actor of X. If it is obligatory for an actor $i \in X$ to perform a positive action, then it is also obligatory for every set with i as an element to perform that action, thus also X.

Finally, we present a proposition that enables us to obtain a better understanding of group events in $DDL(Evt')$, with respect to positive and negative actions.

Proposition 5.5.3 *Let $X, Y \in P^+(I)$ and $\gamma_1, \gamma_2 \in Act_p$, then*

1. $O(X \cup Y : \overline{\gamma_1}) \rightarrow O(X : \overline{\gamma_1})$
2. $O(X : \gamma_1) \rightarrow O(X \cup Y : \gamma_1)$
3. $O(X : \overline{\gamma_1} \cup' Y : \overline{\gamma_1}) \rightarrow O(X \cap Y : \overline{\gamma_1})$, *with* $X \cap Y \neq \emptyset$
4. $O(X : \gamma_1 \cup' Y : \gamma_1) \rightarrow O(X \cup Y : \gamma_1)$
5. $O(X : \overline{\gamma_1} \&' Y : \overline{\gamma_2}) \rightarrow O(X \cap Y : \overline{\gamma_1} \& \overline{\gamma_2})$, *with* $X \cap Y \neq \emptyset$
6. $O(X : \gamma_1 \&' Y : \gamma_2) \rightarrow O(X \cup Y : \gamma_1 \& \gamma_2)$

Proof

1. $O(X \cup Y : \overline{\gamma_1}) \equiv [X \cup Y : \gamma_1]V \rightarrow [X : \gamma_1 \cup' Y : \gamma_1]V \equiv [X : \gamma_1]V \wedge [Y : \gamma_1]V \equiv O(X : \overline{\gamma_1}) \wedge O(Y : \overline{\gamma_1}) \rightarrow O(X : \overline{\gamma_1})$
2. $O(X : \gamma_1) \equiv [X : \overline{\gamma_1}]V \rightarrow [X : \overline{\gamma_1} \&' Y : \overline{\gamma_1}]V \rightarrow [X \cup Y : \overline{\gamma_1}]V \equiv O(X \cup Y : \gamma_1)$
3. $O(X : \overline{\gamma_1}) \vee O(Y : \overline{\gamma_1}) \equiv [X : \gamma_1]V \vee [Y : \gamma_1]V \rightarrow [X : \gamma_1 \&' Y : \gamma_1]V \rightarrow [X \cap Y : \gamma_1]V \equiv O(X \cap Y : \overline{\gamma_1})$

4. $O(X:\gamma_1) \wedge O(Y:\gamma_1) \equiv [X:\overline{\gamma_1}]V \wedge [Y:\overline{\gamma_1}]V \equiv [X:\overline{\gamma_1} \cup' Y:\overline{\gamma_1}]V \rightarrow [X \cap Y:\overline{\gamma_1}]V \equiv O(X \cap Y:\gamma_1)$

5. $O(X:\overline{\gamma_1}\&'Y:\overline{\gamma_2}) \equiv O(X:\overline{\gamma_1}) \wedge O(Y:\overline{\gamma_2}) \rightarrow O(X \cap Y:\overline{\gamma_1}) \wedge O(X \cap Y:\overline{\gamma_2}) \equiv O(X \cap Y:\overline{\gamma_1}\&'X \cap Y:\overline{\gamma_2}) \equiv O(X \cap Y:\overline{\gamma_1}\&\overline{\gamma_2})$

6. $O(X:\gamma_1\&'Y:\gamma_2) \equiv O(X:\gamma_1) \wedge O(Y:\gamma_2) \rightarrow O(X \cup Y:\gamma_1) \wedge O(X \cup Y:\gamma_2) \equiv O(X \cup Y:\gamma_1\&'X \cup Y:\gamma_2) \equiv O(X \cup Y:\gamma_1\&\gamma_2)$

The formulas in proposition 5.5.3 include the following assertions:

1. If a negative action is obligatory for a group, then it is also obligatory for every subgroup.
2. If a positive action is obligatory for a group, then it is also obligatory for every superset of that group.
3. If it is obligatory that a group 'performs' a negative action or that another group 'performs' that action, then that action is obligatory for the intersection of both groups.
4. If it is obligatory that a group performs a positive action or that another group performs that action, then that action is obligatory for the union of both groups.
5. If it is obligatory that a group 'performs' a negative action and another group 'performs' another negative action, then it is obligatory for the intersection of the groups to 'perform' both actions.
6. If it is obligatory that a group performs a positive action and another group performs another positive action, then it is obligatory for the union of the groups to perform both actions.

5.6 From Ought-to-be to Ought-to-do

In this section, we show how the concepts developed in this, and the previous, chapter can help us to formalise and analyse the following two judgements. The first judgement concerns an individual obligation and the second, in our opinion, a weak collective obligation.

The first case reads as follows. According to the 'Reglement van Politie voor de scheepvaart op de Merwede' (Police regulations concerning navigation on the river Merwede), it is prohibited for more than three boats to be moored next to one another breadthways in the river outside harbours.

The Supreme Court specified this norm as follows:[14]

[14] HR, 19-1-1931, *NJ* 1931, 1455.

> It is prohibited to perform an action resulting in an unwanted situation. Such a situation was created by the fourth captain, who moored his boat last.

The second case reads as follows. Under the Dutch Road Traffic Act, it was prohibited for three cyclists to cycle next to one another. In its 1948 ruling, the Supreme Court considered all three cyclists to have broken the law, because each one of them was able to bring an end to the situation.[15]

In the case of the four boats, the person who creates the illegal situation is obliged to bring an end to that situation. We can formalise this by using the system SDL_X:

$$O_{i_4}(\neg p),$$

with p 'more than three boats are moored next to one another breadthways in the river outside the harbour' and i_4 the fourth captain, who moored his boat last. Thus, here we are concerned with a personal obligation.

In the case of the three cyclists, all three are obliged to bring an end to the illegal situation:

$$\forall_{i \in X} O_i(\neg q),$$

with X the set of the three cyclists and q 'more than two cyclists are cycling next to one another'. Here we are concerned with a restricted general obligation. This is very strange, since if one of the cyclists ends the situation, the other cyclists are released from their obligation. A better formalisation would be that they, as a group, are obliged to bring an end to the situation, so

$$O_X(\neg q).$$

Although all three are considered to have broken the law, this does not alter the fact that they, *as a group*, are responsible for bringing an end to the illegal situation.[16] Note that here we are concerned with a weak collective obligation, not with a strict collective obligation. Suppose, for example, that four cyclists are cycling next to one another. In this case, none of them individually can bring an end to the illegal situation, and the general obligation

$$\forall_{i \in Y} O_i(\neg q),$$

with Y the set of four cyclists, would be a void obligation, because each cyclist is not able to bring an end to the illegal situation. The individual is not able to end that situation, the group, however, is:

$$O_Y(\neg q),$$

with Y the group of four cyclists.

---

[15] HR, 9-3-1948, *NJ* 1948, 370.

[16] To bring an end to the illegal situation, the group has to decide how the 'tasks' are to be distributed between the individuals of the group. There has to be a certain regulation of the *coordination of the behaviour* of the individuals to end the illegal situation. Lindahl [1977] has formalised the 'legal' relations (the coordination of the behaviour) between two agents in a group. The intension of his system - which he called the system of collevistic two-agent types - is to facilitate a survey of the various collective regulations of two agents' behaviour. We try to formalise these regulations with the notion of commitment (see the next section).

However, the formalisation is not really satisfactory, since it does not fit in our system of criminal law. The law is geared to unlawful behaviour and illegal situations. Criminal law is concerned with behaviour: if an illegal situation is mentioned in the description of an offence, the question is raised as to who created this situation (by action or by omission) and who is responsible for continuing the situation (omission). From the illegal situation a certain type of behaviour is derived, as it were.

The derivation of an action or a set of actions from a situation is not a clear-cut matter. Take, for instance, obligation $O_X(\neg q)$: 'it is obligatory for group X that no more than two cyclists cycle next to one another.' Now, we want to derive an Ought-to-do statement from this Ought-to-be statement. However, one can think of many actions to be taken by group X that would end the illegal situation.

> Many human actions are described by their results, something on which von Wright in particular has focussed. Thus, according to the suggestion mentioned, in the case of John opening the window, John selects and runs a routine such that at the end of that routine the window is open; in the case of John eating (all of) an apple, John selects and runs a routine at the end of that routine John has eaten an apple; etc. Thus there is a large class of actions of the type 'doing A', where A is a proposition expressing a state-of-affairs. [Segerberg, 1989, p. 327]

In his article 'Bringing it about', Segerberg introduced an operator δ such that '$\delta(p)$' will carry the informal meaning of 'bringing about that p' or 'doing p'. Thus, $\delta(p)$ is the *action* with p as the result (or state of affairs).[17] In general, $\delta(p)$ is a choice between several actions $\beta_1, \ldots, \beta_n$, which all bring about that p. Thus, $\delta(p)$ is equal to $\beta_1 \cup \beta_2 \cup \ldots \cup \beta_n$.

With the help of the operator 'δ', we can smoothly formalise the obligations belonging to the two cases:

1. In the case of the four boats:

$$O(i_4 : \delta(\neg p))$$

2. In the case of the three cyclists:

$$O(X : \delta(\neg q))$$

In section 4.5 we briefly discussed the relativised monadic operator E_i. With the help of this operator - an action operator -, Pörn [1970] developed the *logic of action*. The expression $E_i p$ describes a class of actions that can be performed by actor i to bring it about that p. Thus, the meaning of the expression $O(E_i p)$ corresponds with $O(i : \delta(p))$. However, both approaches allow a certain ambiguity to the interpretation of $i : \delta(p)$ and $E_i p$. Pörn gives the following example, the reading of 'John brings it about that the door is open' is ambiguous in that, since it fails to discriminate between 'John opens the door' and 'John keeps the door open'. Jones and Sergot [1993a] make the following observation about 'brings it about' operators:

[17] For the formal representation of $\delta(p)$ we refer to Segerberg [1989].

> the "brings it about' operator abstracts away details of specific actions performed by the agents, changes of state, and the temporal dimension generally; we have indicated that for certain purposes this abstraction is appropriate. But in the context of computer systems, a specification employing this operator would be a formal specification at an unusually high level of abstraction. (...) [I]t is clear that some aspects of access control mechanisms and some of the behaviour of distributed computer systems need to be modeled at a finer grain of detail. In these cases, it will be necessary to replace or augment use of the "brings it about" operator with more standard approaches to action and time in computer science.

Such a standard approach is dynamic logic. *DDL*, which is based on dynamic logic, is an excellent system for the modelling 'at a finer grain of detail', since it contains the following desirable aspects:

1. Actions and assertions are strictly separated.

2. Actions can be made explicit, so the notion of ambiguity disappears.

3. A notion of time-lag is built in ($[\beta]\Phi$ means that Φ holds after β is performed).

From the above consideration we can conclude that it is important to distinguish Ought-to-do statements (which may be interpreted as expressing imperatives of the form 'an addressee ought to perform an action') and Ought-to-be statements (which express a desired state of affairs without necessarily mentioning addressees and actions bearing relations with that state of affairs). There are situations in which we would like to formalise norms as Ought-to-be statements, and there are situations in which we would like to formalise norms as Ought-to-do statements. In the case of the Penal Code, the formalisation of obligations as Ought-to-do statements fits better than Ought-to-be statements.

5.7 Commitment

The aim of this section is to introduce some notions of commitment to determine the relation between individual agents and their collective obligation to accomplish something. In this and the previous chapter, the collective obligation is formalized in a logical framework, which gives the opportunity to express which group has the responsibility to bring about a certain situation (to express group liability, e.g. liability for a trading partnership) and to express the relation between groups of agents. However, in the theory we cannot express the individual responsibility to achieve the fulfillment of the collective obligation. A consequence is that we cannot indicate which individual is responsible for a violation of a collective obligation. To deal with this, we will investigate the notion of commitment in the context of collective obligation. Commitment links the agents with the joint goal (i.e. the fulfillment of the collective obligation), so that we can express to whom such an agent is committed and to what that agent is committed to [see Dunin-Kęplicz and Verbrugge, 1996; Castelfranchi, 1995].

We will remain very generic, we do not deal with individual motivations, delegations, restrictions on the groups of agents, etc. It has to be seen as a first attempt to combine two notions (collective obligation and commitment) to formalise the individual responsibility and thus achieving a joint goal (the collective obligation, which gives new expressive power and ,therefore, is subject to new intuitions.

Suppose we have the following collective obligation $O(X:\beta)$. The action β represents a set of sequences $<\beta_1,\ldots,\beta_n>$ of individual actions such that the performance of all these individual actions leads to the accomplishment of β. We need a set of sequences, since there are probably many sequences that can accomplish that β will be performed by X. For convenience and for the moment, we assume that there is only one sequence of individual actions that leads to the performance of β. To fulfill a collective obligation $O(X:\beta)$, the group X has to decompose the goal (to perform β) into a number of individual subgoals. For example, if the group X is obligatory that a house is built within three months, the norm can only be fulfilled if the work that has to be done, is shared out in several tasks among the agents of the group X.

A first attempt to formalise the collective obligation is as follows:

$$O(X:\beta) \rightarrow \exists_{i\in X} O(i:\beta_1) \wedge \ldots \wedge \exists_{i\in X} O(i:\beta_n).$$

Thus, if $O(X:\beta)$, then all the individual actions in the sequence presented by β are obligated for some agents of the group X.

However, we must not forget that some individual actions can only be performed after the performance of some other obligated individual actions. For example, the roof of a house cannot be assembled if the foundation of the house is not ready. Thus, an individual obligation can only be fulfilled sometimes if first other obligations are already fulfilled. The responsibility of an individual obligation $O(i:\beta)$ does not always depend on the individual who is committed to fulfill the obligation, but also on agents who have to perform actions that are necessary to fulfill the individual obligation $O(i:\beta)$. This means that the action β not only contains a set of individual actions, but also contains an order of the individual actions, i.e. a sequential composition of the individual actions.[18] We will denote the sequential composition of β_1 and β_2 by $\beta_1;\beta_2$, which we are also going to use in the sequences. This will be done by dividing the individual actions that are performed after other individual actions by ';'. For example, the sequence $<\beta_1,\beta_2;\beta_3;\beta_4>$, has to be read as 'the performance of the individual actions β_1 and β_2, then the performance of action β_3 and then the action β_4'. Let this be the sequence to accomplish that β is performed by X. We then formalise the collective obligation $O_X(p)$ as follows:[19]

$$O(X:\beta) \rightarrow$$

$$\exists_{i\in X} O(i:\beta_1) \wedge \exists_{i\in X} O(i:\beta_2) \wedge \exists_{i\in X}[\beta_1\&\beta_2]O(i:\beta_3) \wedge \exists_{i\in X}[\beta_1\&\beta_2;\beta_3]O(i:\beta_4)$$

[18]For the formal representation of the sequential composition, we refer to Meyer [1988].

[19]Expression $[\beta]\Phi$, with Φ a collective obligation and β an action, means that Φ holds after β is performed.

5.7.1 Individual commitment

Up to now, we have represented a collective obligation as individual obligations, but without specifying which individual has the responsibility to fulfill the obligation. Therefore, we need the notion of commitment. As we already said, the fulfillment of a collective obligation can only be reached if the group decomposes their goal into a number of individual actions by *commitment*. We cannot appropriately influence these individual obligations if we do not exactly know the individual commitments of the group.

> "Commitment" is seen as the glue of the group, of collective activity: it links the agent with the joint goal and the common solution, it links the members' actions with the collective plan, it links the members with each other. [Castelfranchi, 1995]

A formal approach of (collective) commitment is given by Dunin-Kęplicz and Verbrugge [1996].

In this subsection, we are interested in the relation of collective obligation and the individual commitment to indicate the responsibility of the agents to fulfill their obligations. The formula COMM(i, X, β) is meant to stand for 'agent i commits to the group X to perform action β'. With this expression we can formalise that if there is an unspecific individual obligation to perform an action and someone particular of a certain group is committed to that group to perform that action, then this person is obligated to perform that action:

$$\exists_{i \in X} O(i : \beta_1) \wedge COMM(i_1, X, \beta_1) \rightarrow O(i_1 : \beta_1).$$

5.7.2 Collective commitment

For convenience, we had assumed that there is only one sequence of individual actions that brings about that β can be performed by X. However, as we already mentioned, there can be more sequences. So, there has to be a commitment among the group concerning which sequence of individual actions will be chosen to fulfill the collective obligation. This we call the collective commitment: the commitment that is established to fulfill the obligation by performing a particular sequence of individual actions. Therefore, we need the formula C-COMM$_{X,\beta}(< \beta_1, \ldots, \beta_n >)$, meaning that the group X has a collective commitment to perform β by performing the individual actions of sequence $< \beta_1, \ldots \beta_n >$.

Let $< \beta_1; \beta_2, \beta_3 >$ be a sequence of β, then we can formalise

$$O(X : \beta) \wedge \text{C-COMM}_{X,\beta}(< \beta_1; \beta_2, \beta_3 >) \rightarrow$$

$$\exists_{i \in X} O(i : \beta_1) \wedge [\beta_1] \exists_{i \in X} O(i : \beta_2) \wedge [\beta_1] \exists_{i \in X} O(i : \beta_3).$$

Thus, the operator C-COMM$_{X,\beta}$ determines the sequence of individual action by commitment among the group X to perform β.

If we know the collective commitment and the individual commitments of a group X, then we can express the responsibility of all the agents to fulfill the collective obligation precisely:

$$(O(X : \beta) \wedge \text{C-COMM}_{X,\beta}(< \beta_1; \beta_2, \beta_3 >)$$

$$\wedge \text{COMM}(i_1, X, \beta_1) \wedge \text{COMM}(i_2, X, \beta_2) \wedge \text{COMM}(i_3, X, \beta_3))$$
$$\rightarrow O(i_1 : \beta_1) \wedge [\beta_1]O(i_2 : \beta_2) \wedge [\beta_1]O(i_3 : \beta_3)$$

Some authors [Kanger, 1971, 1985; Lindahl, 1977; Makinson, 1986; Herrestad and Krogh, 1995] analysed or described the types of rights relationships between the addressees (or bearers) and counterparties from the classic work by Hohfeld [1964]. The counterparty is an agent or a group of agents that has a 'right' against the addressee, who has a 'duty' (an obligation). 'Right' and 'duty' are correlative terms, i.e. when a right is invaded, a duty is violated.[20] An example of a directed obligation is that John is obliged towards Paul that he shall stay away from Paul's land. In other words, Paul has a *right* against John that the latter will stay away from Paul's land, the correlative (and equivalent) being that John is under a *duty* toward Paul to stay away from the place [cf. Hohfeld, 1964].

In a collective obligation with a collective commitment, the agents of the group are not only bearers, but some of them are counterparties too. If a group X has a collective commitment to perform β by performing the sequence $< \beta_1; \beta_2, \beta_3 >$ and it holds that $O(X : \beta)$, then the agents who have to perform the actions β_2 and β_3 have a right towards an agent, say i, who has to perform the action β_1. If agent i violates his obligation to perform β_1, the other two agents cannot fulfill their obligations. However, they are not responsible for the violation of their obligations, since they have a 'right' to hold agent i responsible for this violation, because of the fact that agent i violates his own duty.

Here, no attempt is made to formalise the relation between addressees and counterparties in collective obligations by directed obligation - which requires further research -, but we only want to note that in the theory presented here a notion of directed obligation is indirectly built in. We have just tried to give a first step to the formalisation of a collectivity as a function of individuals actions.

5.8 Conclusions

In this chapter, we formalised the concept of (groups of) actors in DDL, a deontic system as a variant of dynamic logic. The concept of groups of actors in DDL is new. With the addition of groups of actors, we are able to express who (a group or an actor) has the responsibility for performing certain actions, and when a group or an actor satisfies a norm.

To express the notions of individual obligation (i.e. the general, personal and unspecific obligations) we first used individual events. However, we showed that these notions can also be expressed using collective events. This enabled us to express all the different notions of the individual and collective obligations in the same semantical model. Furthermore, we investigated the relations between these different notions of obligation, analogous to the relations discussed in chapter 4.

With the introduction of collective events, it is now possible to make a distinction between actions performed by all members of a group X and actions performed by a group X

[20] In law, the word 'right' is often used to designate '*legal power*', '*legal claim*', and '*immunity* granted by an authority'.

as a whole. The type of action is very important to indicate when a group fulfills an obligation; e.g. if a group X has to perform a positive action, then some subset of that group has to perform that action, and if a group has to 'perform' a negative action, then every subset of that group has to 'perform' that action.

However, there are more complex and more interesting questions in the logical theory of collective obligation.

> From the point of view of methodological individualism, the action of a collectivity is in some sense composed of or determined by individual actions performed by the members of the collectivity. The general study of the nature of that composition, of the dependence of collective actions on individual ones, could be said to constitute the theory of collective action in a narrower sense. [Pörn, 1970, p. 78]

A first attempt is made to 'constitute the theory of collective action in a narrower sense' by the introduction of commitment and to define an action of a collectivity as a sequence of individual actions. The notion of commitment is very useful to determine which *plan* will be followed to fulfill a collective obligation (collective commitment) and to determine which agent has to perform (or is responsible to perform) a certain action - being part of the committed sequence - to achieve the joint goal (individual commitment).

Finally, we can conclude that it is sometimes important, especially in the case of the Penal Code, to make a reduction of a collective Ought-to-be statement (which expresses a desired state of affairs without necessarily mentioning addressees and actions bearing relations with that state of affairs) to individual Ought-to-do statements (which may be interpreted as expressing imperatives of the form 'an addressee ought to perform an action'). This can be done by using the operator δ introduced by Segerberg or the action operator E_i introduced by Kanger. However, these approaches are sometimes too ambiguous, especially when we want to indicate a special action. Then we need a system that can deal with more detailed specifications, such as *DDL*.

Chapter 6

Enactment of norms

6.1 Introduction

Law changes - the 'dynamic' character of law - as new norms are incorporated by competent normative authorities, and existing norms are repealed and so removed from the legal order. It is our task here to identify of all the norms that were enacted and the validity of these norms at a certain moment. The norms which are used to express and illustrate the issues discussed in this chapter, are norm expressions of *DDL*.[1]

The term 'validity', as it is used in legal discourse, is ambiguous. It is possible to distinguish several meanings in which a legal norm can be said to be valid. In this chapter, we are concerned with two such meanings (two concepts of validity): membership and applicability. Both of them play a central role in law and in legal theories [cf. Bulygin, 1982].

- A norm can be said to be valid in the sense that it belongs to or is a member of a legal system. 'Membership' is a *descriptive* concept, because the sentence '$O(\beta)$ is valid' is a descriptive proposition, not a norm. There are various criteria for membership, but we restrict ourselves to the criterion of competence of the authority that has created the norm: a norm is valid if it has been issued (enacted, promulgated) by a competent authority.

- A norm is often also said to be valid in the sense that it is obligatory or has a 'binding force'. 'Applicability' is also a descriptive concept, for to say that a norm is valid in this sense is not to give a prescription, but to state that there is a prescription according to which the norm must be applied. Here the sentence '$O(\beta)$ is valid' is again a proposition, though referring to a norm.[2]

[1] We might also have used norm expressions of, e.g. *SDL*; however, we have chosen for norm expressions of *DDL* for no particular reason.

[2] A norm has a 'binding force' may also mean that there is a prescription to obey and apply the norm. Then

In legal discourse reference is made to enacted norms and applicable norms. Not all norms that are enacted are applicable or are only applicable in certain circumstances. In most legal support/expert systems only the applicable norms are considered. It is impossible in these systems to talk about the rules that select applicable norms explicitly. Neither is it possible to reason about enacted norms that are not applicable. In this and the next chapter, we present a theory to describe enacted norms and applicable norms separately. In this chapter we discuss the enactment of norms, and we describe how a modality of enactment can be used to express inconsistent enacted norms in a consistent way. The process of filtering out the applicable norms from the set of enacted norms is discussed in chapter 7.

The introduction of a modal operator for enactment is an alternative for the use of non-monotonic logic as is advocated in Meyer and van der Hoek [1988]. Our conjecture is that in general the use of non-monotonic logic can be substituted by the introduction of a modal operator. The preferential models that are used in non-monotonic logics indicate how the default inference rule can be applied. In a logic with a modal operator this preferential ordering is explicitly given. This has the advantage that these orderings can be changed and it is clear on the basis of which criteria inferences take place.

In the presented theory we can reason consistently with enacted norms without requiring all enacted norms to be *normatively consistent*. There are two specific types of normative conflicts [cf. Lindahl, 1992]:

- *disaffirmation conflicts*: these conflicts describe the same behaviour, but the deontic modalities contradict. For example, *it is forbidden to turn left* and *it is not forbidden (permitted) to turn left*.
- *compliance conflicts*: these conflicts occur when the actions which are obliged by different norms are incompatible. For example: *it is obligated to turn left* and *it is obligated to turn right*. Thus, these conflicts describe the same deontic modalities, but the actions conflict (are incompatible).

The normative conflicts are caused, for instance, by the dynamics of the legal system (by the enactment of new norms), by the uncertainty concerning the content of the legal sources (regulations can be vague or ambiguous), etc. [cf. Sartor, 1992a, 1992b].

One way to deal with these type of conflicts is to add sets of authorities enacting the norms to standard deontic logic. Here we use the term authority in an abstract way. They can be seen as real authorities (e.g. government and city council), but also as *source of norms* as in the Penal Code, Traffic Regulations, etc. We treat enactment as a variant of epistemic logic. However, in this theory we cannot adequately express normative inconsistencies. Therefore, we propose an extension of these theories, based on the theory of 'local reasoning' [Fagin and Halpern, 1988]. The basic idea behind this treatment is that authorities may enact several (inconsistent) norms, depending on the frame of reference. The applicability of norms depends on the situation, on the relative importance of the norms,

---

we have a *normative* concept of validity: 'a norm is valid' is to describe that it should be obeyed and applied; so, in this sense, '$O(\beta)$ is valid' is not a proposition, but a prescription, i.e. a norm.

etc. For example, according to Article 15.1 of the Dutch Traffic Regulation vehicles give right of way to vehicles from the right, and according to Article 15.2 bicycles must give right of way to cars. These two norms can conflict, therefore they cannot both be applicable in any situation. We make sets of applicable norms for each situation. For example, in the situation that a car and a bicycle are at a junction and the bicycle is coming from the right, we choose a set of norms with Article 15.2 and other applicable norms (e.g. concerning the maximum speed limit) and not a set of norms consisting Article 15.1, whereas in a situation of two cars we do not choose a set of norms consisting Article 15.2. How this choice can make explicitly in a formalisation, we illustrate in chapter 7. We can view the enacted norms as a society of possible sets of applicable norms, which may contradict each other.

An attempt to express enacted norms is made by Bailhache. First, we discuss a theory, corresponding with the theory from Bailhache [1981, 1991]: a theory for a *coherent deontic system*, i.e. a normative agreement between all (sets of) authorities. A drawback of this theory, however, inherent to the purpose of this theory, is that we cannot express conflicts between enacted norms. These conflicts exist since norms come into being and cease to exist in complex ways, involving different authorities at different times in different places [cf. Prakken, 1993]. Second, we show that this theory has to deal with serious problems concerning the power of expressibility. For instance, in this theory we cannot express that a permission has been enacted by a set of authorities.

To overcome these problems and especially to express normative inconsistencies in a consistent way, we modify the theory. A consequence of this modification is that the theory becomes more powerful, certain formulas acquire new meanings differing from Bailhache's theory. These new meanings are discussed formally in the logic for enactment.

The organisation of this chapter is as follows: in section 6.2, we extend SDL_X to sets of authorities on the basis of Bailhache's theory. This theory excludes the possibility of expressing normative inconsistency, which is discussed in section 6.3. The logic of enactment, based on epistemic logic, is presented in section 6.4 A problem that arises from this theory is the problem of inconsistent enacted norms, which will be solved by the theory of local reasoning for enactment in section 6.5. In the last section, we give some conclusions and suggestions for future research.

6.2 Authorities in SDL_X

In this section, we discuss the addition of sets of authorities on the basis of Bailhache's theory. Bailhache [1981, 1991] wanted to obtain a coherent deontic system, i.e. a normative agreement between all sets of authorities. This is accomplished by avoiding any conflict between the obligations enacted by the sets of authorities. It is necessary and sufficient for each set of authorities not to forbid - in other words to permit - what a set of authorities makes obligatory.

To add authorities to system SDL_X, we have to introduce the set NA of authorities. Let $a \in NA$, then $O^a_X(p)$ can be read as 'a makes it obligatory for X that p'. If there is a normative agreement between all the authorities, then this means that norm $O_X(p)$ holds.

Now it seems natural to make a reduction in statement $O_X(p)$ of SDL_X to statement $O^a_X(p)$: norm $O_X(p)$ holds if and only if there is an authority which enacted that norm. This can be expressed as

$$O_X(p) =_{def} \exists_{a \in NA} O^a_X(p). \tag{6.1}$$

We refer to the two directions of the equivalence of (6.1) as $(6.1)^{\rightarrow}$ and $(6.1)^{\leftarrow}$. There is an argument against the intuitive validity of $(6.1)^{\rightarrow}$.

- Implication $(6.1)^{\leftarrow}$ asserts that if an authority enacts a norm $O_X(p)$, that norm holds. In a coherent deontic system this seems very plausible.
- Implication $(6.1)^{\rightarrow}$ asserts that if norm $O_X(p)$ holds, then an authority enacted that norm. This is simply not true. As a counterexample, consider obligation $O_X(p \wedge q)$, which is equivalent to $O_X(p) \wedge O_X(q)$. Suppose that $O_X(p)$ was enacted by authority a and $O_X(q)$ by authority b, then norm $O_X(p \wedge q)$ was *not* enacted by a single authority, but by the two authorities a and b, in other words by a set of authorities. Thus, the formula

  $$(\exists_{a \in NA} O^a_X(p) \wedge \exists_{a \in NA} O^a_X(q)) \rightarrow \exists_{a \in NA} O^a_X(p \wedge q) \tag{6.2}$$

  is counter-intuitive and it would be strange if it were valid in a formal system [cf. Hansson, 1970, p. 244], in contrast with the formula in SDL_X:

  $$O_X(p) \wedge O_X(q) \rightarrow O_X(p \wedge q). \tag{6.3}$$

  Hence, a norm that holds is not necessarily enacted by one authority.

Thus, the definition for $O_X(p)$ as $\exists_{a \in NA} O^a_X(p)$ is inadequate. This above problem can be solved by using sets of authorities. This leads to an extension of system SDL_X to SDL^A, where the norms are enacted by sets of authorities. Let A be a subset of NA, then $O^A_X(p)$ will be read as 'A makes it obligatory for X that p'.

The system SDL^A is given by the following rules and axioms:

(RO^AM)	$\frac{p \rightarrow q}{O^A_X(p) \rightarrow O^A_X(q)}$
(RO^AM2)	$\frac{B \in P^+(A)}{O^B_X(p) \rightarrow O^A_X(p)}$
(RO^AM3)	$\frac{X \in P^+(Y)}{O^A_X(p) \rightarrow O^A_Y(p)}$

together with the following axiom schemata

(O^AC)	$(O^A_X(p) \wedge O^A_X(q)) \rightarrow O^A_X(p \wedge q)$
(O^AN)	$O^A_X(p \vee \neg p)$
(O^AD)	$\neg O^A_X(p \wedge \neg p)$
$(Df.P^A)$	$P^A_X(p) \equiv \neg O^A_X(\neg p)$

For the semantical interpretation of this system SDL^A we use the following model structure $M = (W, R, P^+(NA), P^+(I), V)$, with R the set of functions $\{R_X^{A_1}, R_X^{A_2}, \ldots\}$ for each set of authorities $A_1, A_2, \ldots \in P^+(NA)$ and for all $X \in P^+(I)$, and the non-empty powerset $P^+(NA)$ of the set of authorities $NA = \{a_1, a_2, \ldots\}$. The function $R_X^A \in R$ on W, which returns the deontically ideal worlds for set A of authorities and for set X of individuals given a world: $R_X^A : W \to 2^W$.

The truth conditions for O_X^A and P_X^A are defined as follows:

$$M, w \models O_X^A(p) \text{ iff } R_X^A(w) \subseteq [\![p]\!] \tag{6.4}$$

and

$$M, w \models P_X^A(p) \text{ iff } R_X^A(w) \cap [\![p]\!] \neq \emptyset. \tag{6.5}$$

The following additional constraint gives schema $O^A D$. Let $R_X^A \in R$, then

$$R_X^A(w) \neq \emptyset \text{ for all } R_X^A \in R \text{ and for all } w \in W. \tag{6.6}$$

The constraints

$$\text{if } R_X^A, R_X^B \in R \text{ and } B \in P^+(A), \text{ then } R_X^A(w) \subseteq R_X^B(w) \text{ for all } w \in W \tag{6.7}$$

and

$$\text{if } R_X^A, R_Y^A \in R \text{ and } X \in P^+(Y), \text{ then } R_Y^A(w) \subseteq R_X^A(w) \text{ for all } w \in W \tag{6.8}$$

validate rules $(RO^A M2)$ and $(RO^A M3)$, respectively.

Rule $(RO^A M2)$ states that if a set of authorities is included in another set, every obligation enacted by the former is also an obligation enacted by the latter. Rule $(RO^A M3)$ states that if a set of authorities makes it obligatory for a set X of individuals that p, then this set of authorities makes it also obligatory for every superset of X that p. Now it follows that[3]

$$O_X^A(p) \equiv \exists_{Y \in P^+(X)} O_Y^A(p).$$

Thus, the collective obligations enacted by sets of authorities are interpreted as weak collective obligations (see section 4.3.2). In the sequel of this book, we will interpret the collective obligation as the weak collective obligation.

From constraint (6.7) we can derive the constraint

$$\text{if } R_X^A \in R, \text{ then } \cap_{B \in P^+(A)} R_X^B(w) = R_X^A(w) \text{ for all } w \in W. \tag{6.9}$$

Hence, $\forall_{A,B \in P^+(NA)}(R_X^A(w) \cap R_X^B(w) \neq \emptyset)$, since $\emptyset \neq R_X^{NA}(w) = \cap_{A \in P^+(NA)} R_X^{NA}(w) \subseteq R_X^A(w) \cap R_X^B(w)$.

[3]Suppose that $O_X^A(p)$ holds, then there is a subset Y of X, such that $O_Y^A(p)$ holds, namely X. Thus, $\exists_{Y \in P^+(X)} O_X^A(p)$. Now suppose that $\exists_{Y \in P^+(X)} O_Y^A(p)$, say Z. Since $Z \in P^+(X)$, it holds by rule $(RO^A M3)$ that $O_X^A(p)$.

Proposition 6.2.1 *Let $X \in P^+(I)$ and $A, B, C \in P^+(NA)$. Then,*

1. $O_X^A(p) \to P_X^B(p)$
2. $O_X^A(p) \wedge O_X^B(q) \to O_X^{A \cup B}(p \wedge q)$
3. $O_X^A(p) \equiv \exists_{B \in P^+(A)} O_X^B(p)$
4. $P_X^A(p) \equiv \forall_{B \in P^+(A)} P_X^B(p)$
5. $O_X^A(p) \wedge O_X^B(q) \to P_X^C(p \wedge q)$

Proof

1. Suppose that $O_X^A(p)$ holds. It follows from rule $(RO^A M2)$ that $O_X^A(p) \to O_X^{A \cup B}(p)$. From $(O^A D)$ and $(O^A C)$ it follows that $O_X^{A \cup B}(p) \to P_X^{A \cup B}(p)$. On the basis of $(Df.P^A)$ and $(RO^A M2)$ it holds that $P_X^{A \cup B}(p) \to P_X^B(p)$. Hence, by modus ponens, it follows that $O_X^A(p) \to P_X^B(p)$.

2. Suppose that $O_X^A(p) \wedge O_X^B(q)$ holds, then by $(RO^A M2)$ $O_X^{A \cup B}(p) \wedge O_X^{A \cup B}(q)$. From $(O^A C)$ it now follows that $O_X^{A \cup B}(p \wedge q)$.

3. Suppose that $O_X^A(p)$ holds, then there is a subset B of A, such that $O_X^B(p)$ holds, namely A. Thus, $\exists_{B \in P^+(A)} O_X^A(p)$. Now suppose that $\exists_{B \in P^+(A)} O_X^B(p)$, say C. Since $C \in P^+(A)$, it holds by rule $(RO^A M2)$ that $O_X^A(p)$.

4. Follows immediately from 6.2.1.3 and $(Df.P^A)$.

5. From 6.2.1.2 it follows that $O_X^A(p) \wedge O_X^B(q) \to O_X^{A \cup B}(p \wedge q)$, and from 6.2.1.1 it follows that $O_X^{A \cup B}(p \wedge q) \to P_X^C(p \wedge q)$. Thus, by MP $O_X^A(p) \wedge O_X^B(q) \to P_X^C(p \wedge q)$.

Proposition 6.2.1.1 expresses the normative agreement between all the possible couples of sets of authorities. Proposition 6.2.1.5 expresses that we have a complete coherent deontic system, i.e. a normative agreement between all sets of authorities [cf. Bailhache, 1991]. Deontic (or normative) coherence makes it necessary that it is not obligatory for all sets of actors that some thing is accomplished as soon as it is obligatory for some set of actors that this thing is accomplished. Thus, if sets of authorities enacted that p and q are obligatory for a certain set of individuals, then every set of authorities has to respect this and *should permit* that $p \wedge q$ for that set of individuals. The question arises how we have to interpret the words 'should permit'. It would be very strange to interpret this as 'enacted the permission', since this is counter-intuitive with the fact that there is a normative agreement between all the sets of authorities. Consider, for example, the formula

$$O_X^A(p) \wedge P_X^B(\neg p) \tag{6.10}$$

and $A \not\subseteq B$. This formula is not contradictory in the system SDL^A. However, if we interpret $P_X^B(\neg p)$ as 'A enacted that it is permitted for X that $\neg p$', then formula (6.10) is counter-intuitive for a coherent deontic system. It expresses that A enacted that $O_X(p)$ and B enacted that $P_X(\neg p)$. Now, there is no normative agreement between these two sets of authorities, since the enacted norms are conflicting: $O_X(p) \wedge P_X(\neg p) \equiv \neg P_X(\neg p) \wedge P_X(\neg p)$.

We have to interpret 'should permit' as 'has not enacted that it is forbidden'. Now the formula (6.10) is not counter-intuitive. It only expresses that A enacted $O_X(p)$ and that B did not enact $F_X(\neg p)$, i.e, $O_X(p)$. Thus, $P_X^A(p)$ has to be read as 'A did not enact that it is forbidden for X that p'.

6.2.1 The relation between SDL_X and SDL^A

Now that we have accomplished a normative agreement between all sets of authorities, we can attempt a reduction in statements of SDL_X to statements of SDL^A: norm $O_X(p)$ holds if and only if there is a set of authorities that enacted that norm. This can be expressed as

$$O_X(p) =_{def} \exists_{A \in P^+(NA)} O_X^A(p), \tag{6.11}$$

and so we can say that norm $P_X(p)$ holds if and only if every set of authorities did not prohibit that p, which corresponds with $P_X(p) \equiv \neg O_X(\neg p)$. Thus,

$$P_X(p) =_{def} \forall_{A \in P^+(NA)} P_X^A(p). \tag{6.12}$$

Note that $\exists_{A \in P^+(NA)} O_X^A(p)$ is equivalent to $O_X^{NA}(p)$ and that $\forall_{A \in P^+(NA)} P_X^A(p)$ is equivalent to $P_X^{NA}(p)$. Thus, $O_X(p) \equiv O_X^{NA}(p)$ and $P_X(p) \equiv P_X^{NA}(p)$.

- Implication $(6.11)^{\rightarrow}$ states that if there is a norm $O_X(p)$ that holds, then there is a set of authorities that enacted that norm. This seems correct, since a norm can only hold if it has been enacted, and a norm can only be enacted by authorities.

- Implication $(6.11)^{\leftarrow}$ states that if a set of authorities enacted a norm $O_X(p)$, this norm holds. This also seems correct in a coherent deontic system.

The semantics can easily cope with both cases when we add the constraint

$$R_X(w) = R_X^{NA}(w) \text{ for all } w \in W \text{ and for all } X \in P^+(I). \tag{6.13}$$

This can be proven as follows. Suppose $O_X(p)$, hence $R_X(w) \subseteq [\![p]\!]$, which is equivalent to $R_X^{NA}(w) \subseteq [\![p]\!]$. Consequently, $\exists_{A \in P^+(NA)}(R_X^A(w) \subseteq [\![p]\!])$, so $\exists_{A \in P^+(NA)} O_X^A(p)$. Now suppose $\exists_{A \in P^+(NA)} O_X^A(p)$, then $\exists_{A \in P^+(NA)}(R_X^A(w) \subseteq [\![p]\!])$, say that this set of authorities is B, thus $R_X^B(w) \subseteq [\![p]\!]$. Since $R_X(w) = R_X^{NA}(w) \subseteq R_X^B(w)$, it follows that $R_X(w) \subseteq [\![p]\!]$, thus $O_X(p)$. The validity of (6.12) follows immediately from $P_X(p) \equiv \neg O_X(\neg p)$ and the proof above.

At first glance, this theory based on Bailhache [1981, 1991], seems a good approach for a coherent deontic system, i.e. a normative agreement between all the sets of authorities. However, this approach has two serious drawbacks. We cannot express that

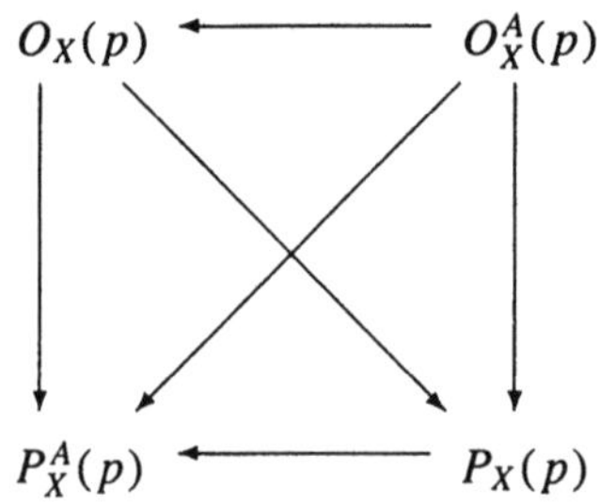

Figure 6.1: The relations between statements $O_X(p)$ and $P_X(p)$ of SDL_X and the statements $O_X^A(p)$ and $P_X^A(p)$

1. A set of authorities enacts a permission. Only obligations (and thus also prohibitions) can be enacted by the sets of authorities. Conversely, we can not express that a set of authorities does not enact an obligation, but only permissions.

2. A set of authorities enacts a combination of collective obligations, e.g. $O_X(p) \vee O_X(q)$. The sets of authorities can only enact an atomic collective obligation, e.g. $O_X(p)$.

Another drawback - although, this drawback is inherent to the developed theory - is that we cannot express normative conflicts, i.e. inconsistencies between enacted norms.

6.3 Normative inconsistencies

In the previous section, we developed a coherent deontic system: a deontic system with a normative agreement between all sets of authorities. However, it is a fact that authorities enact rules that conflict with norms enacted by other authorities; this happens very frequently. The conflicts arise when these norms become part of the same normative system, not if they belong to different systems.

Before we develop a theory that can establish a normative agreement between authorities with several ranks of authorities - in spite of the normative inconsistencies between the norms enacted by the authorities - in chapter 7, we have to develop a theory to allow normative inconsistencies in our system, such as

$$O_X^A(p) \wedge F_X^B(p). \tag{6.14}$$

In SDL^A, this formula is contradictory, since $O_X^A(p) \wedge F_X^B(p) \to O_X^{A \cup B}(p) \wedge O_X^{A \cup B}(\neg p)$, and $O_X^{A \cup B}(p) \wedge O_X^{A \cup B}(\neg p) \to O_X^{A \cup B}(p) \wedge \neg O_X^{A \cup B}(p)$.

To deal with this, we can choose to give up rule $(RO^A M2)$ or schema $(O^A D)$ of system SDL^A.

- If we choose to give up rule (RO^AM2), we can express formula (6.14) if $A \neq B$. However, then we cannot derive formula

$$O_X^A(p) \wedge O_X^B(q) \rightarrow O_X^{A \cup B}(p \wedge q), \tag{6.15}$$

  which is counter-intuitive. Suppose $NA = \{a, b\}$; a has only enacted $O_X(p)$ and b only $O_X(q)$. Then, norm $O_X(p \wedge q)$ intuitively holds, thus the norm has to be enacted. The only possibility is that the norm was enacted by the set $\{a, b\}$. Thus, we cannot give up rule (RO^AM2).

  Furthermore, we would not be able to derive formula

$$O_X^A(p) \wedge F_X^A(p), \tag{6.16}$$

  since this is blocked by axiom (O^AD). A set of authorities can enact conflicting rules; for example, let $A = \{a, b\}$ and a enacted $O_X(p)$ and $F_X(q)$, and b enacted $O_X(p \rightarrow q)$, then A enacts $O_X(q)$ as well as $F_X(q)$. This cannot be expressed if we give up rule (RO^AM2). Thus, we cannot give up rule (RO^AM2).

- It would be preferable to give up axiom (O^AD). (O^AD) removes the possibility of expressing conflicts between norms enacted by sets of authorities, with the result that the deontic system is coherent. By eliminating axiom (O^AD) from SDL^A, we can express formulas (6.14), (6.15) and (6.16).

However, this is not a real solution, since we cannot consistently express that, for example, an authority a enacted $O_X(p)$ and an authority b $\neg O_X(p)$. Then, we can derive $O_X^A(p)$ and $\neg O_X^A(p)$, with $A = \{a, b\}$, and $O_X^A(p) \wedge \neg O_X^A(p)$ is false.

To express these normative conflicts between enacted norms, we choose for another approach. Instead of A modifying $O_X(p)$, we choose to treat N_A as a modal operator. Writing $N_A : O_X(p)$, and instead of $\neg O_X^A(p)$ we write $N_A : \neg O_X(p)$. This seemingly small change has large consequences. The system becomes more powerful, because we can express

- That set A of authorities does not enact a norm, for example, $O_X(p)$:

$$\neg(N_A : O_X(p))$$

- That a set A of authorities enacted a combination of norms, for example, $O_X(p) \vee O_X(q)$:

$$N_A : (O_X(p) \vee O_X(q))$$

- Normative conflicts, for example:

$$N_A : O_X(p) \wedge N_A : \neg O_X(p)$$

Thus, this new approach acquires new meanings, not expressible in SDL^A, and are therefore subject to new intuitions, which we analyse in the following section.

6.4 Logic of enactment

The logic of enactment is independent of the language of the norms, since the addition of sets of authorities is independent of the kind of norms (Ought-to-be statements or Ought-to-do statements) they enact. The theory can be used to order the enacted norms implemented in an expert system. Expert systems should contain rules which of the enacted norms are applicable. These rules can be obtained by several criteria (see chapter 7. The main advantage is that the expert systems can now reason with the use of normal first-order logic in stead of using non-monotonic logic.

The distinction between enacted and applicable norms is explained at length in argumentation approaches [cf. Dung, 1993; Hage, 1996, 1997; Gordon, 1995; Prakken and Sartor, 1995] using applicability predicates in combination with techniques from non-monotonic logic [cf. Brewka, 1991, 1994; Reiter, 1980, 1987]. In these approaches we can reason with inconsistent information, but the level always is that of applicable norms. One cannot reason about enacted norms that are not applicable. Any derivation using these norms is blocked through the implicit consistency requirement of the non-monotonic rule *modus ponens*.

We present a two-step model to describe enacted norms and applicable norms separately. This can be seen as naming the minimal models (which are generally used in modal logics [cf. Chellas, 1980] and in the semantics of non-monotonic logics [cf. Makinson, 1993]) with sets of authorities. Making this explicit in a modal operator enables us to reason about enacted norms that are not applicable (within a non-preferred minimal logic) as well.

To formalise this distinction between the weak and strong permission we add an operator N_{A_i} to the deontic logic. A formula $N_{A_i} : \theta$, with θ a norm, is read as 'the set A_i of authorities enacted the norm θ'. Sets of authorities are needed to determine the consequences of norms enacted by a combination of individual authorities. We define $NA = \{a_1, \ldots, a_n\}$ as the set of normative authorities. Since we consider sets of authorities, we have $2^n - 1$ sets of authorities, instead of considering n authorities. We treat N_{A_i} as a *modal* operator, just as in epistemic logics, e.g. *knowledge* and *belief*. The theory of enactment is based on an extension of epistemic logic. The main reason being that enactment, just as e.g. *belief* and *knowledge* have to deal with reasoning about inconsistent information. So, the similarity mainly concerns this part of reasoning in the present of inconsistencies within a modal operator.

In this section, we briefly review possible-worlds semantics for enactment, corresponding with the semantics for epistemic formulas [cf. Chellas, 1980; Halpern and Moses, 1985; Meyer and van der Hoek, 1995]. The intuitive idea behind the possible-worlds model is that, besides the true state of affairs, there are a number of other possible states of affairs, or possible worlds.

On the one hand, the notion of enactment is a restricted version of the system weak $S5$ or $KD45$, in the sense that we are not dealing with nested enactment. A formula N_{A_i} : $(N_{A_i} : \theta)$, reading that 'A_i enacted that A_i enacted θ', is meaningless. Thus, we restrict the language, so that no N_{A_i} appears within the scope of another. Thus, if θ is a deontic formula, then $N_{A_i} : \theta$ is also a formula. On the other hand, the notion of enactment is an extended version of weak $S5$ or $KD45$, in the sense that we are adding an extra rule. We now present an axiomatic system **Ent** for enactment with respect to set NA of normative authorities, where θ, θ_1 and θ_2 are normative formulas, and Θ_1 and Θ_2 are formulas of system **Ent**:

All tautologies of the propositional calculus. (A1)

$$N_{A_i} : \theta_1 \wedge N_{A_i} : (\theta_1 \rightarrow \theta_2) \rightarrow N_{A_i} : \theta_2 \tag{A2}$$

$$\frac{\Theta_1 \rightarrow \Theta_2, \Theta_1}{\Theta_2} \tag{R1}$$

$$\frac{\theta}{N_{A_i} : \theta} \tag{R2}$$

$$\frac{A_i \subseteq A_j}{N_{A_i} : \theta \rightarrow N_{A_j} : \theta} \tag{R3}$$

The first axiom (A1) and rule (R1) are holdovers from propositional calculus. The second axiom says that enactment is closed under implication. Note that (A2) is equivalent to $N_{A_i} : (\theta_1 \rightarrow \theta_2) \rightarrow (N_{A_i} : \theta_1 \rightarrow N_{A_i} : \theta_2)$, which is sometimes given as an alternative axiom. (A3) says that an authority cannot enact falsehood. The rule (R2) states that every tautology is enacted. The name of this rule, necessitation, stems from the general modal framework, in which N_{A_i} (or denoted usually by $\Box$) has the meaning of necessity. Rule (R3) expresses the relation between the sets of authorities. If a set of authorities enacted a norm, then every superset of authorities of that set also enacted that norm.

The semantics will be given by a Kripke structure $(W, R, V, B_{A_1}, \ldots B_{A_m}, NA)$, where B_{A_i} $(i = 1, \ldots, m$ and $m = 2^n - 1)$ is a binary relation on W for which it holds that if $A_i \subseteq A_j$, then $B_{A_j} \subseteq B_{A_i}$, which validates rule (R3). We do not have the assumptions that B_{A_i} is transitive and euclidean, as in $KD45$ [cf. Chellas, 1980], since we are not dealing with nested enactments. Intuitively, $(w, w') \in B_{A_i}$ if in a world w, the set A_i of authorities considers world w' possible, i.e. A_i considers his enacted norms in w applicable in w' as possible. Thus w' would be considered a possible way to have the enacted norms apply.

The semantics of the formulas is very similar to that of the deontic logic. The clause for the new operator N_{A_i} is as follows, where θ is a normative formula:

$$M, w \models N_{A_i} : \theta \text{ iff } M, w' \models \theta$$

for all w' such that $(w, w') \in B_{A_i}$. The clause is designed to capture the intuition that θ is enacted by A_i exactly if θ is true in all the worlds conform to the norms enacted by A_i. Thus, the sentence 'θ is enacted by A_i' does not say that θ is applicable, instead, it says that θ is applicable in a world that is ideal conform to the enactment by A_i. Thus, the statement 'θ is enacted' describes some idealised world and *not* the actual world. From the semantics it follows that the rules and the first three axioms are valid [cf. Chellas, 1980].

In the theory of knowledge and belief, the natural question arises as to of whether these notions are captured adequately and realistically. The well-known problem of both theories is the problem of *logical omniscience* [cf. Hintikka, 1975]. This problem pertains to a notion of knowledge and belief that is too idealistic: these notions are closed under logical consequences. 'Especially for a notion of belief, which should be more fallible if human everyday beliefs are to be captured, this property is obviously not true' [Meyer and van der Hoek, 1995]. Logical omniscience is not a problem for the notion of enactment. If a norm follows from other enacted norms and does not conflict with another norm, this norm is applicable, even if that norm was not thought of by members of government or parliament when the law was created.

6.4.1 The problem of inconsistent enacted norms

If we assume that the set of enacted norms is consistent, i.e. there are no conflicting norms (deontic coherent system), then we can create an actual world that corresponds with the ideal world: all the enacted norms are applicable. This can be axiomatised by the following formula:

$$(N_{A_i} : \theta) \rightarrow \theta \tag{A3}$$

This corresponds with the axiom $K_i\phi \rightarrow \phi$ of the theory for knowledge: if an agent i knows an assertion ϕ, then that assertion is true, i.e. known facts are true. In our terminology, axiom (A3) is read 'enacted norms are true' or more practically 'enacted norms are applicable'. Axiom (A3) becomes valid by adding the claim that the relation B_{A_i} is reflexive, i.e. if

$$\forall_{w \in W}(w, w) \in B_{A_i}.$$

Axiom (A3) can only be added to a system, if we consider a consistent set of enacted norms.

However, it is a frequently occurring phenomenon that normative authorities enact conflicting norms. As a first and perhaps slightly naive attempt to overcome the problem of inconsistent enacted norms, we have dropped the axiom (D): $\neg N_{A_i} : false$ for system **Ent**, which is an axiom of $KD45$.[4] By dropping this axiom we can now represent inconsistent enactment: $N_{A_i} : \theta \wedge N_{A_i} : \neg\theta$, however there still remains the following modified problem concerning inconsistent enacted norms: $N_{A_i} : \theta \wedge N_{A_i} : \neg\theta \rightarrow N_{A_i} : false$, which already is a theorem in the system - since $N_{A_i} : \theta_1 \wedge N_{A_i} : \theta_2 \rightarrow N_{A_i} : (\theta_1 \wedge \theta_2)$ - stating that, if a norm and its negation are both enacted, every assertion has to be enacted. This problem cannot be solved within the standard modal framework using Kripke-style modal semantics.

Another and perhaps also naive attempt is to solve the problem by distinguishing *implicit* and *explicit* enactment. We have to use an extra modal operator $N^e_{A_i}$, standing for explicit enactment. We define the implicit enacted norms by A_i as the norms that are the

[4] Principle (D) becomes valid by adding the claim that the relation B_{A_i} is serial. The fact that B_{A_i} is serial means that in all worlds, the enacted norms can be applied some way; from this it follows that falsehood cannot be enacted. Note that (D) is a weakening of (A3).

logical consequences of the explicit enacted norms by A_i. Explicit enactment is defined as follows:

$$N^e_{A_i} : \theta := N_{A_i} : \theta \text{ and } \theta \in E_{A_i},$$

with E_{A_i} the set of explicit enacted norms by the set A_i of normative authorities. Implicit enactment is the enactment defined as above:

$$N^i_{A_i} : \theta := N_{A_i} : \theta.$$

Now axiom (A2) does not hold for the explicit enactment. Thus, we can formalise consistently inconsistent enacted norms: $N^e_{A_i} : \theta \wedge N^e_{A_i} : \neg\theta$. This presentation of the explicit and implicit enactment suffers from a serious drawback if the set of explicitly enacted norms is inconsistent: namely, it only deals with the explicitly enacted norms. A viable logic of enactment should be able to capture meta-reasoning - within the logic - about the authority's enacted norms, since one has to reason about the enacted norms that one has and needs to acquire. The notion of implicit enactment still suffers from the problem that then everything is (implicitly) enacted. Only if the set of explicitly enacted norms is consistent, then the notion of implicit enactment has its value. Note that explicit enactment implies implicit enactment.

In Chellas [1980], Chellas argues that an adequate logic of norms should be able to express conflicts of norms, but he also wants to be able to retain the deontic counterparts of (A3). However, one cannot keep (A3) and allow consistent expression of normative conflict (i.e. $O(p) \wedge O(\neg p)$) in a normal modal system. That is why Chellas introduces classical modal systems with minimal models for a revised deontic logic. However, in these systems we cannot explicitly specify the minimal models. Thus, in order to try to solve this problem of inconsistent enacted norms, we have to do something different, and deviate from the standard modal approach even further, by making of the logic of local reasoning presented by Fagin and Halpern [1988].

6.5 Local reasoning

In the logic of local reasoning, there need not necessarily be one set of worlds that a set of authorities thinks possible, but rather a number of sets; each one corresponding to a different set of enacted norms. In a given situation, we specify a *cluster* as a *maximal consistent set* of the set E_{A_i} of explicitly enacted norms by a set A_i of authorities. The basic idea is that a set of authorities may enact inconsistent norms, but these conflicting norms are not applicable at the same time (depending on the situation). In a particular situation, a maximal consistent set of norms (a cluster) represents the applicable norms.

Suppose that a set of authorities enacted the following three norms 'vehicles give right of way to vehicles coming from the right', 'bicycles must give right of way to cars' and 'it is forbidden to drive faster than 50 km/h'. The first two norms cannot both be applicable, since they may conflict. For instance, in the situation that a car and a bicycle are on a junction and that the bicycle is coming from the right. Thus, there are two clusters: the set consisting of the norms 'vehicles give right of way to vehicles from the right' and and 'it is forbidden to drive faster than 50 km/h', and the set consisting of the norms 'bicycles must give right of way to cars' and 'it is forbidden to drive faster than 50 km/h'.

We view a cluster as representing the worlds the set of authorities thinks are possible in a given frame of reference, when he is focusing on a certain set of issues. More formally, a Kripke structure for local reasoning is a tuple $M = (W, V, R, C_{A_1}, \ldots, C_{A_m}, NA)$, where $C_{A_i}(w)$ is a non-empty set of non-empty subsets of W. Intuitively, if $C_{A_i}(w) = \{T_1, \ldots, T_l\}$, then in world w (a certain situation) the set A_i of authorities sometimes thinks that the set of possible worlds is precisely T_1; sometimes the set of possible worlds is precisely T_2, etc. The set $C_{A_i}(w)$ corresponds to the clusters following from the set E_{A_i} of explicitly enacted norms by A_i in world w. Thus, $C_{A_i}(w)$ indicates which clusters (frames of reference) are considered by the set A_i of authorities. We may now distinguish *weak* and *strong* enactment:

$N^w_{A_i} : \theta$: the set A_i of authorities enacted θ in a weak sense, i.e. within *some* cluster considered by A_i.

$N^s_{A_i} : \theta$: the set A_i of authorities enacted θ in a strong sense, i.e. within *all* clusters considered by A_i.

It is easy to gather that strong enactment implies weak enactment. We formally define $\models$ for these structures as follows:

$$\begin{array}{lll} M, w \models N^w_{A_i} : \theta & \text{iff} & \exists_{T \in C_{A_i(w)}} \forall_{w' \in T} M, w' \models \theta \\ M, w \models N^s_{A_i} : \theta & \text{iff} & \forall_{T \in C_{A_i}(w)} \forall_{w' \in T} M, w' \models \theta \end{array}$$

It is easy to see from the semantic definitions given that weak enactment is not closed under logical consequences and that strong enactment is closed under logical consequences. More importantly for our purposes is that a set of authorities may now enact inconsistent norms: $N^w_{A_i} : \theta \wedge N^w_{A_i} : \neg\theta$ is satisfiable[5], since in one cluster the set A_i considers that θ is applicable, while in another the set considers $\neg\theta$ applicable. On the other hand, $N^w_{A_i} : (\theta \wedge \neg\theta)$ is impossible: a set of authorities cannot weakly enact falsehood. It is easy to see that $N^w_{A_i}$ does not satisfy axiom (A2), although $N^w_{A_i}$ satisfies all the others axiom and rules of **Ent**.

$N^s_{A_i} : \theta$ represents that the set A_i of authorities considers that θ is applicable in any frame of reference. This means that θ does not conflict with any other norm enacted by the set A_i of authorities. However, the norm can be conflicting with a norm enacted by a superset A_j of A_i ($A_i \subset A_j$). Suppose that the set A_j explicitly enacted $\neg\theta$, then the norm θ does not appear in all clusters of E_{A_j}, because $\neg\theta$ is also an element of some maximal consistent set (cluster) of E_{A_j}. Thus, $N^s_{A_i}$ does not satisfy rule (R3), although all the axioms and other rules of **Ent** hold. As mentioned above, it holds that $N^s_{A_i} : \theta \rightarrow N^w_{A_i} : \theta$.

Some properties of enactment

The following three propositions show a number of properties for $N^w_{A_i}$ and $N^s_{A_i}$:

[5] Θ is satisfiable in a Kripke structure M if $M, w \models \Theta$ for some world w; Θ is satisfiable if it is satisfiable in some M.

Proposition 6.5.1 *The following formulas are valid:*

1. $N^s_{A_i} : \Theta \rightarrow N^w_{A_i} : \Theta$
2. $N^w_{A_i} : \Theta \rightarrow N^w_{A_i \cup A_j} : \Theta$
3. $\neg N^w_{A_i} : (\Theta \wedge \neg\Theta)$
4. $\neg N^s_{A_i} : (\Theta \wedge \neg\Theta)$
5. $\neg(N^w_{A_i} : \Theta \wedge \neg(N^w_{A_i \cup A_j} : \Theta))$
6. $N^s_{A_i} : \Theta_1 \wedge N^w_{A_i} : \Theta_2 \rightarrow N^w_{A_i} : (\Theta_1 \wedge \Theta_2)$

Proposition 6.5.1.1 says that strong enactment implies weak enactment, and 6.5.1.2 states that if a set of authorities weakly enacted a norm, then all supersets of that set weakly enacted that norm. The propositions 6.5.1.3 and 6.5.1.4 state that falsehood cannot be weakly and strongly enacted. Proposition 6.5.1.5 is equivalent to 6.5.1.2. The last proposition states that $\Theta_1 \wedge \Theta_2$ is weakly enacted if one norm (e.g. Θ_1) is weakly enacted and the other norm (Θ_2) strongly enacted.

To show what formulas we can and cannot express, we give some examples of satisfiable and non-satisfiable formulas:

Proposition 6.5.2 *The following formulas are satisfiable:*

1. $N^w_{A_i} : \Theta \wedge N^w_{A_i} : \neg\Theta$
2. $N^w_{A_i} : \Theta \rightarrow N^w_{A_i \cup A_j} : \neg\Theta$
3. $N^s_{A_i} : \Theta \wedge N^s_{A_j} : \neg\Theta$, *if* $A_i \not\subseteq A_j$ *and* $A_j \not\subseteq A_i$
4. $N^w_{A_i} : (\Theta_1 \wedge \Theta_2) \wedge \neg N^w_{A_i} : \Theta_1 \wedge \neg N^w_{A_i} : \Theta_2$
5. $N^w_{A_i} : (\Theta_1 \wedge \Theta_2) \wedge N^w_{A_i} : \neg\Theta_1 \wedge N^w_{A_i} : \neg\Theta_2$
6. $\neg N^w_{A_i} : \Theta \wedge \neg N^w_{A_i} : \neg\Theta$

Proposition 6.5.3 *The following formulas are not satisfiable:*

1. $N^s_{A_i} : \Theta \wedge N^w_{A_i} : \neg\Theta$
2. $N^s_{A_i} : \Theta \wedge N^s_{A_i} : \neg\Theta$, *if* $A_i \subseteq A_j$ *or* $A_j \subseteq A_i$
3. $N^w_{A_i} : (\Theta \vee \neg\Theta) \wedge \neg N^w_{A_i} : \Theta \wedge \neg N^w_{A_i} : \neg\Theta$

Proof Follows directly from the semantics.

Next, we can formalise the explicit strong enactment with the help of explicit enactment in the previous section. The explicit strong enactment $N^{se}_{A_i}$ is defined as $N^{se}_{A_i} : \theta := N^{s}_{A_i} : \theta$ and $\theta \in E_{A_i}$, meaning that θ is explicitly enacted by the set A_i of authorities and θ does not conflict with any norm or set of norms enacted by the set A_i. Note that the explicit weak enactment corresponds with the weak enactment.

A particularly interesting special case we can capture is the strong enactment of norms by the set NA, the set of all the authorities. These norms are strong enacted by the set of all the authorities, and all these norms do not conflict with other norms enacted by the set NA. So, these norms always are applicable. In other words, these norms are elements of all clusters of the explicitly enacted norms by the set NA. We can formalise this as follows

$$(N^{s}_{NA} : \theta) \rightarrow \theta.$$

Thus, explicitly strong enacted norms by the set NA are applicable, corresponding to the axiom $K_i\phi \rightarrow \phi$ of the theory for knowledge (see subsection 6.4.1). However, an explicitly strong enacted norm is not necessarily applicable (true), only if such a norm is explicitly strong enacted *by the set* NA.

We can extend our semantics with another model operator D_{A_i}, to indicate applicability. The formula $D_{A_i} : \theta$ means that θ is applicable according to A_i in a particular cluster T. The clause for $D_{A_i} : \theta$ is

$$M, w, T \models D_{A_i} : \theta \text{ iff } \forall_{w' \in T} M, w' \models \theta, \text{ for } T \in C_{A_i}.$$

Evidently, from the semantics it follows that $D_{A_i} : \theta \rightarrow N^{w}_{A_i} : \theta$, i.e. if θ is applicable according to A_i in a particular cluster, then θ is weakly enacted by the set A_i. Now we can consistently reason within a cluster, since the set of norms in a cluster is consistent. Within a cluster the property holds that the enacted norms are closed under logical consequences:

$$\text{if } M, w, T \models D_{A_i} : \theta_1 \text{ and } M, w, T \models D_{A_i} : (\theta_1 \rightarrow \theta_2),$$

$$\text{then } M, w, T \models D_{A_i} : \theta_2.$$

This is a first step in determining which norms are valid. The second step would be to determine which clusters are applicable. There are tools developed, which can help to exploit the progress of this research, for example, non-monotonic logic, defeasible reasoning and logic of preference. In the next chapter, we give an example of this determination by the notion of authority-hierarchy.

6.6 Conclusions

First, we discussed system SDL^A, based upon Bailhache's theory. This theory was developed to obtain a coherent deontic system. Inherent to this theory is that we cannot express conflicts between enacted norms. A major innovation of this theory is the use of sets of authorities. Sets of authorities are needed to determine the consequences of obligations, enacted by a combination of individual authorities.

However, we have seen that this theory has some serious drawbacks. We cannot express that

1. A set of authorities enacts a permission. Only obligations can be enacted by the sets of authorities. Conversely, we cannot express that a set of authorities does not enact an obligation, only permissions.

2. A set of authorities enacted a combination of norms, e.g. $O_X(p) \vee O_X(q)$. In this theory, sets of authorities can only enact atomic collective obligations, e.g. $O_X(p)$.

To deal with these drawbacks we have chosen for another approach: instead of the set A of authorities modifying a norm Θ, the set A is treated as a modal operator (within N_{A_i}) enacting the norm Θ, as in the epistemic logic. With the help of this (seemingly small) change, the drawbacks disappear in the logic of enactment.

In the theory of the logic of enactment with local reasoning, we can consistently formalise normative inconsistencies, i.e. conflicting norms enacted by sets of authorities. Consider the following example (see subsection 1.2.2): car driver i_1 is on a major road and approaches a junction, where car driver i_2 approaches from the right. According to Article 15 of the Dutch Traffic Regulation 1990, i_1 has to give way to i_2, who approaches the junction from the right. Also, according to the right-of-way signs (A6 and A9), i_2 has to give way to i_1. On the ground of *the principle of trust*, i_2 does not have to give right of way according to Article 15, and on the grounds of the traffic signs, i_2 has to give right of way. In $DDL(Evt')$,[6] we cannot consistently express this, since this is formalised as follows:

$$\neg O(\{i_2\} : \beta) \wedge O(\{i_2\} : \beta),$$

where β stands for the action 'to give right of way'. This formula is a contradiction. However, now we can express this as follows:

$$N^w_{A_i} : \neg O(\{i_2\} : \beta) \wedge N^w_{A_i} : O(\{i_2\} : \beta),$$

where A_i is the set of authorities that enacted the articles in the Dutch Traffic Regulation 1990. From the natural semantics of enactment it follows that the formula is satisfiable. Thus, this formula expresses, in a consistent way, that the authorities enacted two conflicting norms.

Furthermore, we have shown how we can determine the maximal consistent sets of the enacted norms by local reasoning on the basis of the logic of enactment. The idea is that in spite of the normative conflicts lawyers make use of a consistent set of rules. The choice of such a set depends on the frame of reference, i.e. a particular situation. The determination of this choice - the process of filtering out the applicable set of norms from the maximal consistent sets - will be discussed in the next chapter. This will be done on the basis of

[6]Note that we use system $DDL(Evt')$ instead of SDL_X, since the obligations considered are Ought-to-do statements.

an authority hierarchy. Since we are dealing with enactment by normative authorities, it is possible to indicate the rank of authority between sets of authorities.

Chapter 7

Applicability of norms

7.1 Introduction

The sources of law give rise not only to norms, but also to hierarchical criteria that determine the relative importance of various norms that form part of a legal order. The identification of the material of which a legal system is composed must include a series of relations determining the relative weight of norms. The clearest example is the criterion based on the level of the authority that enacted the norm: for example, a constitutional rule is hierarchically superior to a rule enacted by the ordinary legislature, and the latter, in turn, is superior to a rule enacted by a city council. This criterion is called the 'Lex Superior'. The 'Lex Superior' principle is based on the general hierarchy of a legal system: normative authority is divided along the lines of the hierarchical structure of the normative system; authorities with a lower rank of authority have to respect what was enacted by an authority with a higher rank.

There are more criteria or rules of preference to resolve normative inconsistencies, such as 'Lex Specialis' and 'Lex Posterior'.[1] Thus, when we consider the norms in a legal system, we can often discern some kind of hierarchy among the norms: some are regarded as more basic than others.

> It may be determined in part by considerations arising from the text of the regulations themselves, such as the existence of cross-references from one to another; and it may also be determined in part by factors of a more extrinsic kind, such as the powers and competences of the issuing bodies, dates of promulgation and amendment, and the degree of specificity or generality of the regulations made. [Alchourrón and Makinson, 1981, p. 125]

Each of these principles determines different hierarchical relations between norms and their role is to give a solution in those situations in which one has to choose from among

[1] These rules of preferences are generally not codified.

different norms. For convenience, we will restrict ourselves to the 'Lex Superior' principle, but the theory can easily be extended with other rules of preference.

With the help of a hierarchy of norms, we can solve the problem of conflicting norms in the legal code. In this chapter, we define the hierarchy of norms on the basis of the competences of the normative authorities that enact the norms, following an authority hierarchy. The authority hierarchy is an example of a method for filtering out the applicable set of norms from the maximal N-consistent sets (clusters) obtained by local reasoning and logic of enactment. Thus, we develop a theory to overcome some normative inconsistencies among the norms promulgated (enacted) by the authorities with respect to their hierarchical order, and to determine which norms, members of a given legal system, are applicable; i.e. which norms must be obeyed and applied.

Furthermore, we investigate two types of legislative acts: promulgation and derogation. Law changes by promulgation and derogation: norms are incorporated by promulgation and norms are repealed by derogation. The consequences of these acts will be discussed on the basis of the authority hierarchy.

Another issue we discuss is the way in which universality can be reached by a closure rule, such as *nulla poena sine lege*, expressed in Article 16 of the Dutch Constitution and Article 1 sub 1 of the Dutch Penal Code. A consequence of this closure rule is that we have to take into account the difference between two types of permission: *strong* and *weak permission*. This distinction will be expressed in the axioms of permission.

The organisation of this chapter is as follows. In section 7.2, we determine the hierarchical structure of a legal system on the basis of sets of normative authorities to decide which maximal N-consistent set is applicable of all the maximal N-consistent sets of enacted norms by the authorities. Section 7.3 discusses two basic types of legislative acts of the normative authorities: promulgation and derogation, with respect to the authority hierarchy. Section 7.4 presents (postulated) universality. In the final section we draw some conclusions.

7.2 Authority hierarchy

In this section, we develop a deontic system with normative agreement between the sets of authorities in the same normative system with respect to their hierarchical order, to overcome some normative inconsistencies between the norms enacted by sets of authorities. The authorities will be ordered in a hierarchical system, which helps to determine which norm should be followed in cases of normative inconsistencies. The authorities are thus used to prioritise the norms they enacted.[2] The hierarchy of authorities does not resolve all the inconsistencies; norms with the same priority may still be inconsistent. In such a case, the judge or lawyer may resolve these inconsistencies with the help of interpretative strategies, e.g. the grammatical and the teleological strategies. The theory of authority hierarchy does not solve the latter problem, but indicates and locates this problem.

First, we will introduce a partial ordering of the authorities:

[2] This gives a priority logic [cf. Brewka, 1991]. See also Prakken [1993].

Definition 7.2.1 *Let $a, b \in NA$. We define*

- *$a \sim b$ iff a and b have the same rank of authority*
- *$a \succ b$ iff a has a higher rank of authority than b*
- *$a \succeq b$ iff $a \sim b \vee a \succ b$*

Definition 7.2.2 *Let $A_i, A_j \subseteq NA$. We define*

- *$A_i \succ A_j$ iff $\forall_{a \in A_i} \forall_{b \in A_j}(a \succ b)$*
- *$A_i \sim A_j$ iff $\forall_{a \in A_i} \forall_{b \in A_j}(a \sim b)$*
- *$A_i \succeq A_j$ iff $\forall_{a \in A_i} \exists_{b \in A_j}(a \succ b \vee a \sim b)$*

Proposition 7.2.3 *$\succeq$ over 2NA is transitive and reflexive, but in general not symmetric. $\succ$ over 2NA is transitive and asymmetric, and thus a strict partial ordering of 2NA.*

Definition 7.2.4 *Let $A \subseteq NA$. Then, N_A is defined as the set of norms enacted by the authorities in set A.*

Definition 7.2.5 *Let $A_1, A_2, \ldots, A_n \subseteq NA$. Then, $D(A_1, A_2, \ldots, A_n)$ is an authority hierarchy iff*

$$\forall_{i<j}(A_i \succ A_j) \wedge \forall_i \forall_{a,b \in A_i}(a \sim b).$$

In $D(A_1, \ldots, A_n)$, A_1 is the set of authorithies with the *highest ranking* authority and A_n the set with the *lowest ranking* authority. The ordering of authorities in an authority hierarchy is a total ordering: for every two authorities a and b in $\cup_{i=1}^{n} A_i$ it follows exclusively that $a \succ b$, $b \succ a$ or $a \sim b$.

Example Let $a, b, c, d, e \in NA$, $a \sim b$, $b \succ c$, $c \sim d$ and $d \succ e$. Then an authority hierarchy is $D(\{a, b\}, \{c, d\}, \{e\})$.

Definition 7.2.6 *Let $D(A_1, A_2 \ldots, A_n)$ be an authority hierarchy, $A \subseteq \cup_{i=1}^{n} A_i$, and let $k = max\{i | A \cap A_i \neq \emptyset\}$. Then we define $S(N_A)$ as the set of norms enacted by all the authorities superior or equal to the authorities of A:*

$$S(N_A) = \cup_{i=1}^{k} N_{A_i}.$$

Note that $\forall_{A' \subseteq A \wedge A \succeq A'}(S(N_A) = S(N_{A'}))$.

Example Consider example 6.2.6, and suppose that a enacted $O(\beta_1)$, b enacted $P(\beta_2)$ and $O(\beta_3)$, c enacted $O(\beta_4)$, d enacted $P(\beta_5)$ and $\neg O(\beta_3)$ and e enacted $P(\beta_3)$. Then, we obtain, for example,

1. $S(N_{\{a\}}) = S(N_{\{b\}}) = S(N_{\{a,b\}}) = \{O(\beta_1), P(\beta_2), O(\beta_3)\}$

2. $S(N_{\{c\}}) = S(N_{\{d\}}) = S(N_{\{c,d\}}) = S(N_{\{a,c\}}) = S(N_{\{a,d\}}) = S(N_{\{b,c\}}) = S(N_{\{b,d\}}) = S(N_{\{a,b,c\}}) = S(N_{\{a,b,d\}}) = S(N_{\{a,b,c,d\}}) =$

$$\{O(\beta_1), P(\beta_2), O(\beta_3), O(\beta_4), P(\beta_5), \neg O(\beta_3)\}$$

3. $S(N_{\{e\}}) = S(N_{\{a,b,c,d,e\}}) =$

$$\{O(\beta_1), P(\beta_2), O(\beta_3), O(\beta_4), P(\beta_5), \neg O(\beta_3), P(\beta_3)\}$$

4. $S(N_{\{a\}}) \subseteq S(N_{\{c\}}) \subseteq S(N_{\{e\}})$

To overcome normative inconsistencies among the enacted norms in a normative system, we have to remove at least one of the norms. This can also be achieved by more generous subtractions, such as removing all the norms. However, this is absurd. What is wanted is to remove a *minimum* of norms, on the basis of the authority hierarchy, compatible with the requirement that the resulting set of norms is normative consistent. Before we define this formally, we give a definition of normative consistency (N-consistency).[3]

Definition 7.2.7 *Let N be a set of norms. Then,*

$$N \textit{ is N-consistent iff} \neg\exists_{\beta \in Act}((N \vdash O(\beta)) \wedge (N \vdash O(\overline{\beta}))).$$

Note that if N is N-consistent, then N is also consistent, since if N is inconsistent, everything can be deduced; thus, also $O(\beta)$ *and* $O(\overline{\beta})$. The converse does not hold. Suppose that $N = \{O(\beta), O(\overline{\beta})\}$, then N is consistent, but not N-consistent.

By means of N-consistency, we can define a maximal N-consistent system for a given authority hierarchy as follows:

Definition 7.2.8 *Let $D(A_1, A_2 \ldots, A_n)$ be an authority hierarchy and $A \subseteq \cup_{i=1}^{n} A_i$. Then, the maximal N-consistent system $Sys(D(A_1, A_2, \ldots, A_n))$ is defined as $S(N_A)$, such that*

- *$S(N_A)$ is N-consistent*
- *$\neg\exists_{A' \subseteq \cup_{i=1}^{n} A_i}(A \succ A' \wedge S(N_{A'})$ is N-consistent)*

System $Sys(D(A_1, A_2, \ldots, A_n))$ is based upon the individual normative systems of the authorities in the authority hierarchy, with respect to their ranks of authority. However, this definition does not give acceptable results, because if two 'higher' norms conflict, no norms enacted by lower ranked authorities can be determined.[4]

Example Suppose that a enacted $O(\beta_1)$ and $O(\beta_2)$, that b enacted $\neg O(\beta_1)$ and $P(\beta_3)$, and that c enacted $P(\beta_4)$. Then,

[3] For convenience, we do not consider conditional norms

[4] In the study by Alchourrón and Makinson [1981] the same problem arose. Alchourrón and Makinson suggested that an additional notion of relevance is necessary, but they gave no formal definition.

1. $Sys(D(\{a,b\},\{c\})) = \emptyset$

2. $Sys(D(\{a\},\{b\},\{c\})) = \{O(\beta_1), O(\beta_2)\}$

3. $Sys(D(\{a,c\},\{b\})) = Sys(D(\{a\},\{c\},\{b\})) = \{O(\beta_1), O(\beta_2), P(\beta_4)\}$

We can solve this problem by removing only the norms that are responsible for the normative conflicts. Therefore, we change the definition of *maximal N-consistent system.* A set is maximal N-consistent with respect to system $S(N_A)$ by removing only the norms in $S(N_A)$ which are responsible for the normative conflicts, depending on the authority hierarchy. If two norms, enacted by authorities with different ranks of authority, are conflicting, then the norm enacted by the authority with the lower rank will be removed, and if two norms enacted by authorities with the same rank are conflicting, then we have to choose which norm will be removed.

Definition 7.2.9 *Let $D(A_1, A_2 \ldots, A_n)$ be an authority hierarchy and $A \subseteq \bigcup_{i=1}^{n} A_i$, with the lowest ranking authority coming from A_k. Then, D is a maximal N-consistent set of $S(N_A)$ iff*

1. $D \subseteq S(N_A)$

2. *D is N-consistent*

3. $\neg\exists_{r \in S(N_A) \setminus D}(\{r\} \cup D$ *is N-consistent*$)$

4. $\exists_{D' \in MC(S(N_{A_{k-1}}))}(D' \subseteq D)$

$MC(S(N_A))$ is defined as the set of all the maximal N-consistent sets of $S(N_A)$.

The first three conditions are obvious and are needed to express that D is N-consistent and maximal with respect to $S(N_A)$. Without the fourth condition, the maximal N-consistent sets of $S(N_A)$ would be independent of the given authority hierarchy.

Example Let $D(\{a\},\{b\})$ be an authority hierarchy, $N_{\{a\}} = \{O(\beta_1), F(\beta_2)\}$ and $N_{\{b\}} = \{P(\beta_2), P(\beta_3)\}$. Then,

$$\{O(\beta_1), F(\beta_2), P(\beta_3)\}$$

is the only maximal N-consistent set of $S(N_{\{a,b\}})$. The set $\{O(\beta_1), P(\beta_2), P(\beta_3)\}$ is not an element of $MC(S(N_{\{a,b\}}))$, since it does not satisfy the fourth condition of definition 6.2.12: $\{O(\beta_1), F(\beta_2)\}$ is the only maximal N-consistent set of $S(N_{\{a\}})$, but is not a subset of set $\{O(\beta_1), P(\beta_2), P(\beta_3)\}$.

If $D(\{a,b\})$ is the authority hierarchy, then, we get two maximal N-consistent sets of $N_{\{a,b\}}$:

$$MC(S(N_{\{a,b\}})) = \{\{O(\beta_1), F(\beta_2), P(\beta_3)\}, \{O(\beta_1), P(\beta_2), P(\beta_3)\}\}.$$

Note that $S(N_A)$ is the only maximal N-consistent set of $S(N_A)$ if and only if $S(N_A)$ is N-consistent. If there are at least two maximal N-consistent sets of $S(N_A)$ (so $S(N_A)$ is then N-inconsistent), then there is no logical criterion according to which we can decide which of these sets should be used. This we call *logical indeterminacy* [Navarro and Redondo, 1990]. The decision is a matter of interpretation by the judge or lawyer.

In the introduction we already mentioned that law changes by promulgation and derogation. In the following section, we analyse the consequences of these two legislative acts of the authorities for the validity of the norms, in the sense of membership and applicability, on the basis of the theory developed in this section.

7.3 The promulgation and derogation of norms

Two basic types of legislative acts can be distinguished: promulgation and derogation. Promulgation is referred to as the introduction of a norm into a legal system, and derogation as the removal of a norm from a legal system. We will see that there is more to it than that by investigating what the consequences are for a legal system when an authority enacts or derogates a norm.

According to Alchourrón [1982], an important feature of promulgation is that the resulting system is perfectly identified and that this process differs from derogation since the result of derogation is not always determinate: there is not always one, unique system that can be identified as the result of a process of derogation. We will see that the result of promulgation is not always determinate either, since the result of a promulgated norm can lead to an inconsistent system. To ensure that the normative system becomes consistent again, we sometimes have to decide (determine) which norms are applicable and which are not.

Before we discuss the two legislative acts, we make some assumptions to be used in the sequel. We assume in this section that N is a maximal N-consistent set of $S(N_{A_n})$ with respect to the given authority hierarchy $D(A_1, A_2, \ldots, A_n)$. Further, $Cn(N)$ is the set of norms that embraces N and all its consequences (see subsection 2.6.1).

7.3.1 Promulgation

Legal norms take effect by the promulgation of laws. In the Netherlands, this is done by publication in the *Bulletin of Acts and Decrees*. At the same time, the date of the law's taking effect is determined. Businesses and institutions have their own procedures for the promulgation of current standards. Ethical norms (for example, one should not kill a human being) are not promulgated as such. By way of political discussions, such norms will be reflected in the legislations of most states.

In the promulgation of a norm r to an N-consistent system $Cn(N)$, two cases can be distinguished:

1. System $Cn(N \cup \{r\})$ is N-consistent.

2. System $Cn(N \cup \{r\})$ is N-inconsistent.

System $Cn(N \cup \{r\})$ is N-consistent
In the case of N-consistency, two subcases can be distinguished:

1. $Cn(\{r\}) \subseteq Cn(N)$: this we call *N-consistent redundant promulgation.* The promulgated norm was already deducible and is, therefore, redundant. In other words, norm r was already applicable in system $Cn(N)$. Norm r becomes a *new* member of the system if r has not been enacted explicitly by the authorities before the promulgation. This may be important. Suppose r was not a member of the system, but deduced from norm p. If p is derogated, then r is no longer deduced. Thus, it matters greatly that r becomes a member of the system. Anyway, r becomes a member of the individual normative system of the authority that promulgated norm r. Further, it can restrict the competence of inferior authorities to derogate norm r.

2. $Cn(\{r\}) \not\subseteq Cn(N)$: this we call *N-consistent material promulgation.* The system changes because the number of deducible norms increases. In this resulting system, the new norms are not only the ones pertaining to this norm and its consequences, but also those that can be derived from the promulgated norm *and* the rest of the already existing norms. From this viewpoint of a formal reconstruction, this has consequences for the sum of the two following sets:

   - the existing (explicitly enacted) norms N and
   - the explicitly promulgated norm r.

   Thus, the act of promulgation of r leads from system $Cn(N)$ to system $Cn(N \cup \{r\})$, and not to system $Cn(N) \cup Cn(\{r\})$.[5] In this case, norm r is a new member of the system and is applicable.

We illustrate such cases of promulgation in the following example (for norm expressions of DDL).
Example Let
- $N_{\{a_1\}} = \{O(\beta_1), P(\beta_2)\}$
- $N_{\{a_2\}} = \{O(\beta_3), O(\beta_4 \cup \overline{\beta_1})\}$
- $N_{\{a_3\}} = \{O(\overline{\beta_2})\}$

We define the following authority hierarchy: $D(\{a_1\}, \{a_2\}, \{a_3\})$, thus $A_1 = \{a_1\}$, $A_2 = \{a_2\}$ and $A_3 = \{a_3\}$. Then there is one maximal N-consistent set N for the given authority hierarchy:

$$N = \{O(\beta_1), P(\beta_2), O(\beta_3), O(\beta_4 \cup \overline{\beta_1})\}.$$

Let us consider the following two cases:

1. Authority a_2 promulgates norm $O(\beta_1 \& \beta_3)$.

[5]Note that $Cn(N) \cup Cn(\{r\}) \subseteq Cn(N \cup \{r\})$.

2. Authority a_1 promulgates norm $O(\beta_5)$.

1. If a_2 promulgates $O(\beta_1 \& \beta_3)$, then it holds that $Cn(N \cup \{O(\beta_1 \& \beta_3)\}) = Cn(N)$, since $N \vdash O(\beta_1 \& \beta_3)$. Thus, the promulgation of norm $O(\beta_1 \& \beta_3)$ by authority a_2 is a redundant promulgation.

2. If a_1 promulgates $O(\beta_5)$, then $Cn(N \cup \{O(\beta_5)\})$ is N-consistent and $Cn(\{O(\beta_5)\}) \not\subseteq Cn(N)$. Thus, the promulgation of norm $O(\beta_5)$ by authority a_1 is a material promulgation: norm $O(\beta_5)$ is a new member and also applicable. Further, it holds that $Cn(\{O(\beta_5)\}) \cup Cn(N) \subset Cn(N \cup \{O(\beta_5)\})$, since $O(\beta_3 \& \beta_5)$ is an element of $Cn(N \cup \{O(\beta_5)\})$ and not of $Cn(N) \cup Cn(\{O(\beta_5)\})$.

System $Cn(N \cup \{r\})$ is N-inconsistent
In the case of N-inconsistency, two subcases can be distinguished:

1. $\{N\} = MC(S(N_{A_n}) \cup \{r\})$: this we call *N-inconsistent redundant promulgation*. The negation of the promulgated norm is deducible from a set of norms enacted by a set of authorities with higher ranks of authority than the authority promulgating norm r. Norm r becomes a member of the system, but is not applicable.

2. $\{N\} \neq MC(S(N_{A_n}) \cup \{r\})$: this we call *N-inconsistent material promulgation*. In this case, there is no set of authorities with higher ranks of authority enacting the negation of the promulgated norm than the authority promulgating norm $\{r\}$. This case can again be subdivided into two cases:

   - $N \notin MC(S(N_{A_n}) \cup \{r\})$: the negation of the promulgated norm is only deducible minimally from sets of norms enacted by sets A of authorities with lower ranks of authority than authority a promulgating norm r, i.e. $\{a\} \succ A$. Norm r becomes a member and is also applicable.
   - $N \in MC(S(N_{A_n}) \cup \{r\})$: the negation of the promulgated norm is deducible minimally from a set of norms enacted by a set A of authorities with an authority with the same rank of authority as the authority promulgating norm r. Norm r becomes a *new* member of the system if the norm was not enacted before the promulgation, and is applicable in some, but not all, maximal N-consistent sets in $MC(S(N_{A_n}) \cup \{r\})$. Anyway, norm r becomes a member of the individual normative system of the authority that promulgated norm r.

We illustrate this with the following example.
Example Let
- $N_{\{a_1\}} = \{O(\beta_1), P(\beta_2)\}$
- $N_{\{a_2\}} = \{O(\beta_3), O(\beta_4 \cup \overline{\beta_2}), O(\overline{\beta_2})\}$

- $N_{\{a_3\}} = \{\neg P(\beta_3)\}$

We define the following authority hierarchy: $D(\{a_1\}, \{a_2\}, \{a_3\})$, thus $A_1 = \{a_1\}$, $A_2 = \{a_2\}$ and $A_3 = \{a_3\}$. Then there is one maximal N-consistent set N for the given authority hierarchy:

$$N = \{O(\beta_1), P(\beta_2), O(\beta_3), O(\beta_4 \cup \overline{\beta_2})\}.$$

Let us consider the following three cases:

1. Authority a_2 promulgates norm $\neg P(\beta_2)$.
2. Authority a_1 promulgates norm $\neg O(\beta_3)$.
3. Authority a_2 promulgates norm $O(\overline{\beta_4})$.

1. If authority a_2 promulgates $\neg P(\beta_2)$, then $Cn(N \cup \{\neg P(\beta_2)\})$ is inconsistent, thus also N-inconsistent. There is a set A of authorities with $A \succ \{a_2\}$, namely the set $\{a_1\}$ that enacted $P(\beta_2)$. Thus, the promulgation of norm $\neg P(\beta_2)$ by authority a_2 is an N-inconsistent redundant promulgation. Note that $\neg P(\beta_2)$ is now a member of the system, however.

2. If authority a_1 promulgates $\neg O(\beta_3)$, then $Cn(N \cup \{\neg O(\beta_3)\})$ is inconsistent. There is no set A of authorities with $A \succ \{a_1\}$, such that $A : O(\beta_3)$, thus the promulgation is an N-inconsistent material promulgation. Thus, we have to determine the maximal N-consistent sets of set $S(N_{A_3}) \cup \{\neg O(\beta_3)\}$ for the given authority hierarchy:

$$MC(S(N_{A_3}) \cup \{\neg O(\beta_3)\}) = \{\{\neg O(\beta_3), O(\beta_1), P(\beta_2), O(\beta_4 \cup \overline{\beta_2}), \neg P(\beta_3)\}\}.$$

   The consequences of this promulgation are:

   (a) the membership of $\neg O(\beta_3)$
   (b) the applicability of $\neg O(\beta_3)$
   (c) norm $O(\beta_3)$ is not applicable any more
   (d) norm $\neg P(\beta_3)$ becomes applicable

   Note that $N \notin MC(S(N_{A_n}) \cup \{\neg O(\beta_3)\})$.

3. If authority a_2 promulgates $O(\overline{\beta_4})$, then $Cn(N \cup \{O(\overline{\beta_4})\})$ is inconsistent. There is no set A of authorities with $A \succ \{a_2\}$, such that $A : \neg O(\overline{\beta_4})$, thus the promulgation is an N-inconsistent material promulgation. We have to determine the maximal N-consistent sets of set $S(N_{A_3}) \cup \{O(\overline{\beta_4})\}$ for the given authority hierarchy:

$$MC(S(N_{A_3}) \cup \{O(\overline{\beta_4})\}) = \{\{O(\beta_1), P(\beta_2), O(\beta_3), O(\beta_4 \cup \overline{\beta_2})\},$$
$$\{O(\beta_1), P(\beta_2), O(\beta_3), O(\overline{\beta_4})\}\}.$$

   Norm $O(\overline{\beta_4})$ is now a new member of the system and is applicable in one of the two maximal N-consistent sets. Note that N is still a maximal N-consistent set, though not the only one.

The promulgation by authority a_2 of this last example shows that the result of a promulgation is not determinate since there is not one unique system that can be identified as the result of a process of promulgation. Note that the result of promulgation of a norm to a system $Cn(N)$ is determinate if system $Cn(N \cup \{r\})$ is N-consistent.

7.3.2 Derogation

One important characteristic of legal rules is their persistence over time.[6] This means, among other things, that if a norm belongs to a system S, then it belongs to all successive systems of S, until it is removed from one of them. It is, therefore, possible to ask: when is it true that a norm r has been removed from a system S? The following answers can be given:

1. When a competent authority derogates r.
2. Ahen r is only a logical consequence of a set $\{r_1, r_2, \ldots, r_n\}$ of norms, and one of these norms has been removed from the system.
3. When norm r has restricted the temporal extension of its validity.
4. According to some theories, whether a norm is a member of a legal system not only depends on the actions of the normative authorities, but also on the acts of the addressees of the norm; in this sense, an ineffective norm does not belong to a legal system:

> ... the effectiveness of a norm consists in the fact that it is actually observed by and large ... Effectiveness is a condition for validity to the extent that a single norm and a whole normative order lose their validity - cease to be valid - if they lose their effectiveness or the possibility of effectiveness. [Kelsen, 1991, p. 139]

We do not consider cases 3 and 4, because our purpose here is to look at legislation as a technique for the introduction and removal of legal rules.

Derogation is a common technique for the removal of legal rules from a legal system. A normative authority may decide that a norm r has to be removed, and in order to obtain this result, the authority decides on a *derogatory disposition* d, i.e. a non-normative disposition which has the function of indicating a set of legal dispositions that must leave the system. Thus, the objects of dispositions of type d can be rules, definitions, etc. In this chapter, we consider only the derogation of norms. The decision on a derogatory disposition can be seen as the result of a specific normative act: the rejection of a norm [cf. Navarro, 1993]. Therefore, the derogation process begins with the promulgation of some disposition d. In other words, the process of removing a norm r begins with introducing a disposition d. The promulgation of d by some authority a is important, because it prevents authorities inferior to a from introducing, for example, the norm being the object

[6][Cf. Hart, 1961. 77-78].

of rejection. We formalise the enactment of a derogatory disposition, i.e. the rejection of a norm r, by enacting the negation of that norm (i.e. $\neg r$), on the understanding that this last norm does not become a member of the individual normative system of the authority that decided on the derogatory disposition (if it was not a member of that system already). Such a norm we call a *disposition object*.

We distinguish two cases of derogation of a norm r of a N-consistent system $Cn(N)$:

1. $r \notin Cn(N)$: this we call *derogation in advance*. No norm in N is removed. however, a consequence of this derogation is the restriction of the competence of inferior authorities.

2. $r \in Cn(N)$: in this case, two cases can be distinguished:

   (a) $\{N\} = MC(S(N_{A_n}) \cup \{\neg r\})$: this we call *redundant derogation*. Norm r is deducible from a set of norms enacted by a set of authorities with higher ranks of authority than the one enacting disposition object $\neg r$.

   (b) $\{N\} \neq MC(S(N_{A_n}) \cup \{\neg r\})$: this we call *material derogation*. In this case, there is no set of authorities with higher ranks of authority enacting norm r than the authority enacting disposition object $\neg r$. This case can again be subdivided into two cases:

      - $N \notin MC(S(N_{A_n}) \cup \{\neg r\})$: Norm r is only deducible minimally from sets of norms enacted by sets A of authorities with lower ranks of authority than authority a enacting disposition object $\neg r$, i.e. $\{a\} \succ A$. Note that norm $\neg r$ does not become a member of the system if it was not enacted before the enactment of disposition object $\neg r$, and that norm r is not a member nor applicable any more.
      - $N \in MC(S(N_{A_n}) \cup \{\neg r\})$: Norm r is only deducible minimally from sets of norms enacted by sets A of authorities with an authority with the same rank of authority as the authority enacting disposition object $\neg r$. Norm r will be rejected in some, but not all, maximal N-consistent sets of the set $MC(S(N_{A_n}) \cup \{\neg r\})$.

In the case of material derogation, the question may be raised what norms should be removed from set N in order that norm r is not deducible any more. What is wanted is to remove a minimum of norms in N compatible with the requirement that norm r cannot be derived.[7] This allows us to formulate the following adequacy conditions for the process of derogation:

1. The derogated norm r cannot be derived in the resulting systems.

[7]This is also expressed by the Gärdenfors' postulates [Gärdenfors, 1988]. These postulates are meant for the process of shrinking or contracting a theory to eliminate a norm. For a formal approach of this process, with the notions of *safe contraction* and *partial meet contraction*, we refer to Alchourrón and Makinson [1982] and Alchourrón, Gärdenfors, and Makinson [1985].

2. One should not eliminate more norms in N than is strictly necessary in order to achieve the first condition.

We can accomplish this by determining the maximal N-consistent sets of $S(N_{A_n}) \cup \{\neg r\}$. The resulting systems are these maximal N-consistent sets *without* norm $\neg r$, if norm $\neg r \notin S(N_{A_n})$.

Remarks

1. It is possible to obtain more than one resulting system after a material derogation. Such a derogation, which gives rise to more than one resulting system, will be called *indeterminate derogation* [cf. Alchourrón, 1982].

2. The derogation of a norm r corresponds to the promulgation of $\neg r$ with the exception that $\neg r$ does not become a member of the resulting system if it was not enacted before the enactment of disposition object $\neg r$.

Example Let
- $N_{\{a_1\}} = \{O(\beta_1), P(\beta_2)\}$
- $N_{\{a_2\}} = \{O(\beta_3), O(\beta_4 \cup \overline{\beta_1})\}$
- $N_{\{a_3\}} = \{O(\overline{\beta_2})\}$
- $N_{\{a_4\}} = \{P(\beta_5)\}$

We define the following authority hierarchy: $D(\{a_1\}, \{a_2, a_3\}, \{a_4\})$, thus $A_1 = \{a_1\}$, $A_2 = \{a_2, a_3\}$ and $A_3 = \{a_4\}$. Then there is one maximal N-consistent set N for the given authority hierarchy:

$$N = \{O(\beta_1), P(\beta_2), O(\beta_3), O(\beta_4 \cup \overline{\beta_1}), P(\beta_5)\}.$$

Let us consider the following four cases:

1. Authority a_1 enacts disposition object $\neg O(\beta_6)$.

2. Authority a_4 enacts disposition object $\neg O(\beta_4)$.

3. Authority a_1 enacts disposition object $\neg O(\beta_4)$.

4. Authority a_3 enacts disposition object $\neg O(\beta_3)$.

1. Authority a_1 enacts disposition object $\neg O(\beta_6)$. However, the negation of this norm, i.e. $O(\beta_6)$, is not an element of $Cn(N)$. Thus, this is a derogation in advance. It restricts the competence of authorities a_2, a_3 and a_4. For example, a_3 can promulgate $O(\beta_6)$, but this norm will not belong to the resulting system since the norm has not been promulgated by a 'competent' authority, i.e. an authority with a rank equal to or higher than authority a_1. Thus, derogation by authority a_1 restricts the competence of authority a_3.

2. Authority a_4 enacts disposition object $\neg O(\beta_4)$. Norm $O(\beta_4) \in Cn(N)$, since $\{a_1\} : O(\beta_1) \wedge \{a_2\} : O(\beta_4 \cup \overline{\beta_1}) \rightarrow \{a_1, a_2\} : O(\beta_4)$. This is a redundant derogation, since norm $O(\beta_4)$ is enacted by a set of authorities with higher ranks of authority than the one enacting disposition object $\neg O(\beta_4)$. Thus, $O(\beta_4)$ is still a member of the system and applicable.

3. Authority a_1 enacts disposition object $\neg O(\beta_4)$. Norm $O(\beta_4) \in Cn(N)$. This is a material derogation since there is no set of norms enacting by a set of authorities with higher ranks of authority than the one enacting disposition object $\neg O(\beta_4)$. Further, it holds that

$$MC(S(N_{A_3}) \cup \{\neg O(\beta_4)\}) = \{\{O(\beta_1), P(\beta_2), O(\beta_3), \neg O(\beta_4), P(\beta_5)\}\}.$$

Thus, $N \notin MC(S(N_{A_3}) \cup \{\neg O(\beta_4)\})$. Note that $\neg O(\beta_4)$ will not belong to the resulting system, i.e. the set

$$\{O(\beta_1), P(\beta_2), O(\beta_3), P(\beta_5)\}.$$

The consequences of this derogation are:

(a) Norm $O(\beta_4 \cup \overline{\beta_1})$ will be removed from the normative system; thus, is not applicable any more.

(b) It restricts the competence of authorities a_2, a_3 and a_4, since it prevents these authorities, for example, from introducing the derogated norm.

4. Authority a_3 enacts disposition object $\neg O(\beta_3)$. Norm $O(\beta_3) \in Cn(N)$. This is a material derogation since norm $O(\beta_3)$ is only enacted minimally by authority a_2 with the same rank as the one enacting disposition object $\neg O(\beta_3)$. Thus, norm $O(\beta_3)$ will be rejected in some, but not all, maximal N-consistent sets of the set $MC(S(N_{A_3}) \cup \{\neg O(\beta_3)\})$:

$$\{N, \{O(\beta_1), P(\beta_2), \neg O(\beta_3), O(\beta_4 \cup \overline{\beta_1}), P(\beta_5)\}\}.$$

Note that N in an element of $MC(S(N_{A_3}) \cup \{\neg O(\beta_3)\})$. The resulting systems are N and $\{O(\beta_1), P(\beta_2), O(\beta_4 \cup \overline{\beta_1}), P(\beta_5)\}\}$.

7.3.3 Evaluation

The relationship between 'promulgation entrance' of norms into a system and 'derogation departure' of norms from a system is only one aspect of the process of introduction and removal of norms. On the one hand, through the promulgation of a norm r, we not only introduce r into a system, but also restrict the competence of inferior authorities, i.e. authorities with a lower rank of authority than the authority promulgating norm r, as regards the set of norms which enters the system as a consequence of the promulgation of r. On the other hand, the derogation of a norm usually takes place through the promulgation of a derogatory disposition d. The promulgation of d modifies the normative system in two ways:

1. A disposition enters the system.
2. The set of norms indicated in d is removed from it.

Besides modifying the system, the derogation of a set of norms has the function of preventing any authority inferior to the one enacting disposition d from introducing the derogated norm(s) into the system. Therefore, derogation and promulgation have two features in common:

1. The modification of the applicable norms.
2. The restriction of the competence of inferior authorities.

Promulgation and derogation of norms are structurally similar processes: both operations may result in norms being introduced into or removed from a normative system.

Sometimes the promulgation or derogation of a norm leads to an undecided situation with respect to the norms of a normative system N.

Example Let
- $N_{\{a_1\}} = \{P(\beta_2)\}$
- $N_{\{a_2\}} = \{O(\overline{\beta_1}), O(\beta_1 \cup \overline{\beta_3})\}$

We define the following authority hierarchy: $D(\{a_1\}, \{a_2\})$. Then there is one maximal N-consistent set N for the given authority hierarchy:

$$N = \{P(\beta_2), O(\overline{\beta_1}), O(\beta_1 \cup \overline{\beta_3})\}.$$

Suppose authority a_1 promulgates norm $O(\beta_3)$ or enacts disposition object $\neg O(\overline{\beta_3})$. Norm $O(\overline{\beta_3})$ is an element of $Cn(N)$. In both cases, one of the two norms enacted by a_2 becomes inapplicable; however, which one is undetermined. This is called the 'logische Unbestimmtheit des Normensystems'[8] or logical indeterminacy.

In the following section, we discuss the notion of *universality*. A universal system is a normative-consistent system, such that all actions are prescribed, prohibited or permitted. Thus, for every action there is a norm enacted by a set of authorities, which is applicable.

7.4 Universality

The question whether universality can be reached can be formulated as follows: is it possible to set norms for all actions such that the obtained set of norms is N-consistent? In other

[8][Bulygin, 1976, p.619].

words: can all actions be prescribed, prohibited or permitted in a normative-consistent way?

Of course, the set of norms concerned has to be consistent. In the case of an inconsistent set, the question of universality would lose its meaning: everything would be deducible and, in particular, every norm that prescribes, prohibits or permits an action would be deducible. In order to deal with the question of universality, some concepts need to be introduced. We have to keep in mind that universality concerns three sets:

1. The set of norms that prescribes, prohibits or permits actions.
2. The set of actions (Act).
3. The set of actions that are actually regulated (Act^*).

A system N is universal if there is a norm for every action $\beta \in Act$, that is $Act^* = Act$ and if N is N-consistent. Usually, Act^* is only a real subset: $Act^* \subset Act$. To give a more precise formulation (cf. definition 2.6.5):

Definition 7.4.1 *N is universal iff for every $\beta \in Act$ it holds (exclusively) that:*
$O(\beta) \in Cn(N)$, or
$F(\beta) \in Cn(N)$, or
$(P(\overline{\beta}) \wedge P(\beta)) \in Cn(N)$.

From this definition it follows that a universal set is N-consistent (cf. proposition 2.6.6).

Proposition 7.4.2 *If N is universal, then N is N-consistent.*

Proof Assume that N is N-inconsistent. Then it holds for an action β that $N \vdash O(\beta)$ and $N \vdash O(\overline{\beta})$. Hence, $O(\beta) \in Cn(N)$ *and* $F(\beta) \in Cn(N)$. Thus, N is not universal.

Proposition 7.4.3 *Every N-consistent set N can be extended to a universal set N^*.*

The extension is based on the countability (countdown) of the formulas (cf. subsection 2.6.2). The notion of countability does not establish the precise order of the formulas. It has been avoided, however, that both $O(\beta)$ and $O(\overline{\beta})$ occur in the universal set. From the above it also is clear that this possibility is purely a logical one, and in practice may entail a very difficult (promulgation) process (for example, in legal practice or in the practice of making a traffic system universal). The contents of N^* have indeed not been determined unambiguously. This appears from the nature of the construction process of N^*. On the basis of purely logical considerations, a certain order in counting cannot be enforced: *logical indeterminacy*. But in practice, that is where important decisions will be made as to the norms that are to be promulgated or not.

From this it appears that, starting from a certain set of norms, many different universal sets can be obtained. In this sense, the concept is ambiguous. However, it has to be stated that a universal set cannot be constructed in practice,

- because of the incredibly great number of actions in *Act*;
- because some actions do not need to be regulated according to a legislator;
- because of the creation of ever more new actions, and so also new - and thus not yet regulated - actions.

As a result, all actions that have been regulated by law constitute a subset of the set of actions that are possible: $Act^* \subset Act$.

Thus, the introduction of a universal system of norms meets with practical difficulties. These difficulties are, in fact, well known, and one tries to get round them by formulating general closure rules such as:

- All acts that are not forbidden, are permitted.
- All acts that are not expressly permitted, are forbidden.

The former corresponds with the legal expression *nulla poena sine lege*, stated in Article 1 sub 1 of the Dutch Penal Code. The latter is used in the rules of certain games (such as chess, checkers and football). To show that the general rules mentioned above are not altogether unproblematic, we concentrate on the former rule.

7.4.1 Postulated Universality

When we want to examine different kinds of forms of acts within the framework of the description of the Dutch criminal law and whether an act is permitted or not permitted, we can encounter certain distinctions. On the one hand, it could be the case that a particular act is permitted by a competent normative authority. For example, the Dutch Code of Criminal Procedure teems with such regulations. On the other hand, it could be the case that in the Dutch criminal law a certain act is *weakly* permitted without a competent normative authority having enacted that permission. Nevertheless, the act in the last case is also permitted in the Dutch criminal law on the basis of Feuerbach's legal expression *nullum crimen, nulla poena sine praevia lege poenali*, stated in Article 1 sub 1 of the Dutch Penal Code. In jurisprudence this principle is usually labelled as the 'sealing legal principle', often formulated as 'whatever is not forbidden, is permitted' [cf. Tammelo, 1969; Brouwer, 1979]. This regulation 'does not function here through logical necessity, but because of legislation, in this way making absence of norms within these systems impossible' [Soeteman, 1989]. We call these systems *closed legal systems*, also called universal normative systems. Within these systems there is a positive legal norm - a general closure rule - governing all acts that are not subject to other legal norms [Alchourrón and Bulygin, 1971].

In the Dutch Traffic Regulation - part of the Dutch criminal law - a regulation concerning a permission is always an exception to an obligation or a prohibition [Langemeijer, 1987]. Otherwise, the permission would be superfluous, because of the sealing legal principle 'whatever is not forbidden, is permitted'. In what way are we to interpret this rule?

The obvious thing would be to accept the following principle:

$$\neg F(\beta) \rightarrow P(\beta).$$

This principle seems to be in accordance with what is meant, but does not add anything, because it is already incorporated in our system. If interpreted in this way, the rule mentioned does not guarantee universality, since axioms, theorems and definitions have to be applicable to non-universal systems.

The principle

> 'what is forbidden is permitted' addresses the judge and forbids him to extend the whole of legal prohibitions on the grounds of his own or someone else's political or moral conviction. [Soeteman, 1989, p. 189]

So, we can distinguish two types of permission:

- The permission which is an exception of an obligation or a prohibition: *the strong permission.*
- The permission which follows from the absence of a prohibition: *the weak permission* [cf. Wright, 1963].

A consequence of the strong permission is that the negation of the permitted act is permitted too, since the strong permission is an exception to a general article (rule), and one does not break the law by following that general article nevertheless. So, this implies a choice for the norm subjects to perform that act or not, without a liability to sanction.

7.4.2 The strong and weak permission

Strong permission
We will give an example concerning 'overtaking' taken from the Dutch Traffic Regulation:

Section 11. 1. Overtaking occurs on the left.
2. ...
3. Cyclists and moped-drivers should overtake other cyclists and moped-drivers on the left; they are permitted to overtake other drivers on the right.
4. Drivers who are on the right of a block-signposting are permitted to overtake drivers on the right, who are on the left of that signposting.
5. Drivers are permitted to overtake trams on the right.

All the permissions mentioned in section 11 are exceptions of the general rule 'overtaking occurs on the left'. This rule does not contain any deontic operator. However, it is easy to model this in a regulation model. For instance, 'overtaking on the right is forbidden'. The permission in the Dutch Traffic Regulation has a higher priority than the obligations and prohibitions which are incompatible with that permission. The consequence of the fact that an enacted permission is always an exception of a prohibition or obligation is that the addressees (to whom the permission is directed) always have a choice to perform the permitted act or not. For example, from the permission that drivers are allowed to overtake trams on the right it follows that drivers are also allowed *not* to overtake trams on the right. This does not mean that drivers are allowed to overtake trams on the left. It only means that it is permitted not to overtake a tram on the right in at least one way. Probably, there are many ways of performing the act 'not to overtake a tram on the right', some of which are forbidden. In contrast with the permission, the prohibition means that *all ways* of performing an act are forbidden. From the above-mentioned consequence, it is tempting to add the following formula to a deontic system:

$$P(\beta) \rightarrow P(\overline{\beta}).$$

However, this is unacceptable, since from this it follows that $O(p) \rightarrow F(p)$ - because $(P(p) \rightarrow P(\neg p)) \equiv (\neg O(\neg p) \rightarrow \neg O(p)) \equiv (O(p) \rightarrow F(p))$ - which says that if p is obligatory, then p also is forbidden. We have to make a distinction for this type of permission, the *strong* permission and the *weak* permission in our formalisation, since for the weak permission it does not hold that the negation of a weakly permitted act is permitted.

Weak permission

An example of a weak permission is the permission to drive at a speed of 95 km/h on a motorway. According to the Dutch Traffic Regulation a speed limit of 120 km/h holds on motorways. Nothing is said about a speed of 95 km/h. Consequently, because of the sealing legal principle (or because of the absence of a prohibition to that act), this act (to drive at a speed of 95 km/h on a motorway) is permitted: weak permission. However, the prohibition to exceed the speed limit of 120 km/h clearly does not imply that all speeds below the 120 km/h are *by definition* permitted: one has to take other speed prohibitions and orders into account, such as Article 25 of the Traffic Act: On the road, it is prohibited to act in such a way that the freedom of traffic is hindered without reason or that road security is jeopardised or may reasonably be expected to be jeopardised. It would be absurd to stick to this meaning when one considers the following example. There is a traffic jam on the motorway, and a car is driving at a speed of 100 km/h. The driver breaks the law in this situation, and he cannot maintain that it was permitted to drive at a speed of 100 km/h on this section of the road.

As stated before, a permission is weak (in the sense relevant here) if the act (proposition) is not forbidden. The permission is strong if the act is not forbidden, though subject to norm [cf. Soeteman, 1989]. This means that a permission is strong if and only if it is enacted by a normative authority (explicitly enacted permission) or if the permission is a logical consequence from a norm or set of norms enacted by a normative authority (implicitly enacted permission). Consequently, if an act is strongly permitted, then the negation of that act is too. From the fact that an authority enacted that an act is permitted, which is an exception of a prohibition or obligation, it follows that the authority also enacted (although implicitly) that the negation of that act is permitted. This does not hold for the weak permission. For instance, if no authority enacted that a certain act is forbidden and some authority enacted that that act is obligatory, then that act is simultaneously weakly permitted and obligatory. Thus, the negation of that act is *not* permitted, since it is forbidden by the obligation $O(\beta)$ ($O(\beta) \equiv F(\overline{\beta})$). So, the weak permission entails no choice, unlike the strong permission [cf. Royakkers, 1997].

The legal difference between these two types of permission is quite obvious. The idea is that a later enacted prohibition could be in conflict with a strong permission, but not with a weak permission. If an act is weakly permitted then the prohibition of that act can be given with any conflict [cf. Weinberger, 1970]. In standard deontic logic, we cannot distinguish between the strong and weak permission, since there is no explicit indication to the enactment of norms (they are God given). In the next section we will formalise these two types of permission with the help of the logic of enactment [cf. Royakkers, 1997]. The basic idea of the treatment is that a norm enacted by a normative authority is not always applicable, since, for example, the norm can be ineffective [Kelsen, 1960] or the norm can be overruled (derogated) by a norm enacted by a superior authority or by a norm enacted at a later point in time. Thus, a strong permission is not always applicable, but a weak permission is.

7.4.3 The axioms of permission

We will now introduce two axioms, which enables us to make a distinction between weak and strong permission.

$$N_{A_i} : P(\beta) \rightarrow N_{A_i} : P(\overline{\beta}) \tag{A4}$$

$$(\forall_{i \in \{1,\ldots,2^n-1\}} \neg(N_{A_i} : F(\beta))) \rightarrow P(\beta) \tag{A5}$$

These two axioms are the added to **Ent**, which we have developed in the previous chapter. Axiom (A4) we call *the axiom of the strong permission* and axiom (A5) we will call *the axiom of the weak permission*. The axiom of the strong permission says that if an authority A_i or a set A_i of authorities enacted that an act is permitted, A_i also enacted that the negation of that act is permitted. Thus, the addressee to whom the enacted permission is enacted, has a choice to perform the permitted act or not, (without a liability of sanction). The axiom of the weak permission says that the absence of a prohibition implies a permission, i.e. set A of authorities enacted that something is forbidden, then it is permitted. The difference between the strong and weak permission reveals itself in these axioms. A strong permission owes its existence to the fact that it is enacted, and a weak permission owes its existence to the absence of a prohibition.

To validate the axioms (A4) and (A5) we have to add two clauses. (A4) becomes valid by adding the clause:

$$\forall_{w' \in \{w'' | (w,w'') \in B_{A_i}} (R(w') \cap [\![p]\!] = \emptyset) \text{ or } \forall_{w' \in \{w'' | (w,w'') \in B_{A_i}} (R(w') \cap \overline{[\![p]\!]} \neq \emptyset)$$

Axiom (A5) becomes valid by adding the clause

$$\text{if } \forall_{w' \in \{w'' | (w,w'') \in B_{A_i}} (\forall_{i \in \{1,\ldots,m\}} (R(w') \subseteq [\![\neg p]\!])) \text{ then } R(w) \cap [\![p]\!] \neq \emptyset$$

Note that the formula $P(\beta) \wedge O(\beta)$ is *satisfiable* in system DDL, in contrast to the formula $N_{A_i} : P(\beta) \wedge N_{A_i} : O(\beta)$. The last formula is inconsistent, since $N_{A_i} : P(\beta) \wedge N_{A_i} : O(\beta)$ implies $N_{A_i} : P(\overline{\beta}) \wedge N_{A_i} : \neg P(\overline{\beta})$, and this in its turn implies, according (A6), $P(\overline{\beta}) \wedge \neg P(\overline{\beta})$, which is equivalent with falsehood. Conversely, formula $P(\beta) \wedge O(\beta)$ can hold: if $P(\beta)$ follows from the absence of prohibition $F(\beta)$ (i.e. (A5)) and $O(\beta)$ follows from (A6).

As we mentioned in chapter 3, we dropped axiom (OD), i.e. $\neg O(\beta \& \overline{\beta})$ for our deontic system. Suppose we do not drop this axiom, then we can derive $O(\beta) \rightarrow P(\beta)$. This would be a menace to our theory, since if an obligation is enacted, then this implies falsehood. Suppose that $N_{A_i} : O(\beta)$ holds, then consequently $N_{A_i} : \neg P(\overline{\beta})$ and $N_{A_i} : P(\beta)$. This can easily be proved by the following rule (N_{A_i}*-distribution*), which is derivable in system **Ent:**

$$\frac{\theta_1 \rightarrow \theta_2}{N_{A_i} : \theta_1 \rightarrow N_{A_i} : \theta_2}.$$

From $N_{A_i} : P(\beta)$ we can derive $N_{A_i} : P(\overline{\beta})$. Thus now with axiom (A6) it follows that $P(\overline{\beta})$ and $\neg P(\overline{\beta})$ both can be derived, which leads to falsehood. However, axiom (OD) is controversial nowadays - as we already mentioned -, so this is not a drawback in our system. Now we can easily check whether a permission is weak or strong. Suppose $P(\beta)$ is derivable, then this permission is strong if $N_{A_i} : P(\beta)$ is derivable for some i, and weak if the permission is strong or $N_{A_i} : P(\beta)$ is not derivable for all i. Thus, the strong permission implies the weak permission.

7.4.4 The danger of postulated universality

The general closure rule, which is supposed to guarantee universality, also poses a problem of an entirely different nature. If we interpret the rule to mean that every action is permitted unless it is explicitly or implicitly prohibited, then we encourage people to find loopholes in the law. Yet, this kind of practice is considered to be against the spirit of the law. It cannot be the intention of legal principles (such as the rule mentioned above) to encourage acting against *the spirit of the law* (the danger of postulated universality). There are cases, that the general principle which states that everything is permitted that is not prohibited,[9] is limited by the rule that it is not permitted to violate the 'spirit' of the (criminal) law.[10]

In the construction of universality, it appears that the interpretation of norms plays an important role. The conclusion that 'this act is not explicitly provided for by the legislator' can be drawn prematurely. We have to look for the cause 'in den semantischen Eigenschaften der Sprache (aktuelle und potentielle Vagheit der Begriffe)' [Alchourrón and Bulygin, 1977, p. 25].[11] Then the set of possible instances of a concept is not determined

[9]This principle can, in the context of criminal law, be associated with the principle of no punishment without preceding statutory law.

[10]See HR, 24-6-1935, *NJ* 1936, 91, in which the Supreme Court considered that cases that were not thought of by members of government or parliament when the law was created can still be dealt with under that law on the basis of the consideration that they are determined by the spirit of a certain (criminal) law.

[11]In English: 'in the semantic properties of language (topical and potential vagueness of concepts).'

in advance of the application of that concept. Only a judge can decide whether an object is an instance of a certain concept or not, e.g. is a 'surfboard' an instance of the concept 'boat'?

In the philosophical literature [see Alchourrón and Bulygin, 1971, especially chapter 7], it has been mentioned that universal systems of norms restrict the freedom and responsibility of the individual. Do individuals still possess the personal intellectual freedom to develop systems of norms for themselves on the basis of which they can responsibly act in a certain manner? In our opinion, this question springs from an incorrect application of the notion of universality. Not universality of a legal system restricts the freedom and responsibility of individuals, but the extensions of obligations and prohibitions to that legal system.[12] Permissions do not restrict personal intellectual freedom. In a legal sense, it is manifest that the legislator leaves room for an individual system of norms: according to the Supreme Court's judgement, abusing a mentally handicapped woman was permitted in the sense that it was not a punishable act.[13] It will, however, be clear that personal, normative judgements may differ.

7.5 Conclusions

A normative system $Cn(N)$ can be (normative) inconsistent since norms are enacted, for example, by different authorities. To obtain a maximal normative-consistent system of a normative system $Cn(N)$, we introduced an ordering of the authorities with respect to their competence, i.e. an authority hierarchy. For example, a norm $O(\beta)$, enacted by an authority a, is not applicable if there is a set A of authorities all with higher ranks of authority than a which enacted $O(\overline{\beta})$ or $\neg O(\beta)$.

The theory of the authority hierarchy illustrates a workable framework for reasoning with orderings. In this chapter, $D(A_1, \ldots, A_n)$ represented an authority-hierarchy, but it can also be interpreted as, e.g. a specificity hierarchy. A_k stands for the rank of specificity of a certain norm. Take, for example, a norm with rank A_1 of specificity which has a higher priority than a norm with rank A_2 of specificity. This can easily be applied to a deontic system, in this chapter system DDL. Suppose A_1 stands for the rank of specificity of traffic signs, and A_2 stands for the rank of specificity of traffic rules. According to Article 63 of the Dutch Traffic Regulation 1990, traffic signs override traffic rules in as far as specific rules are incompatible with specific signs.[14] Thus, we can state that $A_1 \succ A_2$. Consider the following example: car driver i_1 is on a major road and approaches a junction, where car driver i_2 approaches from the right. On the ground of Article 15 of the Dutch Traffic Regulation 1990, i_1 has to give way to i_2, who approaches the junction from the right. But,

[12] A good example of this can be found in the replacement of the Dutch Traffic Regulation 1966 by the Dutch Traffic Regulation 1990. In the explanatory memorandum it is stated: 'Because of the unequivocal formulation of many rules for relatively uncomplicated situations the road user is deprived of part of his responsibility. There is no need for him to think; the government has done that for him.' (Dutch Traffic Regulation 1990, explanatory memorandum, pp. II-B-7).

[13] HR, 21-6-1943, *NJ* 1943, 559.

[14] The expressing of such a meta-statement requires further research [cf. Prakken, 1993].

on the grounds of the right-of-way signs (A6 and A9) and the principle of trust, i_1 does not have to give way to i_1. We can formalise this as follows:

$$A_1 : \neg O(\{i_1\} : \beta) \wedge A_2 : O(\{i_1\} : \beta),$$

where β stands for the action 'to give right of way'. Thus, we can consistently express these conflicting norms with the addition of specificity. Also, norm $\neg O(\{i_1\} : \beta)$ is applicable - in contrast to norm $O(\{i_1\} : \beta)$, since norm $\neg O(\{i_1\} : \beta)$ has a higher rank of specificity than norm $O(\{i_1\} : \beta)$.

We have seen how we can deal with normative inconsistencies on the basis of an authority hierarchy. A drawback of our approach is that we can only deal with norms and, more precisely, with unconditional norms. We cannot deal with, for example, inconsistencies between 'classification rules' (interpretation rules). To deal with such inconsistencies, all sorts of consistency-based approaches have been developed, such as the argumentation theories [cf. Dung, 1993; Hage, 1996, 1997; Prakken and Sartor, 1995; Royakkers and Dignum, 1997; Sartor, 1993], non-monotonic reasoning [cf. Brewka, 1991; Poole, 1988; Prakken, 1993; Shoham, 1988], default logics [cf. Delgrande, 1988; McDermott and Doyle, 1980; Pollock, 1987] and defeasible deontic logics [cf. Nute, 1997; Tan and van der Torre, 1994].

Furthermore, a normative system changes by promulgation (the introduction of a norm into a legal system) and derogation (the removal of a norm from a legal system), i.e. the dynamic character of law. We have seen that these two legislative acts by authorities have two features in common: the modification of the applicable norms and the restriction of the competence of inferior authorities. Furthermore, we have seen that both derogation and promulgation may lead to logical indeterminacy.

Finally, we discussed (postulated) universality, and the way in which universality can be reached by a closure rule, such as *nulla poena sine lege*, expressed in Article 16 of the Dutch Constitution and Article 1 sub 1 of the Dutch Penal Code. The importance of the distinction between strong and weak permission is revealed in this context of postulated universality. The distinction can be expressed by the addition of a modal operator N_{A_i}, which expresses *enactment* in a deontic system. A strong permission is always enacted (implicitly or explicitly) and a weak permission owes its existence to the absence of a prohibition. Thus, a weak permission is not enacted. Another difference is that the strong permission implies a giving choice to the addressees.

Chapter 8

Conclusion

Assuming that logic, especially deontic logic, can provide foundations for the construction of expert systems and knowledge-based systems in law, the purpose of this book was to give a logical analysis of the representation of legal rules and legal reasoning. We investigated three concepts with respect to deontic logic:

- The addition of (groups) of actors.
- Enactment of norms.
- Applicability of norms.

A first aim has been to clarify the addition of (groups of) actors and authorities in deontic logic in order to represent legal rules. This showed that the extensions of deontic logic have more expressive power and that formulas acquire new meanings, not expressible in SDL and DDL. A second aim has been to reason with conflicting legal rules/inconsistent information. Therefore we presented a two-step model to describe enacted and apllicable norms separately. With the theory of enactment we are able to express inconsistent enacted norms in a consistent way and with the theory of applicability we have developed a process of filtering out the applicable norms from a set of enacted norms with the help of an authority hierarchy. An authority hierarchy implicitly determines which norm should be followed in cases of conflict, since the priority of norms depends on this hierarchy.

Both aims were attained and we can safely conclude that we can improve the representation of legal texts and of legal knowledge in general with the theories presented here. Such an improvement of formalisation forms a basis for the improvement of legal expert systems and knowledge based systems in law.

This research was meant to be a contribution to developments initiated by others, partly by applying these developments to the legal domain and partly by adding something new to the developments themselves.

8.1 The Dutch Traffic Regulation 1990 revisited

In this section, we formalise some cases related to the case concerning speed limits discussed in chapter 1. Before we present the cases, we will give the formal representation of Articles 20, 21 and 22 of the Dutch Traffic Regulation 1990 concerning the speed limit. We use the following abbreviations:
$Q_1(i)$: i is within built-up areas
$Q_2(i)$: i is outside built-up areas
$Q_3(i)$: i is on motorways
$Q_4(i)$: i is on national routes

$\underline{a_l}$: to drive l km/h, for $l = 0, 1, 2, \ldots, 300$
$\underline{b_l}$: $\underline{a_{l+1}} \cup \underline{a_{l+2}} \cup \ldots \cup \underline{a_{300}}$
$\underline{c(i)}$: to give right of way to i.

M: the group of motor-vehicle drivers
C_1: the group of moped drivers
C_2: the group of motorised wheelchair drivers
E_1: the group of lorry drivers
E_2: the group of bus drivers
E_3: the group of tractor drivers
E_4: the group of construction vehicle drivers
E_5: the group of motor vehicles with trailers drivers

The formalisation of the articles is as follows:

Article 20. Within built-up areas the following speed limits hold:
for motor vehicles 50 km/h;
for mopeds and motorised wheelchairs 30 km/h.

$$\forall_{i \in M}(Q_1(i) \Rightarrow F(i : b_{50}));$$

$$\forall_{i \in C_1 \cup C_2}(Q_1(i) \Rightarrow F(i : b_{30})).$$

Article 21. Outside built-up areas the following speed limits hold:
a. for motor vehicles on motorways 120 km/h, on national routes 100 km/h and on other roads 80 km/h;
b. for mopeds and motorised wheelchairs 40 km/h.

$$\forall_{i \in M}((Q_2(i) \wedge Q_3(i)) \Rightarrow F(i : b_{120}));$$

$$\forall_{i \in M}((Q_2(i) \wedge Q_4(i)) \Rightarrow F(i : b_{100}));$$

$$\forall_{i \in M}((Q_2(i) \wedge \neg(Q_3(i) \vee Q_4(i))) \Rightarrow F(i : b_{80}));$$

$$\forall_{i \in C_1 \cup C_2}(Q_2(i) \Rightarrow F(i : b_{40})).$$

Article 22. Assuming that, in accordance with other sections, no lower speed limit holds, the following speed limits hold for the following vehicles:

a. for lorries, buses and motor vehicles with trailers 80 km/h;
b. for tractors and construction vehicles 25 km/h.

$$\forall_{i \in E_1 \cup E_2 \cup E_5} F(i : b_{80});$$

$$\forall_{i \in E_3 \cup E_4} F(i : b_{25}).$$

Speed limit

The main case in chapter 1 was as follows. On a national route, a lorry driver drove at a speed of 96 km/h. The lorry driver was imposed an administrative sanction on the ground of 'a lorry exceeding the speed limit by 15 to 20 km/h'. However, the lorry driver was of the opinion that, on the road in question, traffic signs indicating a speed limit of 100 km/h were in force, and that, therefore, no sanctionable act had been committed, for traffic signs override traffic rules according to Article 63 of the Dutch Traffic Regulation 1990.

In Article 22 of the Dutch Traffic Regulation 1990, it is laid down that for lorries the special speed limit of 80 km/h holds, which can be formalised as follows:

$$\forall_{i \in E_1} F(i : b_{80}).$$

According to traffic sign A1(100), it is forbidden to drive faster than 100 km/h:

$$\forall_{i \in M} F(i : b_{100}).$$

Let i_1 be the lorry driver. Then, the following statement holds

$$F(i_1 : b_{80}) \wedge F(i_1 : b_{100}),$$

since $i_1 \in E_1$ and $i_1 \in M$. Note that $E_1 \subset M$. This formula is equivalent to[1]

$$F(i_1 : b_{80});$$

thus, the two prohibitions are not in conflict. Hence, Article 63 is not applicable in this case, since traffic signs override traffic rules in as far as these rules are *incompatible* with the signs.

However, as we have seen in chapter 1, the letter of the law with regard to the speed limit is not in agreement with the spirit of the law in the Dutch Traffic Regulation 1990. In built-up areas, there are, for example, A1(70) traffic signs on circular roads, indicating that it is prohibited to drive faster than 70 km/h:

$$\forall_{i \in M} F(i : b_{70}).$$

Many drivers will, and justifiably, take this sign to mean that it is permitted to drive at a speed of 70 km per hour. This is, however, in disagreement with the motivation by the

[1] $F(i_1 : b_{80}) \wedge F(i_1 : b_{100}) \equiv F(i_1 : a_{81} \cup \ldots \cup a_{300}) \wedge F(i_1 : a_{101} \cup \ldots \cup a_{300}) \equiv F(i_1 : a_{81}) \wedge \ldots \wedge F(i_1 : a_{300}) \wedge F(i_1 : a_{101}) \wedge \ldots \wedge F(i_1 : a_{300}) \equiv F(i_1 : a_{81}) \wedge \ldots \wedge F(i_1 : a_{300}) \equiv F(i_1 : b_{80})$.

district court judge and the Advocate-General. According to Article 20 of the Dutch Traffic Regulation 1990, a speed limit of 50 km/h holds for motor vehicles inside built-up areas. Thus, the following norm holds

$$\forall_{i \in M} F(i : b_{50}).$$

In this case, the following combination of the two general prohibitions holds:

$$\forall_{i \in M} F(i : b_{70}) \wedge \forall_{i \in M} F(i : b_{50}),$$

which is equivalent to

$$\forall_{i \in M} F(i : b_{50}).$$

In chapter 1, we solved this problem by replacing Articles 20, 21 and 22 by the following Article

> The following speed limits hold:
> a. for motor vehicles on motorways 120 km/h, on national routes 100 km/h and on other roads 80 km/h;
> b. for lorries, buses and motor vehicles with trailers 80 km/h;
> c. for mopeds and motorised wheelchairs inside built-up areas 30 km/h and outside built-up areas 40 km/h;
> d. for tractors and construction vehicles 25 km/h.

Thus, the speed limit of 50 km/h for motor vehicles inside built-up areas is removed, and speed has to be regulated by means of A1 signs. Then, the above case can be formalised as follows:

$$\forall_{i \in M} F(i : b_{80}) \wedge \forall_{i \in M} F(i : b_{70}),$$

which is equivalent to

$$\forall_{i \in M} F(i : b_{70}).$$

This alternative has two advantages: first, the rules can be applied consistently, and second, the legislator's wish is expressed in a clearer way. The legislator's intention is stated precisely in these rules. In the Dutch Traffic Regulation 1990, this is definitely not the case.

Right of way

In chapter 1, we saw that traffic signs and traffic rules can be incompatible in cases concerning 'right of way'. We gave the following example. Car driver i_1 is on a major road and approaches a junction, where car driver i_2 approaches from the right.

On the grounds of the rule in Article 15, i_1 has to give right of way to i_2; on the grounds of the right-of-way signs (A6 and A9) and the principle of trust, i_1 does not have to give right of way to i_2. In this formulation, i_1 both has to give right of way and does not have to give right of way, which is clearly a case of incompatibility, which can be expressed as follows on the basis of the principle of trust:

$$O(i_1 : \underline{c(i_2)}) \wedge \neg O(i_1 : \underline{c(i_2)}).$$

It is obvious, that here we have an inconsistency. We can express this consistently with the addition of articles and signs, in the same way as the addition of authorities in chapter 6:

$$N^{w}_{\mathrm{Art.15}} : O(i_1 : \underline{c(i_2)}) \wedge N^{w}_{\mathrm{sign(A6/9)}} : \neg O(i_1 : \underline{c(i_2)}),$$

meaning that according to Article 15, i_1 is obliged to give right of way to i_2, and according to signs A6 and A9, i_1 is not obliged to give right of way to i_2. In this formalisation, there is clearly a case of incompatibility, thus Article 63 is applicable. Since signs A6 and A9 have a higher priority than Article 15, the norm $\neg O(i_1 : \underline{c(i_2)})$ is followed in this situation.

Just as we define an authority hierarchy, we can define an article/sign hierarchy, i.e., an ordering of articles and signs. This is not only a hierarchy concerning two sets, the set of articles and the set of traffic signs; articles are also ordered among themselves. For example, according to Article 15.1 a driver has to give right of way to another driver who approaches the junction from the right, and according to Article 15.2 a driver on a dirt road has to give right of way to another driver on a paver road. Article 15.2 has a higher priority than Article 15.1 in case of incompatibility.

Emergency service vehicles

As we saw in chapter 1, there is one case in which Article 63 has a nasty consequence. A passenger car driving on a major road approaches a junction, and at the same time a police car with flashing light and sirens approaches from the left. On the ground of Article 50, driver i_1 of the passenger car has to give way to driver i_2 of the police car, but on the ground of Article 15 and right-of-way signs A6 and A9, i_2 has to give way to i_1. This can be formalised as follows on the basis of the principle of trust:

$$O(i_1 : \underline{c(i_2)}) \wedge \neg O(i_1 : \underline{c(i_2)}).$$

It is obvious, that we have an inconsistency; however, this can be consistently expressed with the addition of articles and signs:

$$N^{w}_{\mathrm{Art.50}} : O(i_1 : \underline{c(i_2)}) \wedge N^{w}_{\mathrm{Art.15}} : \neg O(i_1 : \underline{c(i_2)}) \wedge N^{w}_{\mathrm{sign(A6/9)}} : \neg O(i_1 : \underline{c(i_2)}).$$

Article 50 has a higher priority than Article 15, and signs A6 and A9 have a higher priority than Article 50. Hence, on the ground of Article 63, the norm $\neg O(i_1 : \underline{c(i_2)})$ is chosen. We solved this problem by replacing Article 50 by:

> Yielding right of way by road users to drivers of emergency service vehicles overrides traffic lights and traffic signs and rules that regulate right of way.

Then, the above case can be formalised as follows:

$$N^{w}_{\mathrm{e.s.v.}} : O(i_1 : \underline{c(i_2)}) \wedge N^{w}_{\mathrm{Art.15}} : \neg O(i_1 : \underline{c(i_2)}) \wedge N^{w}_{\mathrm{sign(A6/9)}} : \neg O(i_1 : \underline{c(i_2)}).$$

Now, norm $O(i_1 : \underline{c(i_2)})$ is chosen, since emergency service vehicles have a higher priority than signs and articles.

The above cases show that we can smoothly represent articles in the Dutch Traffic Regulation 1990 in our 'extended' deontic logic. Using this representation, we can analyse legal reasoning with conflicting norms or inconsistent information.

8.2 Further research

This book invites further research in several areas:

- The incorporation and implementation of the theories discussed in this book, in legal expert systems.
- The representation of meta-statements, such as Article 63 of the Dutch Traffic Regulation. These statements are not explicitly expressed in our representation of legal rules.
- The representation of *open-textured concepts*. Open texture is one of the ways in which a judge (or a lawyer) deals with unforeseen change, and is essential to facilitate legal change. However, this is one of the hardest problem of representation.
- The role of the individuals in a group with respect to collective obligations are indeterminate; every individual plays the same part in the group. In reality, there is more structure in a group, like goalkeeper, defenders, midfield players and attackers in a football team, but they all have the same goal, i.e., to win.
- The combination of Ought-to-do and Ought-to-be statements. There are situations in which we would like to relate the two Oughts with each other.

Bibliography

Alchourrón, C. (1969). Logic of norms and logic of normative propositions. *Logique et Analyse*, **12**, 242–268.

Alchourrón, C. (1982). Normative order and derogation. In A. Martino, editor, *Deontic Logic, Computational Linguistics and Legal Information Systems*, volume 2, pages 51–63. North-Holland, Amsterdam.

Alchourrón, C. (1986). Conditionality and the representation of legal norms. In A. Martino and F. Socci Natali, editors, *Automated Analysis of Legal Texts*, pages 175–186. North-Holland, Amsterdam.

Alchourrón, C. and Bulygin, E. (1971). *Normative Systems*. Springer, Wien.

Alchourrón, C. and Bulygin, E. (1977). Unvollständigkeit, widersprüchlichkeit und unbestimmtheit der normenordnungen. In A. Conte, R. Hilpinen, and G. von Wright, editors, *Deontische Logik und Semantik*, pages 20–32. Athenaion, Wiesbaden.

Alchourrón, C. and Bulygin, E. (1981). The expressive conception of norms. In R. Hilpinen, editor, *New Studies in Deontic Logic*, pages 95–124. Reidel, Dordrecht.

Alchourrón, C. and Bulygin, E. (1984). Pragmatic foundations for a logic of norms. *Rechtstheorie*, pages 453–464.

Alchourrón, C. and Makinson, D. (1981). Hierarchies of regulations and their logic. In R. Hilpinen, editor, *New Studies in Deontic Logic*, pages 125–148. Reidel, Dordrecht.

Alchourrón, C. and Makinson, D. (1982). On the logic of theory change: Contraction functions and their associated revision functions. *Theoria*, **48**, 14–37.

Alchourrón, C., Gärdenfors, P., and Makinson, D. (1985). On the logic of theory change: Partial meet contraction and revision functions. *Journal of Symbolic Logic*, **50**, 510–530.

Altan, d', P., Meyer, J.-J., and Wieringa, R. (1993). An integrated framework for ought-to-be and ought-to-do constraints. In Y. Tan, editor, *Working Papers of the Workshop on Deontic and Non-Monotonic Logics*, pages 14–45. EURIDIS, Rotterdam.

Anderson, A. (1967). Some nasty problems in the formalization of ethics. *Noûs*, **1**, 345–360.

Åqvist, L. (1967). Good samaritans, contrary-to-duty imperatives, and epistemic obligations. *Noûs*, **1**, 361–379.

Bailhache, P. (1981). Analytical deontic logic: Authorities and addressees. *Logique et Analyse*, **93**, 65–80.

Bailhache, P. (1991). Authorities and addressees in deontic logic: Indexed operators and action. In J.-J. Meyer and R. Wieringa, editors, *ΔEON'91, Proceedings of the First International Workshop on Deontic Logic in Computer Science*, pages 72–88, Amsterdam.

Bakker, de, J., Kok, J., Meyer, J.-J., Olderog, E.-R., and Zucker, J. (1986). Contrasting themes in the semantics of imperative concurrency. In J. de Bakker, W. de Roever, and G. Rozenberg, editors, *Current Trends in Concurrency: Overviews and Tutorials*, pages 15–121. Springer, Berlin.

Bench-Capon, T. (1989). Deep models, normative reasoning and legal expert systems. In *Proc. Second International Conference on Artificial Intelligence and Law*, pages 37–45. ACM Press.

Beth, E. (1971). *Aspects of modern logic*. Reidel, Dordrecht.

Brewka, G. (1991). Preferred subtheories: An extended logical framework for default reasoning. In *Proceedings IJCAI-1991*, pages 1043–1048.

Brewka, G. (1994). Reasoning about priorities in default logic. In *Proceedings AAAI-94*, pages 247–260.

Brouwer, P. (1979). Openheid van en in rechtsordes. *Rechtsfilosofie en Rechtstheorie*, **8**, 128–149.

Brouwer, P. (1990). *Samenhang in Recht. Een Analytische Studie*. Wolters-Noordhoff, Groningen.

Brouwer, P. (1992). Over coherentie in recht. *Rechtsfilosofie en Rechtstheorie*, **21**, 178–192.

Brouwer, P., Soeteman, A., and Wild, de, A., editors (1982). *Logica en Recht*. Tjeenk Willink, Zwolle.

Brown, M. and Carmo, J., editors (1996). *Deontic Logic, Agency and Normative Systems*. Springer, Berlin.

Broy, M. (1986). A theory for nondeterminism, parallelism, communication and concurrency. *Theoretical Computer Science*, **45**, 1–62.

Bulygin, E. (1976). Logische fragen der gesetzgebungstechnik. In J. Rödig, editor, *Studien zu einer Theorie der Gesetzgebung*, pages 612–627. Springer, Berlin.

Bulygin, E. (1982). Time and validity. In A. Martino, editor, *Deontic Logic, Computational Linguistics and Legal Information Systems*, volume 2, pages 51–63. North-Holland, Amsterdam.

Castañeda, H.-N. (1970). On the semantics of the ought-to-do. *Synthese*, **21**, 449–468.

Castañeda, H.-N. (1981). The paradoxes of deontic logic. In R. Hilpinen, editor, *New Studies in Deontic Logic*, pages 37–85. Reidel, Dordrecht.

Castelfranchi, C. (1995). Commitments: From individual intentions to groups and organizations. In V. Lesser, editor, *Proceedings First International Conference on Multi-Agent Systems*. AAAI-Press and MIT Press, San Francisco.

Chellas, B. (1980). *Modal Logic: An Introduction*. Cambridge University Press, Cambridge.

Chisholm, R. (1963). Contrary-to-duty imperatives and deontic logic. *Analysis*, **24**, 33–36.

Delgrande, J. (1988). An approach to default reasoning based on a first-order conditional logic. *Artificial Intelligence*, **36**, 63–90.

Dignum, F. (1989). *A Language for Modelling Knowledge Bases. Based on Linguistics, Founded in Logic*. Free University, Amsterdam.

Dignum, F. and Meyer, J.-J. (1990). Negations of transactions and their use in the specification of dynamic and deontic integrity constraints. In M. Z. Kwiatkowska, M. Shields, and R. Thomas, editors, *Semantics for Concurrency*, pages 61–80. Springer, London.

Dung, P. (1993). On the acceptability of arguments and its fundamental role in nonmonotonic reasoning and logic programming. In *Proceedings IJCAI-93*, pages 852–857.

Dunin-Kęplicz, B. and Verbrugge, R. (1996). Collective commitments. In M. Tokora, editor, *Proceedings Second International Conference on Multi-Agent Systems*. AAAI-Press, California.

Eck, van, J. (1982). A system of temporally relative modal and deontic predicate logic and its philosophical application. *Logique et Analyse*, **100**, 249–381.

Eemeren, van, G. and Grootendorst, R. (1992). *Argumentation, Communication and Fallacies*. Erlbaum.

Fagin, R. and Halpern, J. (1988). Belief, awareness and limited reasoning. *Artificial Intelligence*, **34**, 39–76.

Føllesdal, D. and Hilpinen, R. (1971). Deontic logic: An introduction. In R. Hilpinen, editor, *Deontic Logic: Introductory and Systematic Readings*, pages 1–35. Reidel, Dordrecht.

Freundenthal, H. (1971). Euklid. In K. Fassmann, editor, *Die Grossen der Weltgeschichte 1*, pages 710–715. Kindler, Zürich.

Frost, R. (1986). *Introduction to Knowledge Base Systems*. Collins, London.

Gärdenfors, P. (1988). *Knowledge in Flux*. MIT press, Cambridge.

Gordon, T. (1995). *The Pleadings Game. An Artificial Intelligence Model of Procedural Justice*. Kluwer, Dordrecht.

Hage, J. (1996). A theory of legal reasoning and a logic to match. *Artificial Intelligence and Law*, **4**, 199–273.

Hage, J. (1997). *Reasoning with Rules*. Kluwer Academic Publishers, Dordrecht.

Halpern, J. and Moses, Y. (1985). A guide to the modal logics of knowledge and belief. In *Proceedings of the 9th International Joint Conference on Artificial Intelligence*, pages 480–490.

Hamilton, A. (1988). *Logic for Mathematicians*. Cambridge University Press, Cambridge.

Hansson, B. (1970). Deontic logic and different levels of generality. *Theoria*, **36**, 241–248.

Harel, D. (1984). Dynamic logic. In D. Gabbay and F. Guenther, editors, *Handbook of Philosophical Logic*, volume 2, pages 497–604. Reidel, Dordrecht.

Hart, H. (1961). *The Concept of Law*. Clarendon Press, Oxford.

Herrestad, H. (1991). Norms and formalization. In *The Third International Conference on Artificial Intelligence and Law. Proceedings of the Conference*, pages 175–184, New York.

Herrestad, H. and Krogh, C. (1995). Deontic logic relativised to bearers and counterparties. In J. Bing and O. Torrund, editors, *Anniversary Anthology in Computers and Law*, pages 453–522. Tano A.S., Oslo.

Hilpinen, R. (1973). On the semantics of personal directives. *Ajatus*, **35**, 140–157.

Hintikka, J. (1970). Some main problems of deontic logic. In R. Hilpinen, editor, *Deontic Logic: Introductory and Systematic Readings*, pages 59–104. Reidel, Dordrecht.

Hintikka, J. (1975). Impossible possible worlds vindicated. *Journal of Philosophical Logic*, **4**, 475–484.

Hohfeld, W. (1964). *Fundamental Legal Conceptions*. Yale University Press, New Haven-London. edited by W.W. Cook.

Horty, J. (1994). Moral dilemmas and nonmonotonic logic. *Journal of Philosophical Logic*, **23**, 35–66.

Jones, A. (1990). Deontic logic and legal knowledge representation. *Ratio Juris*, **3**, 237–244.

Jones, A. and Sergot, M. (1992). Deontic logic in the representation of law: Towards a methodology. *Artificial Intelligence and Law*, **1**, 45–64.

Jones, A. and Sergot, M. (1993a). On the characterization of law and computer systems: The normative systems perspective. In J.-J. Meyer and R. Wieringa, editors, *Deontic Logic in Computer Science, Normative System Specification*. Wiley, Chichester.

Jones, A. and Sergot, M., editors (1993b). *Second International Workshop on Deontic Logic in Computer Science*. Tano A.S., Oslo.

Kanger, S. (1971). New foundations for ethical theory. In R. Hilpinen, editor, *Deontic Logic: Introductory and Systematic Readings.*, pages 1–35. Reidel, Dordrecht.

Kanger, S. (1985). On realization of human rights. In G. Holmström and A. Jones, editors, *Action, Logic, and Social Theory - Acta Philosophica Fennica*, **38**, pages 71–78. Philosophical Society of Finland, Helsinki.

Kanger, S. and Kanger, H. (1966). Rights and parliamentarism. *Theoria*, **32**, 85–115.

Kelsen, H. (1960). *Reine Rechtslehre*. Verlag Deuticke, Wien.

Kelsen, H. (1991). *General Theory of Norms*. Clarendon Press, Oxford. translated by M. Hartney.

Kloosterhuis, H. (1994). De rationele reconstructie van a contrario-argumentatie: een pragmadialectische benadering. *Tijdschrift voor Taalbeheersing*, **16**, 106–116.

Koers, A., Kracht, D., Smith, M., Smits, J., and Weusten, M., editors (1989). *Knowledge Based Systems in Law: in Search of Methodologies and Tools*. Kluwer, Deventer.

Kordig, C. (1975). Relativised deontic modalities. In A. Anderson, R. Marcus, and R. Martin, editors, *The Logical Enterprise*, pages 221–257. Yale University Press, New Haven.

Kutschera, von, F. (1973). *Einführung in die Logik der Normen, Werte und Entscheidungen*. Verlag Karl Alber, Freiburg/München.

Kutschera, von, F. (1982). *Grundlagen der Ethik*. De Gruyter, Berlin.

Langemeijer, G. (1987). De betekenis van veroorlovende normen in het strafrecht voor het privaatrecht. In J. Remmelink, editor, *Naar eer en geweten*, pages 301–307. Gouda Quint, Arnhem.

Lindahl, L. (1977). *Position and Change*. Reidel, Dordrecht.

Lindahl, L. (1992). Conflicts in systems of legal norms: A logical point of view. In B. Brouwer, T. Hol, A. Soeteman, W. van der Velden, and A. de Wild, editors, *Coherence and Conflict in Law*, pages 39–64. Kluwer Law and Taxation Publishers, Deventer.

Linden, van, B., Hoek, van der, W., and Meyer, J.-J. (1996). How to motivate your agents. on formalising preference, goals and commitments. In J. Fiadeiro and P.-Y. Schobbens, editors, *Proceedings of the 2nd Workshop of the ModelAgeproject*, pages 151–166.

MacCormick, D. (1984). Coherence in legal justification. In W. K. et al, editor, *Theorie der Normen*. Duncker & Humblot, Berlin.

Makinson, D. (1986). On the formal representation of rights relations. *Journal of Philosophical Logic*, **15**, 403–425.

Makinson, D. (1993). Five faces of minimality. *Studia Logica*, **52**, 339–379.

Martino, A. and Natali, F. S., editors (1986). *Automated Analysis of Legal Texts*. North-Holland, Amsterdam.

McCarty, L. (1986). Permissions and obligations: An informal introduction. In A. Martino and F. S. Natali, editors, *Automated Analysis of Legal Texts*, pages 307–337. North-Holland, Amsterdam.

McCarty, L. (1989). A language for legal discourse 1: Basic features. In *The Second International Conference on Artificial Intelligence and Law*, pages 180–189. Association for Computing Machinery.

McDermott, D. and Doyle, J. (1980). Non-monotonic logic 1. *Artificial Intelligence*, **13**, 41–72.

McLaughlin, R. (1955). Further problems of derived obligation. *Mind*, **64**, 400–402.

Meyer, J.-J. (1987). A different aproach to the 'deepest' paradox in deontic logic. *Logique et Analyse*, **30**, 81–90.

Meyer, J.-J. (1988). A different approach to deontic logic: Deontic logic viewed as a variant of dynamic logic. *Notre Dame Journal of Formal Logic*, **29**, 109–136.

Meyer, J.-J. (1989). Using programming concepts in deontic reasoning. In R. Bartsch, J. van Benthem, and P. van Emde Boas, editors, *Semantics and Contextual Expression*, pages 117–145. FORIS publications, Dordrecht.

Meyer, J.-J. and van der Hoek, W. (1988). Non-monotonic reasoning by monotonic means; technical report ir-171. Technical report, Free University, Amsterdam.

Meyer, J.-J. and van der Hoek, W. (1995). *Epistemic Logic for AI and Computer Science*. Cambridge University Press, Cambridge.

Meyer, J.-J. and Wieringa, R., editors (1991). *ΔEON'91, Proceedings of the First International Workshop on Deontic Logic in Computer Science*, Amsterdam.

Meyer, J.-J., Dignum, F., and Wieringa, R. (1994). The paradoxes of deontic logic revisited: A computer science perspective; technical report uu-cs-1994-38. Technical report, Utrecht University.

Navarro, P. (1993). Promulgation and derogation of legal rules. *Law and Philosophy*, **21**, 385–394.

Navarro, P. and Redondo, M. (1990). Derogation, logical indeterminacy and legal expressivism. *Rechtstheorie*, **21**, 233–239.

Nute, D., editor (1997). *Defeasible Deontic Logic*. Kluwer Academic Publishers, Dordrecht.

Otte, M. (1993). *Het Stelsel van Gedragsregels in het Wegverkeer*. Gouda Quint, Arnhem.

Otte, M. and Simmelink, J. (1993). Kronkels in het rvv 1990. de bijzondere snelheidsmaxima in het rvv 1990. *Verkeersrecht 1993*, page 167.

Pollock, J. (1987). Defeasible reasoning. *Cognitive Science*, **11**, 481–518.

Poole, D. (1988). A logical framework for default reasoning. *Artificial Intelligence*, **36**, 27–47.

Pörn, I. (1970). *The Logic of Power*. Basil Blackwell, Oxford.

Prakken, H. (1993). *Logical Tools for Modelling Legal Argument*. Free University, Amsterdam.

Prakken, H. (1996). Two approaches to the formalisation of defeasible deontic reasoning. *Studia Logica*, **57**, 73–90.

Prakken, H. and Sartor, G. (1995). On the relation between legal language and legal argument: Assumptions, applicability and dynamic priorities. In *Proceedings of the Fifth International Conference on Artificial Intelligence and Law.*, pages 1–11. University of Maryland, MD USA.

Reisinger, L. (1977). *Rechtsinformatik.* De Gruyter, Berlin.

Reiter, R. (1980). A logic for default reasoning. *Artificial Intelligence*, **13**, 81–132.

Reiter, R. (1987). Nonmonotonic reasoning. *Annual Review Computer Science*, **2**, 147–186.

Rescher, N. (1966). *The Logic of Commands.* Dover, New York.

Ross, A. (1941). Imperatives and logic. *Theoria*, **7**, 53–71.

Royakkers, L. (1995). Kunnen maximumsnelheden conflicteren? over de notie van 'onverenigbaarheid' in artikel 63 rvv 1990. *Verkeersrecht 1995*, pages 39–42.

Royakkers, L. (1996). *Representing Legal Rules in Deontic Logic.* University of Tilburg, Tilburg.

Royakkers, L. (1997). Giving permission implies giving choice. In *Eighth International Workshop on Database and Expert Systems Applicaions (DEXA'97)*, pages 198–203.

Royakkers, L. and Dignum, F. (1995). Actors and norms. In R. Wieringa and R. Feenstra, editors, *Information Systems. Correctness and Reusability.* World Scientific.

Royakkers, L. and Dignum, F. (1997). Defeasible reasoning with legal rules. In D. Nute, editor, *Defeasible Deontic Reasoning*, pages 263–286. Kluwer Academic Publishers, Dordrecht.

Ruiter, D. (1989). Deontic-logical relations and speech act theory. *Rechtsfilosofie en Rechtstheorie*, **18**, 75–107.

Sarlemijn, A. and Royakkers, L. (1997). *Logica: grondbeginselen en toepassingen.* Van Gorcum, Assen.

Sartor, G. (1992a). Artificial intelligence in law and legal theory. In *Current Legal Theory*, volume 2, pages 1–59. Tilburg University Press.

Sartor, G. (1992b). Normative conflicts in legal reasoning. *Artificial Intelligence and Law*, **1**, 209–235.

Sartor, G. (1993). Defeasibility in legal reasoning. *Rechtstheorie*, **24**, 281–316.

Segerberg, K. (1989). Bringing it about. *Journal of Philosophical Logic*, **18**, 327–347.

Sergot, M., Sadri, F., Kowalski, R., Kriwaczek, F., Hammond, P., and Cory, H. (1986). The british nationality act as a logic program. *Communications of the ACM*, **29(5)**, 370–386.

Shoham, Y. (1988). *Reasoning about Change.* MIT Press, Cambridge.

Simmelink, J. (1995). *Algemeenheden in het Wegenverkeersrecht.* Gouda Quint, Arnhem.

Smith, M. (1994). *Legal Expert Systems: Discussion of Theoretical Assumptions.* Utrecht University, Utrecht.

Soeteman, A. (1989). *Logic in Law. Remarks on Logic and Rationality in Normative Reasoning, Especially in Law.* Kluwer Academic Publishers, Dordrecht.

Susskind, R. (1987). *Expert Systems in Law.* Clarendon, Oxford.

Tammelo, I. (1969). *Outlines of Modern Legal Logic.* Athenaion, Wiesbaden.

Tan, Y.-H. and van der Torre, L. (1994). Multi preference semantics for a defeasible deontic logic. In H. Prakken, A. Muntjewerff, A. Soeteman, and R. Winkels, editors, *Legal Knowledge Based Systems. The Relation with Legal Theory.*, pages 115–126. Koninklijke Vermande, Lelystad.

Torre, van der, L. (1997). *Reasoning about Obligations, Defeasibility in Preference-based Deontic Logic*. Erasmus University of Rotterdam, Rotterdam.

Urmson, J. (1969). Saints and heroes. In J. Feinberg, editor, *Moral Concepts*, pages 60–73. Oxford University Press, London.

Weinberger, O. (1970). *Rechtlogik*. Springer, Wien.

Wieringa, R. and Meyer, J.-J. C. (1993). Actors, actions and initiative in normative system specification. *Annals of Mathematics and Artificial Intelligence*, **7**, 289–346.

Wild, de, A. (1979). *De Rationaliteit van het Rechtelijk Oordeel*. Kluwer, Deventer.

Wright, von, G. (1951). Deontic logic. *Mind*, **60**, 1–15.

Wright, von, G. (1963). *Norm and Action: a Logical Enquiry*. Routledge & Kegan Paul, London.

Index

Law and Philosophy Library

1. E. Bulygin, J.-L. Gardies and I. Niiniluoto (eds.): *Man, Law and Modern Forms of Life*. With an Introduction by M.D. Bayles. 1985 ISBN 90-277-1869-5
2. W. Sadurski: *Giving Desert Its Due*. Social Justice and Legal Theory. 1985 ISBN 90-277-1941-1
3. N. MacCormick and O. Weinberger: *An Institutional Theory of Law*. New Approaches to Legal Positivism. 1986 ISBN 90-277-2079-7
4. A. Aarnio: *The Rational as Reasonable*. A Treatise on Legal Justification. 1987 ISBN 90-277-2276-5
5. M.D. Bayles: *Principles of Law*. A Normative Analysis. 1987 ISBN 90-277-2412-1; Pb: 90-277-2413-X
6. A. Soeteman: *Logic in Law*. Remarks on Logic and Rationality in Normative Reasoning, Especially in Law. 1989 ISBN 0-7923-0042-4
7. C.T. Sistare: *Responsibility and Criminal Liability*. 1989 ISBN 0-7923-0396-2
8. A. Peczenik: *On Law and Reason*. 1989 ISBN 0-7923-0444-6
9. W. Sadurski: *Moral Pluralism and Legal Neutrality*. 1990 ISBN 0-7923-0565-5
10. M.D. Bayles: *Procedural Justice*. Allocating to Individuals. 1990 ISBN 0-7923-0567-1
11. P. Nerhot (ed.): *Law, Interpretation and Reality*. Essays in Epistemology, Hermeneutics and Jurisprudence. 1990 ISBN 0-7923-0593-0
12. A.W. Norrie: *Law, Ideology and Punishment*. Retrieval and Critique of the Liberal Ideal of Criminal Justice. 1991 ISBN 0-7923-1013-6
13. P. Nerhot (ed.): *Legal Knowledge and Analogy*. Fragments of Legal Epistemology, Hermeneutics and Linguistics. 1991 ISBN 0-7923-1065-9
14. O. Weinberger: *Law, Institution and Legal Politics*. Fundamental Problems of Legal Theory and Social Philosophy. 1991 ISBN 0-7923-1143-4
15. J. Wróblewski: *The Judicial Application of Law*. Edited by Z. Bańkowski and N. MacCormick. 1992 ISBN 0-7923-1569-3
16. T. Wilhelmsson: *Critical Studies in Private Law*. A Treatise on Need-Rational Principles in Modern Law. 1992 ISBN 0-7923-1659-2
17. M.D. Bayles: *Hart's Legal Philosophy*. An Examination. 1992 ISBN 0-7923-1981-8
18. D.W.P. Ruiter: *Institutional Legal Facts*. Legal Powers and their Effects. 1993 ISBN 0-7923-2441-2
19. J. Schonsheck: *On Criminalization*. An Essay in the Philosophy of the Criminal Law. 1994 ISBN 0-7923-2663-6
20. R.P. Malloy and J. Evensky (eds.): *Adam Smith and the Philosophy of Law and Economics*. 1994 ISBN 0-7923-2796-9
21. Z. Bankowski, I. White and U. Hahn (eds.): *Informatics and the Foundations of Legal Reasoning*. 1995 ISBN 0-7923-3455-8
22. E. Lagerspetz: *The Opposite Mirrors*. An Essay on the Conventionalist Theory of Institutions. 1995 ISBN 0-7923-3325-X
23. M. van Hees: *Rights and Decisions*. Formal Models of Law and Liberalism. 1995 ISBN 0-7923-3754-9
24. B. Anderson: *"Discovery" in Legal Decision-Making*. 1996 ISBN 0-7923-3981-9

Law and Philosophy Library

25. S. Urbina: *Reason, Democracy, Society.* A Study on the Basis of Legal Thinking. 1996 ISBN 0-7923-4262-3
26. E. Attwooll: *The Tapestry of the Law.* Scotland, Legal Culture and Legal Theory. 1997 ISBN 0-7923-4310-7
27. J.C. Hage: *Reasoning with Rules.* An Essay on Legal Reasoning and Its Underlying Logic. 1997 ISBN 0-7923-4325-5
28. R.A. Hillman: *The Richness of Contract Law.* An Analysis and Critique of Contemporary Theories of Contract Law. 1997 ISBN 0-7923-4336-0
29. C. Wellman: *An Approach to Rights.* Studies in the Philosophy of Law and Morals. 1997 ISBN 0-7923-4467-7
30. B. van Roermund: *Law, Narrative and Reality.* An Essay in Intercepting Politics. 1997 ISBN 0-7923-4621-1
31. I. Ward: *Kantianism, Postmodernism and Critical Legal Thought.* 1997 ISBN 0-7923-4745-5
32. H. Prakken: *Logical Tools for Modelling Legal Argument.* A Study of Defeasible Reasoning in Law. 1997 ISBN 0-7923-4776-5
33. T. May: *Autonomy, Authority and Moral Responsibility.* 1998 ISBN 0-7923-4851-6
34. M. Atienza and J.R. Manero: *A Theory of Legal Sentences.* 1997 ISBN 0-7923-4856-7
35. E.A. Christodoulidis: *Law and Reflexive Politics.* 1998 ISBN 0-7923-4954-7
36. L.M.M. Royakkers: *Extending Deontic Logic for the Formalisation of Legal Rules.* 1998 ISBN 0-7923-4982-2

KLUWER ACADEMIC PUBLISHERS – DORDRECHT / BOSTON / LONDON

MIX
Papier aus verantwortungsvollen Quellen
Paper from responsible sources
FSC® C105338

If you have any concerns about our products,
you can contact us on
ProductSafety@springernature.com

In case Publisher is established outside the EU,
the EU authorized representative is:
Springer Nature Customer Service Center GmbH
Europaplatz 3, 69115 Heidelberg, Germany

Printed by Libri Plureos GmbH
in Hamburg, Germany